MINORITY EDUCATION:

Anthropological Perspectives

Social and Policy Issues in Education: The University of Cincinnati Series

Kathryn M. Borman, *Series Editor*

Contemporary Issues in U.S. Education, *edited by Kathryn M. Borman, Piyush Swami, and Lonnie D. Wagstaff*

Early Childhood Education: Policy Issue for the 1990s, *edited by Dolores Stegelin*

Effective Schooling for Disadvantaged Students: School-based Strategies for Diverse Student Populations, *edited by Howard Johnston and Kathryn M. Borman*

Home Schooling: Political, Historical, and Pedagogical Perspectives, *edited by Jane Van Galen and Mary Anne Pitman*

Minority Education: Anthropological Perspectives, *edited by Evelyn Jacob and Cathie Jordan*

in preparation

Assessment Testing and Evaluation in Teacher Education, *edited by Suzanne W. Soled*

Basil Bernstein: Consensus and Controversy, *edited by Alan R. Sadovnik*

Children Who Challenge the System, *edited by Anne M. Bauer and Ellen M. Lynch*

The New American Schools: Alternative Concepts and Practices, *edited by Bruce A. Jones and Kathryn M. Borman*

Minority Education:

Anthropological Perspectives

Edited by

Evelyn Jacob

George Mason University

and

Cathie Jordan

Kamehameha Schools

ABLEX PUBLISHING CORPORATION
NORWOOD, NEW JERSEY

Library of Congress Cataloging-in-Publication Data

Minority education : anthropological perspectives / edited by Evelyn Jacob, Cathie Jordan.
   p.   cm. — (Social and policy issues in education)
Includes bibliographical references and index.
ISBN 0-89391-868-7. — ISBN 0-89391-937-3 (pbk.)
   1. Minorities—Education—Social aspects—United States. 2. Educational anthropology—United States. I. Jacob, Evelyn. II. Jordan, Cathie. III. Series.
LC3731.M5587 1992   92-27519
371.97′00973—dc20   CIP

Ablex Publishing Corporation
355 Chestnut Street
Norwood, New Jersey 07648

Contents

Preface

This volume presents an overview of current anthropological thinking on a central educational concern: the education of minority students.

Most children in the United States have greatly benefited from free, mandatory, public education. However, like any large, highly organized social institution, public schools have had their problems as well as their successes. One of the most persistent problem areas has been minority education. Although the children of some minority groups fare well in school, the children of other minority groups do not. These discrepancies represent a major challenge as schools attempt to reach the goal of providing all students with equal educational opportunity.

Scholars from many disciplines have employed a variety of perspectives in their efforts to understand and resolve problematic issues in minority education. This book brings the perspectives of educational anthropology to bear on understanding minority education and resolving its inequities.

Within the field of educational anthropology there have been two major approaches to understanding minority education: the cultural difference theory and the theory of secondary cultural discontinuity. Until recently, these two approaches have existed more or less in parallel, seldom addressing one another directly. About five years ago, the editors of this volume felt that it was time to explore the relationships between the approaches. In 1985, Jacob organized and chaired a session at the meetings of the Society for Applied Anthropology, in which Frederick Erickson and John Ogbu presented papers concerning the two approaches and possible relationships between them. This session generated so much interest that Jordan organized a special invited session on the same topic, sponsored by the Council on Anthropology and Education, at the meetings of the American Anthropological Association later that same year. To broaden the base of discussion, she included, in addition to theoretical papers by Ogbu and Erickson, four case studies and two discussion papers. In 1987, revised versions of these papers appeared in a theme issue (18:4) of *The Anthropology & Education Quarterly (AEQ)*.

The present volume carries the anthropological exploration of the topic of minority education and its problems a step further. At the core of the book (Sections II and III) are papers from the *AEQ* issue: the theoretical works by Erickson and Ogbu and the four case studies, two of which tend to support each theoretical stance. The other sections expand on this core. The introductory chapters present the theoretical, conceptual, and practical framework of the volume. Section IV presents additional viewpoints on minority education, raising issues not attended to or not central to Ogbu's and Erickson's stances. Section V addresses applied issues and policy implications. The chapters in the Introduction as well as Section IV and Section V appear here for the first time and make new contributions to the field of educational anthropology.

This volume is intended to address a larger audience than the *AEQ* theme issue, which was addressed primarily to educational anthropologists. We hope that it will be of interest to educational researchers, practitioners, and policymakers who are concerned with minority education. To this end, the first chapter in the Introduction presents the theoretical context of anthropological views, and the second chapter in the Introduction provides background in the concepts, methods, and perspectives of educational anthropology, which may be new to some readers. To help make the theoretical discussions more explicitly relevant to educators, the final section of the book turns to applied concerns. We hope that the volume will help to generate increased dialogue between educational anthropologists and others interested in minority education, especially the practitioners and policymakers who are able to influence its current and future course.

We owe thanks to a number of people who have contributed to the process leading to this volume. We would like to thank Frederick Erickson, who, as editor of the *AEQ*, published the original theme issue. David Fetterman was instrumental in prompting us to develop this book, and Kathryn Borman was heartening in her interest in our ideas. Barbara Bernstein, our editor at Ablex, has been supportive, patient, and encouraging from the beginning. We also would like to thank the American Anthropological Association for permission to reprint the papers from the *AEQ* theme issue.

Contributors

John D'Amato
Kamehameha Schools

Stephen Diaz
California State University, San Bernadino

Margaret Eisenhart
University of Colorado, Boulder

Frederick Erickson
University of Pennsylvania

David Fetterman
Stanford University

Margaret Gibson
University of California, Santa Cruz

Perry Gillmore
University of Alaska, Fairbanks

Shelley Goldman
Institute for Research on Learning, Palo Alto

M. Elizabeth Graue
University of Wisconsin, Madison

Barbara Harrison
University of Waikato, Hamilton, New
    Zealand

Evelyn Jacob
George Mason University

Cathie Jordan
Kamehameha Schools

Ray McDermott
Stanford University

Luis Moll
University of Arizona

John Ogbu
University of California, Berkeley

David Smith
University of Alaska, Fairbanks

Marcelo Suarez-Orozco
University of California, San Diego

Roland Tharp
University of California, Santa Cruz

Lynn Vogt
Kamehameha Schools

I
Introduction

1

Understanding Minority Education: Framing the Issues

Evelyn Jacob and Cathie Jordan

Students who come from backgrounds that are ethnically, linguistically or socioculturally distinct from the white majority, form an increasingly large proportion of the public school population in the United States today. In 1986 minority students comprised 30 percent of all students in public elementary and secondary schools (National Center for Educational Statistics 1990:62). However, in some areas they constitute a much larger proportion of the student population: "Minority students today outnumber white students in twenty-five of the nation's twenty-six largest urban school systems" ("Cultural Differences" 1988:1). *Time* magazine estimates that if recent trends continue, minority groups, taken together, will outnumber the current white majority in the overall population by 2056 (Henry 1990:30).

Educating minority students poses a challenge to our society because students from minority backgrounds frequently fare poorly in school. This is evidenced by a number of indices. For example, black and Hispanic students drop out at a higher rate than white students, and they score lower on standardized tests of reading and writing (National Center for Educational Statistics 1990:20, 26–29). In mathematics and science the gap between majority students and minority (black and Hispanic) students is large and widens as the complexity of the skill measured increases (National Center for Educational Statistics 1989:115,117).

This book brings anthropological perspectives to bear on the education of minority children in the United States. Drawing on the field of educational anthropology, the authors in this anthology offer insights that may be helpful in the continuing effort to understand and cope with the great variety of groups and cultures that our schools undertake to serve.

In order to place anthropological perspectives in their larger context, we begin this chapter with a review of a number of nonanthropological views of minority education which have been important during the past 30 years. We then turn to anthropological approaches to minority education which are discussed in this volume, concluding with an outline of the unique contributions of these approaches.

MINORITY EDUCATION: BIOLOGICAL, PSYCHOLOGICAL AND SOCIOLOGICAL VIEWS

Since the 1960s a number of theories have emerged which attempt to explain the problems of minority education. Many of these explanations have framed the problems in terms of explaining the "limited achievement" of minority students (Banks 1985:5401) and many have focused on students from lower socioeconomic backgrounds in which most ethnic minority students find themselves. Three of the most prominent explanations place the responsibility for the low achievement and other problems that many minority students experience in school on the minority groups themselves. Of these three explanations, one stresses their genetic heritage (termed the genetic explanation) and two focus on their home environment (termed the cultural deficit explanation and the status attainment approach). A fourth explanation focuses primarily on the role of society and schools.

The genetic explanation is that social class and racial differences in IQ scores are largely the result of genetic differences. For example, Jensen (1969) asserts that compensatory education programs fail because they are based on the false premise that IQ differences are the result of environmental differences and biases in the tests. He argues that eighty percent of individual variance in intelligence has a genetic base, and, therefore, genes affect intelligence more than environment does.

The genetic explanation was much discussed for several years (e.g., Brace, Gamble and Bond 1971), and is now widely discredited. For example, Jencks and his colleagues (1972) discuss some of the limitations on the concept of heritability on which this approach rests. One limitation is that heritability does not take into account the fact that genes can influence test scores indirectly by interacting with the environment in which an individual develops.

If, for example, a nation refuses to send children with red hair to school, the genes that cause red hair can be said to lower reading scores...If an individual's genotype affects his environment, for whatever rational or irrational reason, and if this in turn affects his cognitive development, conventional methods of estimating heritability automatically attribute the entire effect to genes and none to environment (Jencks et al. 1972:66-67)

Another limitation is that estimates of heritability apply only to populations. "The heritability of IQ for the general population....tells us almost nothing about the likely cause of the difference between subpopulations [such as minority groups]" (Jencks et al. 1972:68).

In contrast to the genetic explanation, the cultural deficit explanation stresses the importance of environment as a causal factor. This approach focuses on a "culture of poverty" which poor people are posited to share by virtue of their economic condition (e.g., Riessman 1962). Although proponents of this view see *all* poor people as participating in a culture of poverty, many discussions focus on the black poor. Holding middle-class white culture as the norm, the culture of poverty is viewed as deficient in providing the experiences, attitudes or values children need to succeed in school (e.g., Deutsch and Associates 1967). Theorists in the cultural deprivation approach argue that "a major goal of school programs for 'culturally deprived' students should be to provide them with cultural and other experiences designed to compensate for their cognitive and intellectual deficits" (Banks 1985:5401).

Several aspects of the culture of poverty are emphasized as central deficiencies for the children's "retarded" language, psychological, and social development. Followers of the cultural deficit approach assert that the home environment of the poor does not provide sufficient stimulation for normal development (Deutsch and Associates 1967; Hunt 1969). Poor children are viewed as having a narrower range of stimuli and less systematic ordering of that stimuli than middle-class children (Deutsch 1967). This stimulation deficit purportedly leads to deficits in many areas: cognitive development, attention span, expectations of reward from knowledge and task completion, ability to use adults as sources of information, ability to delay gratification, and linguistic and symbolic development. The language used in poor homes is also seen as deficient (Bereiter and Englemann 1966; Deutsch 1967; Hunt 1967; Riessman 1962). Drawing partly on the work of Bernstein (1964), proponents of this approach see the speech of the poor as limited, simple, poorly structured syntactically, and not supportive of abstract thought. In addition, the homes of the poor are characterized as exhibiting little direct instruction:

> The culture appears to center around attitudes, interests, a style of life, and a scattering of unorganized beliefs and superstitions so unformalized that they may be transmitted without explanation, argument, or detailed exposition. Deliberate teaching is not a normal or necessary part of the adult role in such cultural groups, and neither the skills nor the language peculiar to teaching are developed and maintained (Bereiter and Englemann 1966:33).

Many scholars have criticized the cultural deficit approach. Some criticisms have focused on the notion of a "culture of poverty" itself (e.g., Leacock 1971; Valentine 1968). These critics argue that those discussing the culture of poverty apply the concept of culture inappropriately, approaching lower-class groups from an ethnocentric, middle-class point of view rather than attempting to understand the group's behavior from its own perspectives. According to the critics such an approach ignores the heterogeneity of ethnicity, language, and culture that exists among people with low incomes. Also, it is premature in that it asserts, on little evidence, specific characteristics for the culture of poverty and thus makes a "prejudgment of empirical questions" (Valentine 1968:16), rather than carrying out close investigation of whether such characteristics indeed exist and what their nature might in fact be.

Other scholars have attacked specific characterizations of the culture of poverty. For example, sociolinguists (Labov 1969, 1972; Wolfram 1969) have documented that black working-class speech is a well-ordered and highly structured separate dialect, not a deficient version of white middle-class speech. Others (e.g., Baratz and Baratz 1970; Leacock 1971) have challenged assertions about the lack of stimulation and teaching in lower-class homes.

A third approach, termed the status attainment or production function approach, examines the issue of minority education within the larger question of which factors (such as family background, innate abilities, peers, and school characteristics) affect educational achievement. To explore these issues, scholars adapt economists' production function model to examine assumed deterministic relationships between input variables and an output variable such as performance on a standardized test. They use statistical procedures such as regression analysis to examine large samples of quantitative data to determine which factors explain more variance in standardized test scores. The overall findings of this body of work are that family background is highly related to student performance on standardized tests and that school variables, except for some characteristics of teachers, are not significantly related to student test performance (Coleman et al. 1966; Hanushek 1972, 1985; Jencks et al. 1972).

Since the mid-1970s the status attainment approach has been seen as being inadequate for explaining differential academic achievement. Hanushek (1985) summarizes the criticisms of this approach as follows: Some researchers question the appropriateness of the assumptions underlying the model, and others point out that empirical studies rarely correspond to the conceptual models guiding the work. Many have criticized the measures used and the accuracy with which variables are measured. Moreover, the measures often are selected because of availability rather than conceptual appropriateness. Finally, this approach pays no attention to the processes by which inputs supposedly cause outputs. These models ignore "micro" processes and decisions that mediate between inputs and outcomes.

A fourth explanation, social reproduction theory, shifts the focus of responsibility from the minority groups themselves to society and schools. Social reproduction theory has many forms. An early form, termed correspondence theory, sees members of the working class (who are largely members of minority groups) as passive, shaped largely by structural forces beyond their control. Social reproduction theorists argue that schools replicate the hierarchical division of labor by reproducing the hierarchical social relations of the economy in the schools (Bowles and Gintis 1976:131). Moreover, the schools specifically channel different groups into different economic slots through different social relationships within and among schools:

> Different levels of education feed workers into different levels within the occupational structure and correspondingly, tend toward an internal organization comparable to levels in the hierarchical division of labor....Thus blacks and other minorities are concentrated in schools whose repressive, arbitrary, generally chaotic internal order, coercive authority structures, and minimal possibilities for advancement mirror the characteristics of inferior job situations. Similarly, predominantly working-class schools tend to emphasize behavioral control and rule-following, while schools in well-to-do suburbs employ relatively open systems that favor greater student participation, less direct supervision, more student electives, and, in general, a value system stressing internalized standards of control. (Bowles and Gintis 1976:132)

Mehan (1989) summarizes the major criticisms of this work. The theory (1) is deterministic, (2) exaggerates the degree of integration between the demands of the capitalist elites and the organization of schooling, and (3) presents a functionalist's argument similar to what it is trying to replace.

Bourdieu (Bourdieu and Passeron 1977) tries to deal with these criticisms within the basic framework of the social reproduction approach by suggesting that cultural elements mediate between economic structures, schooling, and the lives of students. Cultural elements are discussed in terms of cultural capital (Bourdieu and Passeron 1977), which refers to the general cultural background of a group. This includes "ways of talking, acting, modes of style, moving, socializing, forms of knowledge, language practices, and values" [underlined in original] (McLaren 1989:190). Schools contribute to the reproduction of inequality by valuing and rewarding the cultural capital of the dominant classes and devaluing that of the lower classes. "Academic performance represents, therefore, not individual competence or the lack of ability on the part of disadvantaged students but the school's depreciation of their cultural capital" [last phrase underlined in original] (McLaren 1989:191).

While Bourdieu's account softens the determinism in traditional reproduction theory, he has been criticized for "depicting cultural forms and practices as largely the reflection of structural forces conceptualized at the societal level" (Mehan 1989:13). Moreover, neither Bowles and Gintis nor Bourdieu examines the school processes that produce inequalities (Mehan 1989).

Some recent empirical studies (Willis 1977; MacLeod 1987) have begun to examine the processes by which the school's approach to cultural capital leads to differential achievement. Willis' research (1977) among British working-class male students, for example, has documented that lower-class students often resist this devaluation of their cultural capital through oppositional behavior and attitudes. Moreover, he has shown that by rejecting the cultural capital of the school (particularly through their rejection of "mental labor" in favor of manual labor) they contribute to their continued status in the working class by foreclosing other career options that success in school might have opened to them. Thus, in this view, the students themselves unwittingly contribute to the maintenance of their position in the lowest economic stratum of society.

Educational anthropology has shared in many of these debates. However, the work done by educational anthropologists has tended to produce somewhat different views of minority schooling and the problems related to it, and therefore has generated somewhat different kinds of attempts at solution.

MINORITY EDUCATION: ANTHROPOLOGICAL VIEWS

Since the 1960s, educational anthropology has developed two major approaches to problems associated with minority education, with various alternatives or refinements emerging along the way. The two major approaches have been called the cultural difference approach and the secondary cultural discontinuity approach (termed "communication process explanation" and "perceived labor market explanation," respectively, by Erickson in this volume).

Proponents of the cultural difference approach argue that differences between majority and minority cultures in interaction, linguistic, and cognitive styles can lead to conflicts between school and child that interfere with effective education. Erickson (this volume) offers a contemporary discussion of this perspective, combining the traditional focus on cultural differences with a new concern for power relationships among teachers and students in classrooms. Case studies by Vogt, Jordan and Tharp and by Moll and Diaz in this volume tend to illustrate and support the position taken by the cultural difference approach. They report on situations in which schools are ordinarily not very successful in educating the children of a minority group, but in which changes in classrooms and schools have reduced problems and produced more effective education.

The secondary cultural discontinuity approach differs from the cultural difference approach in two ways. First, it examines variations in school performance among minority groups. Ogbu (1974) distinguishes between minority groups (termed subordinate or castelike) who were incorporated into U.S. society against their will and tend to do poorly in school, and minority groups (termed immigrant) who came to the U.S. by their own choice and frequently do well in school. Second, the cultural discontinuity approach consciously looks beyond the school and home settings to the larger society in which these settings are embedded, focusing on minority groups' adaptations to the larger society. Ogbu (1974:12) argues that the poor school performance among subordinate minorities "is both a reaction and an adaptation to the limited opportunity available to them to benefit from their education" because the same economic opportunities are not open to them as to Anglos. This adaptation leads to what Ogbu (this volume) calls "secondary cultural discontinuities." The case studies by Gibson and by Suarez-Orozco in this volume tend to support Ogbu's approach. They report on situations in which schools are relatively successful in educating students from immigrant minority groups.

Recently, as we shall see in Part IV, anthropologists have begun to modify these approaches, to raise new questions, and to emphasize other ways of looking at the problem. While the viewpoints espoused in these chapters may accept and utilize some or all of the insights offered by the cultural difference or secondary discontinuity stances, they add something to these approaches or go beyond them. They remind us of additional factors that must be considered if we wish to understand problems in minority education and especially if we wish to produce solutions to those problems, or they ask us to look at minority education from a different perspective altogether. Harrison (this volume) draws on her experience in Alaska and New Zealand to suggest that minority education is never going to be successful until minority group adults themselves are vested with real decision-making power with respect to how their children shall be educated. Eisenhart and Graue (this volume) demonstrate that the "groups" that are relevant to school are not always or not only those that can be associated with markers of ethnicity, but that cultural groupings form in direct and indirect response to schools themselves. D'Amato (this volume) offers an explanation for the variation in minority children's compliance with school which incorporates and melds the cultural difference and secondary discontinuity stances and focuses attention on school children as active decision makers in school who are responding to a different agenda than are teachers, administrators or parents. Gilmore, Goldman, McDermott and Smith focus attention on how schools' emphasis on competition requires that some students fail and on how researchers' focus on school failure also contributes to the problem. To counteract these forces, Gilmore et al. discuss examples of teaching practices that may help eliminate failure.

Moreover, some scholars have combined an anthropological perspective with perspectives with reproduction theory. For example, as mentioned above, Erickson (this volume) combines ideas from cultural difference theory with the emphasis on power from the social reproduction approach; D'Amato offers a model to explain variability in student resistance; Gilmore et al. use the social reproduction approach in a reflexive stance to examine the very questions that researchers ask.

The various anthropological approaches to minority education discussed in this volume have implications for research, practice, and policy. Examples of research motivated by the different approaches appear throughout the volume. The last part of the volume turns to applied concerns. Fetterman discusses policy implications of the anthropological perspective on minority education. Using case material from his own work, he offers examples and advice about how to effectively make the leap from research or practice to influencing educational policy and policy makers. Jordan and Jacob conclude with a discussion of the different contexts in which anthropological knowledge may affect educational practice, and the goals and possible outcomes of such intervention.

CONTRIBUTIONS OF ANTHROPOLOGICAL VIEWS

What can educational anthropology contribute to understanding minority education? How do anthropological perspectives differ from other perspectives in ways that may be significant for our understanding of issues in that arena and for our ability to effectively respond to its problems?

We would like to suggest three contributions as worthy of note.

1. Educational anthropology views minority students and their families and communities as no less well endowed, in basic intelligence, talents, language, culture, or life experience, than members of the majority population. Therefore, clashes with majority culture schools, when they occur, are matters not of deficit, but of difference (whether viewed as primary or secondary discontinuity, or resistance).
2. Educational anthropology broadens the focus of attention and inquiry beyond the low scores on tests that emerge from the encounters of the

children of some minority groups with the majority culture schools. This broadening involves attention to the range of variation in cultural meanings and behavior within and between minority groups which are associated with schooling. It also involves attention to what the whole of the schooling experience is like and to the specifics of what actually happens in classrooms for the children of any particular minority in any particular community. And it involves attention to the wide variability in school performance of minority groups within the United States and abroad.

3. Educational anthropology views education as a process in which all participants contribute to shaping the outcomes, influenced not only by the immediate contexts but also by their past experience and culture. This view leads to insights into the processes (cultural, social, political, historical, interactional, and psychological) that contribute to the various outcomes of minority education.

As a corollary to these views, there is an emerging awareness that debates about who is responsible for the problems plaguing minority education are of little profit. Such arguments are pointless because no one group of participants in minority education (whether society as a whole, researchers, school officials, teachers, local communities, parents or students) is responsible in the sense of being culpable. While each group can be shown to be a significant player in the processes of minority education, the only sense in which it seems worthwhile to talk about responsibility for problems in minority education is to ask what can be done to help change the current situation and who is in a position to make the changes. This a question to which we will return at the end of the volume.

REFERENCES

Banks, J. A.
   1985   Urban Education: Educational Programs. *In* The International Encyclopedia of Education. Vol. 9. T. Husen and T. N. Postlethwaite, eds. Pp. 5400–5402. Oxford: Pergamon.
Baratz, S., and J. Baratz
   1970   Early Childhood Intervention: The Social Science Base for Institutional Racism. Harvard Educational Review 40:29–50.
Bereiter, C., and S. Englemann
   1966   Teaching Disadvantaged Children in the Preschool. Englewood Cliffs, NJ: Prentice-Hall.
Bernstein, B.
   1964   Elaborated and Restricted Codes: Their Social Origins and Some Consequences. American Anthropologist 66 (no.6, part 2):55–70.

Bourdieu, P. and J-C. Passeron
  1977 Reproduction in Education, Society and Culture. London: Sage.
Bowles, S., and H. Gintis
  1976 Schooling in Capitalist America. New York: Basic Books.
Brace, C. Loring, G. R. Gamble, and James T. Bond
  1971 Race and Intelligence. Washington, DC: American Anthropological
        Association.
Coleman, James, E. Campbell, C. Hobson, J. McPartland, A. Mood, F. Weinfeld, and
R. York
  1966 Equality of Educational Opportunity. Washington, DC: U.S. Government
        Printing Office.
Cultural Differences in the Classroom
  1988 Harvard Education Letter (March), Pp. 1–4.
Deutsch, M.
  1967 The Disadvantaged Child and the Learning Process. In The Disadvantaged
        Child: Selected Papers of Martin Deutsch and Associates. Martin Deutsch
        and Associates, eds. Pp. 39–57. New York: Basic Books.
Deutsch, M., and Associates
  1967 The Disadvantaged Child: Selected Papers of Martin Deutsch and Associ-
        ates. New York: Basic Books.
Hanushek, E.
  1972 Education and Race: An Analysis of the Educational Production Process.
        Lexington, Massachusetts: D.C. Heath and Company
Henry, W.
  1990 Beyond the Melting Pot. Time (April 9):28–31.
Hunt, J. Mc V.
  1967 The Psychological Basis for Preschool Cultural Enrichment Programs. In
        Social class, Race, and Psychological Development, M. Deutsch et al., eds.
        New York: Holt.
  1969 The Challenge of Incompetence and Poverty: Papers on the Role of Early
        Education. Urbana, IL: University of Illinois Press.
Jencks, C., M. Smith, H. Acland, M. J. Bane, D. Cohen, H. Gintis, B. Heyns, and S.
Michelson
  1972 Inequality. New York: Basic Books
Jensen, A.
  1969 How Much Can We Boost IQ and Scholastic Achievement? Harvard
        Educational Review 39:1–123.
Labov, W.
  1969 The Logic of Nonstandard English. Georgetown Monographs on Language
        and Linguistics 22:1–22,26–31.
  1972 Language in the Inner City: Studies in the Black English Vernacular.
        Philadelphia: University of Pennsylvania Press.
Leacock, E., ed.
  1971 The Culture of Poverty: A Critique. New York: Simon and Schuster.
MacLeod, J.
  1987 Ain't No Makin It. Boulder, CO: Westview Press.

McLaren, P.
   1989   Life in Schools: An Introduction to Critical Pedagogy in the Foundations of Education. New York: Longman.
Mehan, H.
   1989   Understanding Inequality in Schools: The Contribution of Interpretive Studies. Paper presented at the meetings of the American Sociological Association, August.
National Center for Educational Statistics
   1989   Digest of Educational Statistics. Washington, DC: U.S. Government Printing Office.
   1990   The Condition of Education: 1990. Vol. 1. Elementary and Secondary Education. Washington, DC: U.S. Government Printing Office.
Ogbu, J.
   1974   The Next Generation: An Ethnography of Education in an Urban Neighborhood. New York: Academic Press.
Riessman, F.
   1962   The Culturally Deprived Child. New York: Harper.
Valentine, C.
   1968   Culture and Poverty: Critique and Counter-proposals. Chicago: University of Chicago Press.
Willis, P.
   1977   Learning to Labor. New York: Columbia University Press.
Wolfram, W.
   1969   A Sociolinguistic Description of Detroit Negro Speech. Urban Language series, no.5. Washington, DC: Center for Applied Linguistics.

2

Understanding Educational Anthropology: Concepts and Methods*

Evelyn Jacob and Cathie Jordan

The chapters in the remainder of the book draw on concepts and methods from anthropology in presenting their views of minority education. Within anthropology, concern for minority education is part of the study of the full range of educational settings which is the domain of educational anthropology. For readers who may not be familiar with anthropology, this chapter summarizes key concepts, perspectives and methods which are important in educational anthropology and its approach to minority education.

ANTHROPOLOGICAL CONCEPTS AND PERSPECTIVES

Most anthropologists share certain basic perspectives. They move beyond a focus on individual psychology to examine issues in social and cultural frameworks. Some basic concepts of anthropology are culture, context, holism, and the comparative perspective.

Culture

Anthropologists use the concept of culture in a variety of ways. Most broadly, culture refers to all that humans learn, in contrast to what is genetically endowed (Keesing and Keesing 1971:20). What is learned encompasses both patterns *for* behavior and patterns *of* behavior.

* Portions of this chapter were reprinted from Evelyn Jacob, 1990, Alternative Approaches for Studying Naturally Occurring Human Behavior and Thought in Special Education Research, *The Journal of Special Education*, Vol. 42, pp. 195–211. Reprinted by permission from Pro-Ed Journals.

Patterns *for* behavior are mental phenomena, "meanings" shared by members of a social group. They comprise "standards for deciding what is, standards for deciding what can be, standards for deciding how one feels about it, standards for deciding what to do about it, and standards for deciding how to go about doing it" (Goodenough 1971:21, 22). Anthropologists infer these shared standards from the speech and behavior of members of a culture.

Patterns *of* behavior are directly observable phenomena. They include shared patterns in such diverse areas as social interaction, dress, literacy activities, political behavior, and social interaction. When anthropologists use the term culture they may refer to both patterns of behavior and patterns for behavior, or, more narrowly, they may use the term to refer only to shared meanings.

Anthropologists view shared cultural meanings as crucial for understanding behavior because the same behavior can "mean" different things in different cultures. For example, Gibson (this volume) contrasts teachers' and parents' varying interpretations of Punjabi students' participation in extracurricular activities in a California high school. To their non-Punjabi teachers, Punjabi student participation in these activities is a sign that the students fit in socially and are a "success." To Punjabi parents this same behavior constitutes dishonorable socializing between the sexes.

While individuals are aware of some aspects of their culture, they are frequently unaware of other, "implicit" aspects of culture. For example, rules and patterns of face-to-face social interaction (e.g., how far one stands from another person when having a conversation) are not usually at the level of conscious awareness. Although such aspects of culture are outside conscious awareness, they can have powerful effects in education. For example, Vogt, Jordan and Tharp (this volume) suggest that teachers' incorporation of features of the Hawaiian-American "talk story" pattern of conversation into reading lessons with Hawaiian children contributed to dramatic improvements in the students' reading scores. Such patterns of and rules for verbal interaction are not things that most people are aware of or can talk about readily, but they are very important to peoples' ability to participate effectively in a conversation, and in this case, seem to have had important effects on the success of efforts to teach children to read.

Anthropologists assume that there is a significant regularity in cultural meanings and behavior across individuals within a cultural group (Goodenough 1971; Pelto 1970). However, diversity also exists *within* a cultural group. One reason for this diversity is that individuals are socialized into cultural norms in different ways and are influenced by different subgroups within their society. (See Weisner, Gallimore and Jordan [1988] for a discussion of this in the Hawaiian case.) Second, although cultural norms exert a powerful influence on behavior, these norms do not *determine* behavior since individuals must decide whether and how to apply cultural guidelines for behavior in specific situations. Third, shared cultural meanings and behaviors are not static. Shared meanings are created, continued, changed and transmitted through social interaction.

Although anthropologists assume that certain categories of activity are important in all cultures (e.g., how children are socialized), they also assume that each culture is unique. They do not know in advance what cultural meanings particular behaviors have to members of the society, nor do they know the specific relationships among the parts of the culture (Mead 1973:246).

Anthropologists originally applied the notion of culture to self-contained societies and ethnic groups, and many people are comfortable thinking about concepts such as "Japanese culture" or "Puerto Rican culture." However, anthropologists also apply the concept to the to patterns shared by other regularly interacting groups of people. For example, educational anthropologists use it to speak of the culture(s) of schools (e.g., Peshkin 1986), of classrooms (Jacob 1989), and of groups of students who interact regularly for educational purposes (Eisenhart and Graue, this volume).

Two terms that anthropologists often use related to the learning of culture are enculturation and acculturation. "Enculturation" (sometimes also called socialization) refers to a child learning cultural norms and behaviors for the first time. "Acculturation" refers to the learning that occurs when people from different cultures come into contact with one another. Thus, a child living in El Salvador is enculturated into the Salvadoran culture, and if the child comes to the United States she then becomes, to a greater or lesser extent, acculturated into U.S. culture.

Context

The notion of context is related to the concept of culture. In an anthropological sense, contexts are settings created by people in which certain behaviors are defined as appropriate and others as inappropriate. Institutions, such as churches, offices and schools, provide examples of one level of context. Within these larger contexts are other "embedded" contexts. For example, Mrs. Jones' history class is one context and Mrs. Smith's art class is another context. While each shares some cultural norms for school, each also has some specific contextual rules. Within these contexts, individuals create smaller and smaller contexts. Thus, in Mrs. Jones' class "taking a test" is one context and "reviewing for the test" is another context. While observable features of the environment (type of building, different classrooms, etc.) can signal different contexts, the crucial thing is how people interactionally define the context. Thus, while a church is a physical context, people can define what is going on in the physical structure as "holding a religious service" or "having a party," and different behavior is appropriate in each context.

In studying education, anthropologists have demonstrated that context influences student performance dramatically. For example, Moll and Diaz (this volume) show that modifying the context of instruction results in dramatically different performance by minority students. Vogt, Jordan and Tharp (this volume) find similar results in working with Hawaiian children and their teachers.

Holism

Anthropologists see culture as pervading all aspects of human life. Culture is represented not only in behavior and speech, but also in physical artifacts. For anthropologists these would include the physical organization of a classroom, the decorations put up on the walls, and the texts of books. Thus, anthropologists are interested in the entirety of a setting such as a classroom or school because culture is manifested in all aspects of life.

Various parts of a culture are interdependent. This means that similar themes or patterns can be expected to appear in many aspects of a culture. It means also that change in one area of a culture often will result in changes in others. Because of these interrelationships, any single aspect of a culture needs always to be described and explained in relation to the larger system of which it is a part.

Some scholars (Erickson 1982; Cole and Griffin 1987) have used the image of concentric circles to visualize the mutual influence of different "layers" of society and culture on one another. In this view a child doing a particular task is situated within the larger contexts of a lesson, a classroom, and a school. These settings are further influenced by the bureaucracy of the school system, the organization of the local community, the city, the state, and the country. Many anthropologists do not stop at the contemporary scene, but also take the historical context into consideration.

Ogbu's framework (this volume) exemplifies the holistic perspective of anthropology. He argues that a student's performance in school is influenced by the cultural norms and values for school performance in the student's community, which in turn is influenced by the perceptions the community has of the "payoff" school has for its members. Ogbu's analysis thus takes into account the local community context, the larger society, and the historical relationships between a cultural group and the larger society.

The Comparative Perspective

The "comparative perspective" involves understanding the range of cultural variation that exists for a particular topic of inquiry. A principal benefit of this kind of knowledge is that it expands researchers' awareness beyond their own cultural assumptions, broadening their view of the possible and helping them become more explicitly conscious of the assumptions of their own culture and how these may be affecting their analyses. Another benefit is that identification of patterns that exist *across* cultures can help strengthen an argument.

Several chapters in this volume illustrate the comparative perspective. Chapters by Ogbu, by Gibson and by Suarez-Orozco demonstrate the value of examining minority groups who do well in U.S. schools rather than solely focusing on those who do poorly. Harrison illustrates how looking at minority control of education in New Zealand can expand the sense of the possible in the United States. D'Amato strengthens his argument by documenting cross-cultural patterns in students' stance toward school. Vogt and her colleagues demonstrate that similar-looking patterns of school achievement and behavior (e.g., reluctance to answer questions in class) may, upon close examination, be found to arise from quite different cultural roots and therefore require somewhat different response on the level of educational practice.

ANTHROPOLOGICAL RESEARCH METHODS

Because of the perspectives outlined above, anthropologists tend to collect and analyze their data through in-depth case studies that preserve to a maximum extent the detail and complexity of naturally occurring settings. Because anthropologists assume that each culture is unique and that it is critical to understand cultural meanings, researchers take a broad focus and an "open" theoretical stance at the beginning of their work in order to identify cultural meanings and determine the significance of behaviors to culture members before narrowing their research focus. In this sense, research is seen as "exploration into the unknown, in which the investigator must acquire firsthand acquaintance with the background facts of ecology, language, social organization and culture of a people before formulating more specific research goals" (LeVine 1973:183).

The most basic goal of anthropological research is to accurately describe the cultural behavior and meanings of a cultural group (which could be a village in a foreign country or a school or classroom in the investigator's own society). Anthropological studies of cultures are commonly called *ethnographies,* that is, writings about a culture or people. When anthropologists work in schools, they often produce "classroom ethnographies."

Because research goals are emergent, research design in anthropology is also frequently emergent. Researchers analyze ethnographic data to determine cultural meanings, and build on their understanding of those meanings to collect additional data and to focus their study. Data collection and data analysis occur simultaneously and continually inform one another.

Although there is no single standard anthropological research design, most long-term projects follow a common pattern. This involves starting with a broad focus building on analysis in the "field" to select a more narrow focus or foci, and then collecting data on a more limited topic. When quantitative data are collected as part of an anthropological study, design of the quantitative instruments builds on previous qualitative research that has identified relevant cultural categories and meanings.

Most anthropologists hold the basic tenet that it is crucial for researchers to gather data directly themselves through "fieldwork" in the culture they are studying (which for educational anthropologists could be a school or a classroom). Fieldwork involves a broad combination of methods, including participant observation and informal interviews. As its name implies, participant observation involves a dual role. The researcher is both a participant, that is, operating within a culture, and an observer, that is, standing outside the culture. Participation is viewed as crucial for several reasons. First, long-term direct involvement with culture members allows rapport and trust to develop, which is important if researchers are to form an accurate understanding of another culture. Second, participant observation permits anthropologists to develop and test hypotheses concerning cultural meanings through their direct experiences. Because much of culture is *implicit,* members of a culture often cannot explicitly talk about some of their cultural assumptions. Researchers can become aware that the implicit assumptions of others differ from their own when the behavior of culture members does not make sense to them or when they have strong emotional reactions to the behavior of others (because it does not fit their own automatically applied standards and expectations). By reflecting on these personal experiences and reactions anthropologists generate hypotheses about implicit cultural meanings, which they then test through explicit data collection. Anthropologists can begin to test their formulations of cultural meanings through their participation, that is, by the degree to which they can "behave appropriately as a member of the society or social group...or, more modestly, they can anticipate and interpret what occurs in the group as appropriately as its own members can" (Wolcott 1975:112).

The relative emphasis on participation and observation varies across studies and at different times within a given study. Sometimes the researcher is more observer than participant. For example, an educational ant gist might spend at least some of her time sitting in the back of a cla simply observing the children and the classroom activity, and delil avoiding any interaction, so as to change the usual classroom culture a. ittle as possible. It is difficult for such an observer to be truly unobtrusive as far as other adults in the classroom are concerned. However, it does seem that a noninteracting, nonresponsive adult can become uninteresting and almost "not there" as far as the children (especially if they are quite young) are concerned, and thus something close to a pure observer role becomes possible. In any case, participant observers record narrative observations in as detailed and concrete manner as possible, trying to keep inferences to a minimum (Pelto 1970).

In some studies, particularly those concerned with culturally patterned social interactions, anthropologists may use videotape as an observation tool. The use of videotape allows the researcher to review the same interactions repeatedly to identify and analyze the implicit culture revealed in them. This data collection method is especially useful for providing an accurate record of interaction in complex settings in which there are several related interactions involving a number of people going on simultaneously, as is frequently the case in classrooms. Also, in classrooms students often intend many of their interactions with each other to go unnoticed by teachers and other adults; videotape is particularly useful in catching and recording such *sub rosa* interactions.

Interviewing is the other principal method used in fieldwork. The general goal of the interview is to encourage members of a culture to talk about things of interest to them and to cover matters of importance to the researcher in a way that allows the cultural members to use their own concepts and terms (Whyte 1982). To do this, anthropologists try to listen more than they talk, and they attempt to listen with a "sympathetic and lively interest" (Whyte 1982:111).

Anthropological interviews can vary from casual, unplanned discussions, to open-ended formal interviews, to longterm, indepth discussions with selected individuals called "key informants." In educational settings, a key informant might be a teacher, a principal or the leader of a playground gang. In casual discussions anthropologists do not have a written list of questions. They take the opportunity within normal social discourse to follow up on or probe culture members' statements. In interviews, anthropologists usually have some general, open-ended questions or a list of topics to be covered. At times, they may then go on to develop more structured instruments based on results from the open-ended interviews.

One methodological tenet that spans all fieldwork is that it is important to document cultural meanings in the words of a culture's members. Since cultural meanings are represented through language, verbatim records of culture members' language provide important clues to categories and ideas in the culture. Without such records researchers can easily fall into the trap of "translating" ideas expressed by culture members into the researchers' own cultural understandings, without even realizing that they are doing so (Spradley 1979). Another common tenet is that it is important to collect a wide range of data using a wide range of methods, in order to form as complete a picture of the culture as possible. Thus, besides collecting data through participant observation, videotaping and interviewing, anthropologists commonly collect other data such as artifacts, documents, and photographic records.

Narrative descriptions from participant observation, and transcripts and notes from ethnographic interviews are usually analyzed qualitatively with an emphasis on elucidating the complex relationships that exist. As mentioned above, anthropologists begin preliminary analyses even while they are still collecting data. This strategy allows them to identify cultural meanings and categories for use in ongoing data collection. Further analysis occurs after data collection has been finished. Unlike the *coding* procedures followed by traditional educational researchers, anthropologists usually *index* their qualitative data, assigning as many categories as are relevant to every segment of text, much as in indexing a book. Data analysis is iterative, with initial indexing leading to preliminary analyses that generate new categories that are then applied to the data, analyzed, and so on. Preliminary categories are often descriptive or derived from culture members' language, with subsequent categories becoming increasingly analytic.

Data analysis usually generates further questions which often can be answered only by collecting additional data focused on those particular questions. So, it is not unusual for anthropologists to return to the same field site several times, sometimes over the course of a lifetime, trying to further check, refine and expand their understanding of a culture. While an educational anthropologist cannot repeatedly return to the "same" classroom since children grow up and move one, there are anthropologists who have spent 10 or even 20 years looking at the same educational system or the same aspect of education in a particular society. Such in-depth and iterative studies produce a fuller and richer understanding of educational phenomena than do the short-term and controlled studies more typical in traditional educational research.

SUMMARY

Although anthropologists approach education in a variety of ways they share some basic concepts, perspectives, and methods. Educational anthropology examines education from the viewpoint of culture, with culture being a complex and multifaceted concept. Within a cultural frame of reference educational anthropologists tend to conduct in-depth case studies that preserve the detail and complexity of naturally occurring settings such as classrooms. Using methods such as participant observation and in-depth interviewing, educational anthropologists document cultural meanings and behavior, structural and contextual influences on meanings and behavior, and the various processes involved in education. In addition, they attempt to place their local studies in the context of the range of variability that occurs cross-culturally. Drawing on these concepts and methods, the remaining chapters present the perspectives of educational anthropology on minority education.

REFERENCES

Cole, M. and P. Griffin, eds.
    1987   Contextual Factors in Education: Improving Science and Mathematics Education for Minorities and Women. Madison, Wisconsin: Wisconsin Center for Educational Research, University of Wisconsin-Madison.

Erickson, F.
    1982   Taught Cognitive Learning in its Immediate Environments: A Neglected Topic in the Anthropology of Education. Anthropology & Education Quarterly 13(2):149–180.

Goodenough, W.
    1971   Culture, Language, and Society (Addison-Wesley Module). Reading, MA: Addison-Wesley.

Jacob, E.
    1989   Students Creating Culture: Cooperative Learning in a Multi-ethnic Elementary School. Paper presented at the annual meetings of the American Anthropological Association, Washington, DC.

Keesing, R. and F. Keesing
    1971   New Perspectives in Cultural Anthropology. New York: Holt, Rinehart and Winston.

LeVine, R.
    1973   Research Design in Anthropological Fieldwork. In A Handbook of Method in Cultural Anthropology. R. Naroll and R. Cohen, eds. Pp. 183–195. New York: Columbia University Press.

Mead, M.
    1973   The Art and Technology of Fieldwork. In A Handbook of Method in Cultural Anthropology. R. Naroll and R. Cohen, eds. Pp. 264–265. New York: Columbia University Press.

Pelto, P.
    1970   Anthropological Research: The Structure of Inquiry. New York: Harper and Row.

Peshkin, A.
  1986   God's Choice: The Total World of a Fundamentalist Christian School. Chicago: University of Chicago Press.
Spradley, J.
  1979   The Ethnographic Interview. New York: Holt, Rinehart and Winston.
Weisner, T., R. Gallimore and C. Jordan
  1988   Unpackaging Cultural Effects on Classroom Learning: Native Hawaiian Peer Assistance and Child-Generated Activity. Anthropology & Education Quarterly 19:327–353.
Whyte, W. F.
  1982   Interviewing in Field Research. *In* Field Research: A Sourcebook and Field Manual. R. G. Burgess, ed. Pp. 111–122. London: Allen & Unwin. (Original work published 1960)
Wolcott, H.
  1975   Criteria for an Ethnographic Approach to Research in Schools. Human Organization 34:111–127.

Part II

Cultural Continuity and Discontinuity

3

Transformation and School Success: The Politics and Culture of Educational Achievement*

Frederick Erickson

There are numerous explanations for the generally low school achievement of minority students and working-class students in schools in the United States and other developed societies. A common explanation has been that of genetic deficit—poor children of color or of minority cultural or language background have been seen as inherently inferior, intellectually and morally, to the children of the middle class. In the 1960s, among professional educators, cultural deficit explanations began to replace the genetic deficit explanation. Nurture replaced nature as the main reason for school failure. Minority children, it was argued, did not achieve because they did not experience a cognitively stimulating environment (Bereiter and Engelmann 1966; Deutsch et al. 1967; Hess and Shipman 1965). Their language and lifestyle were intellectually impoverished. They were "culturally deprived" or "socially disadvantaged."

As the anthropology of education became a distinct field in the mid-1960s, its members were generally appalled by the ethnocentrism of the cultural deficit explanation. It was not literally racist, in the sense of a genetic deficit explanation. Yet it seemed culturally biased. The poor were still being characterized invidiously as not only deprived but depraved. The cultural deficit explanation seemed especially reprehensible to many because its ethnocentricism was cloaked in the legitimacy of social science. Various

---

* I wish to thank Cathie Jordan, Evelyn Jacob, and Marge Murray for editorial suggestions. The contributions from Howard van Ness and James Collins are acknowledged in the text itself. Defects in the interpretation presented are my own responsibility.

critiques were presented (e.g., Baratz and Baratz 1970; Valentine 1968). These did not receive much attention within the community of professional educators, perhaps because the cultural deficit explanation was so attractive. It enabled educators, frustrated by their difficulties in working with minority children, to place the responsibility for school failure outside the school.

In the late 1960s, sociolinguistically oriented anthropologists identified a factor inside the school as playing an important role in the low school achievement and morale of minority students. This was the factor of cultural difference in communication style between teachers and their students. This was a culturally relativist position. It blamed neither the children of the poor nor the school staff. Rather, it provided a way of seeing classroom troubles as inadvertent misunderstanding—teachers and students playing into each other's cultural blind spots.

In the middle 1970s the sociolinguistic position began to be criticized strongly by Ogbu (1978a, 1982). He identified a cause of school failure outside the school itself. Inequity in access to employment, he argued, had over many generations made minority people cynical about their life chances in American society. They communicated this cynicism to their children, and that accounted for the children's school failure.

In this chapter I will review the sociolinguistically oriented position and that of Ogbu. I will characterize the sociolinguistic position as a "communication process explanation" and Ogbu's position as a "perceived labor market explanation." I will then discuss both explanations in terms of a more comprehensive frame of reference, within which the two lines of explanation can be seen to be complementary in some ways although contradictory in others. I will also consider the nature of school failure and success. *School failure* in this discussion is used in two senses. It refers to the reflexive ways in which schools "work at" failing their students and students "work at" failing to achieve in school. School success is used in a similarly reflexive sense, as something the school does as well as what the student does. I will conclude by arguing that, whatever the reasons for school failure may be in schools, it is necessary for educators to transform routine practice and symbol systems in their own school settings as well as to work for change in the larger society. Changing society is a big order, and changing school societies is also a big order, in that it involves reorienting the daily struggles of doing school from collective work at failure toward collective work at success.

THESIS: THE COMMUNICATION PROCESS EXPLANATION

This position emphasizes the role of culturally learned verbal and nonverbal communication styles in explaining the high rates of school failure by students of low socioeconomic status and minority ethnic and cultural background. The argument is that, especially in the early grades, when teachers and students differ in implicit expectations of appropriateness in behavior, they act in ways that each misinterprets. Their expectations are derived from their experience outside school in what sociolinguists have called *speech communities* (Gumperz 1972) or, more recently, *speech networks*. The networks are sets of people who associate closely and who come to share similar assumptions about the appropriate uses and styles of communication. Culturally distinctive *ways of speaking* (Hymes 1974) differ from one speech network to the next. Boundaries between networks tend to run along the lines of major social divisions in modern mass societies, such as class, race or ethnicity, and first language background. Thus while many people in the United States belong to the same language community (i.e., they know the sound system, grammar, and vocabulary of English), they are members of differing speech networks (i.e., they have differing assumptions about ways of communicating that show functional intentions such as irony, sincerity, approval and positive concern, rapt attention, disinterest, disapproval, and the like). In addition, other subtle cultural differences obtain across networks—differences in assumptions regarding how much emotion should be displayed or felt, how social control should be exercised. There are differences in preferred room arrangements, body ornaments, and clothing styles. However, since it is the verbal and nonverbal aspects of interactional style that have been most intensively studied in recent sociolinguistically oriented educational anthropology, it is these differences that are mainly addressed here.

Cultural differences in ways of speaking and listening between the child's speech network and the teacher's speech network, according to the communication process explanation, lead to systematic and recurrent miscommunication in the classroom (Hymes 1972: xix–xxv). For example, if a child comes from a speech network in which direct questions are avoided because they are regarded as intrusive, when a teacher routinely asks that child a direct question in the classroom the child may be puzzled by the teacher's strange behavior, and assume that the teacher is angry. If the teacher comes from a speech network in which it is expected that listeners will show attention by direct eye contact while listening, and a child comes from a speech network in which it is considered impolite to look directly at a speaker, the teacher may infer that the child who is listening with averted eyes may be bored, confused, or angry.

To the extent that either party in these routine interactional engagements reflects on the situation, cultural explanations for what is happening do not occur to them. The teacher tends to use clinical labels and to attribute internal traits to students (e.g., "unmotivated") rather than seeing what is happening in terms of invisible cultural differences. Nor does the teacher see student behavior as interactionally generated—a dialectical relation in which the teacher is inadvertently coproducing with students the very behavior that he or she is taking as evidence of an individual characteristic of the student. Given the power difference between teacher and student, what could be seen as an interactional phenomenon to which teacher and student both contribute ends up institutionalized as an official diagnosis of student deficiency (Mehan 1978, 1980, 1987).

There is considerable empirical support for the communication process explanation. Numerous studies have documented interactional difficulty in elementary classrooms that is related to cultural differences in communication style (e.g., Barnhardt 1982, Erickson and Mohatt 1982, and Philips 1983, reporting studies of Native Americans in Alaska, Northern Ontario, and Oregon; and Heath 1983, Michaels and Collins 1984, and Piestrup 1973, reporting studies of urban and rural black Americans). In addition, Barnhardt and Heath, among others, have gone beyond documenting the existence of trouble that is related to cultural difference. They have also claimed that culturally responsive pedagogy resulted in higher school achievement and morale than was typical of Native American and black students in most schools. It should be emphasized, however, that the relationship between cultural difference in communication and actual school achievement is not clear, since most of the research that has been done on cultural differences in communication style between home and school was not designed to test directly a cause and effect relationship with school achievement. (Indeed, many ethnographers would argue that such inference is not possible in social science.)

One set of studies (Au and Mason 1981) comes as close as one can get toward demonstrating a causal connection between the cultural communication patterns of classroom discourse and academic achievement. This work was part of the research and development effort at the Kamehameha Elementary Education Program in Hawaii (see the discussion in Jordan 1985). In controlled experiments, two culturally differing ways of teaching reading were done with native Hawaiian first graders. In one way of teaching, the students followed mainstream Anglo patterns for the conduct of turn-taking while discussing reading stories. Those patterns required that only one child speak at a time. The other way of teaching was to allow students to overlap in speaking while others were speaking. This allowed students to comment and build on each other's comments. Overlapping talk of this kind was characteristic of certain kinds of speech situations that were common in students' experience in family and community life, especially in a named speech event, "talk-story." The way of teaching that incorporated talk-storylike ways of speaking can be called a culturally responsive pedagogy because it accommodated community cultural norms for conversation.

When conversation in reading lessons was organized in a talk-storylike way the students' participation was manifestly more enthusiastic than it was when overlapping turns at speaking were prohibited. Moreover, the students' understanding of the reading texts, as measured by tests given immediately after each lesson, was markedly greater when the talk-storylike conversational format was used by the teachers.

Why might so seemingly simple an adaptation as altering the structure of conversational turn-taking in a lesson enhance the school achievement of minority students? One line of explanation comes from anthropology—the cultural adaptation may reduce cultural shock in the classroom, enabling students to feel conversationally competent in familiar ways in an otherwise unfamiliar setting. In addition, the school's acceptance of ways of acting that the children employ in a mode of interaction that is positively regarded in their community may, even for young children, be perceived by them at some level as a symbolic affirmation of themselves and their community by the school. There may be a chance to feel a bit at home, to feel you know what you are doing, that what others do makes sense. You can feel that there is some safety in this new world, and that the teacher likes you.

Another line of explanation comes from cognitive psychology and cognitively oriented theories of reading instruction. By using a familiar conversational organization to approach the practice of unfamiliar concepts and skills (those of reading a text) the overall cognitive task structure is made simpler than it would be if both the social organizational aspects of the task and the academic subject matter organizational aspects of the task were unfamiliar. Thus students are able to concentrate mental effort on the reading rather than on the reading and the talking simultaneously. Moreover, the nature of talk-storylike conversation, in which conversational partners repeat and amplify each other's ideas, makes for a conversational environment appropriate for the kind of reading that was being asked of the children—"comprehension" of full sentences and of even larger discourse units in the written text, as constrasted to "decoding" of smaller text units, such as letter/sound combinations, morphemes, and words. When students talk overlapping above the sense of the story, echoing each other and adding ideas in a conversational "Dagwood sandwich" of many layers, they may, by the very repetition and overlapping in their talk, provide mutually constructed cognitive scaffolding for each other. This form of conversation may make it easier for students to grasp the idea of the story than if those ideas were strung out one by one, in more linear fashion, with less repetition.

In sum, the communication process explanation seems reasonable. It is warranted by theory in anthropology and psychology and by empirical evidence. Let us now turn to what has been presented as a competing explanation for school failure and success.

ANTITHESIS: THE PERCEIVED LABOR MARKET
EXPLANATION

This position, as articulated by its chief proponent, John Ogbu (1974, 1978a, 1982, 1987), argues that the main reason for the low school achievement of many minority students in the United States is that those students (and their parents and peers) are convinced that school success will not help them break out of a cycle of poverty that they attribute to the racism that is endemic in American society. Such minority students are members of what Ogbu calls "castelike" minority groups (e.g., blacks, Chicanos, Puerto Ricans) who have resided for generations in the United States in situations of oppression. Such groups are distinguished from immigrant minority groups who have not yet experienced oppression across many generations (e.g., Punjabis, Southeast Asians). In the castelike minority group, according to Ogbu, members share a fatalistic perspective—there will never be jobs (because of racism), so why try had to succeed at school? Ogbu sees the members of immigrant minority groups as much more optimistic about their life chances in American society. Things may be bad here, but not as bad as in the old country. Immigrant minority people in the United States may still be committed to their ethnic heritage yet also see the United States in a basically positive light. Since conditions in the United States are better than the extremely negative conditions they left when departing their home countries, the immigrants experience America, despite its flaws, as being a land of opportunity for them. Consequently, immigrant minority students and their parents believe that effort devoted to school success is likely to pay off in future employment. Students persist in their school work, encouraged in this by their parents, and this persistence accounts for their school success.

The labor market explanation has much to recommend it. First, there appears to be empirical support for it. In cross-cultural demographic and school achievement data (Ogbu 1978b), it appears that domestic minority students fare less well in school than do immigrant minority students. Indeed, immigrant minority students who come from groups that were in the position of being a domestic minority group in their country of origin in some cases seem to have done better in school in the United States than did comparable students from that ethnic group in the home country.

There seems also to be evidence that goes beyond that of formal research. The recent dramatic success in American schools of many students who were refugees from Southeast Asia is being mentioned in the press and in political debate as evidence that culturally differing students whose first language is not English can succeed in school without the special assistance of bilingual or multicultural education programs. Asian-American students represent an ever-increasing proportion of the graduate student population in American universities. This is also pointed to as evidence that cultural difference is not necessarily a barrier to school success.

Ogbu's demographic evidence appears to be borne out in ethnographic case studies of immigrant minority groups. For example, a study of Punjabi immigrants in a California town (Gibson 1987b, this volume) reports that despite linguistic and cultural differences between home and school and despite overt stigmatizing of Punjabi students in high school, those students showed higher graduation rates and academic performance than did domestic minority students within that same school system. Analogous case studies have been conducted in other immigrant ethnic communities.

The labor market explanation can also be justified because of its theoretical force. It is comprehensive in scope, linking phenomena across diverse levels of social organization. Ogbu's analysis shows how labor market conditions can be related to the local decisions of individuals in everyday life, as mediated by socially shared perceptions derived from experience as members of a social group that is either a domestic or an immigrant minority ethnic community. The explanation connects individual thought and action with the situation of individuals at the local school and community level and in the wider society and political economy.

In sum, on both theoretical and empirical grounds, it would seem that the perceived labor market explanation for school failure has much to recommend it. Yet so does the communication process explanation. The two positions are not mutually exclusive. Ogbu has repeatedly claimed that they are, however, arguing that the labor market explanation is the far more powerful factor (Ogbu 1982). He has distinguished between primary and secondary cultural differences—those characterizing domestic and immigrant minority groups, respectively. Using this distinction. he has argued that the cultural differences between speech networks in a mass society are so slight as to be trivial. (Ogbu 1982, 1987b:276). This seems too extreme a claim. It is necessary to reexamine to reexamine the two positions in relation to each other.

SYNTHESIS: THE POLITICS AND CULTURE OF SCHOOL FAILURE AND SUCCESS

One way to reconcile the two positions is to consider school motivation and achievement as a political process in which issues of institutional and personal legitimacy, identity, and economic interest are central. To do this we must also consider the nature of the symbolic discourse through which issues of legitimacy, identity, and interest are apprehended and framed by individual students and teachers in local communities and schools. Social theory as related to pedagogical theory—more especially, implication of resistance theory—provide a framework within which the alternative explanations can be reconsidered (see Giroux 1983; see also Apple and Weis 1983; Everhart 1983). I will begin the synthesis with a negative critique of the two positions as originally stated. Within that critique some facets of resistance theory will be mentioned. These will be elaborated later in the discussion.

Both the communication process explanation and the labor market explanation have some inadequacies. The first type of inadequacy involves accounting for certain kinds of school success. The kinds of school success that go unaccounted for differ for the two explanations. First I will consider the communication process explanation. That explanation can account for the success of strategies for teaching caste-like minority students that involve culturally responsive pedagogy. But some teaching strategies have been successful that do not involve culturally responsive pedagogy—at least the strategies do not involve use of communication styles found in children's homes.

We can find instances of teaching domestic minority students (Ogbu's "castelike" minority students) in which teachers go to great lengths not to have classroom interaction resemble interaction patterns found in the students' homes and communities. One thinks immediately of Black Muslim schools, of inner-city Roman Catholic parochial schools with white teachers, of special nonsectarian schools such as that of Marva Collins in Chicago (in which a curriculum is built on classic literature of Western Europe), and of special programs designed for minority populations, such as the intense drill and practice sessions conducted according to predetermined scripts in the DISTAR model for early grades education. One thinks as well of the countless cases of individual teachers who are unusually effective with domestic minority students but who know very little about the students' home cultural communication patterns and who do not teach by making use of those patterns instructionally. There are the cases, already discussed, of immigrant minority students who achieve in school without special bilingual instruction or culturally responsive pedagogy. These are very different kinds of instances. At some level, however, each does "work," in that students rise to the challenge, put forth effort, and appear to be doing well academically, in terms of achievement as measured by standardized test scores. (That such measurements can be criticized as too narrow and too literal a way of defining achievement is an issue beyond the scope of this chapter.) How is such a school success possible, if the instructional processes violate the expectations of students regarding communicative routines and norms? The communication process explanation as presented above cannot account for any school success save that attributed to culturally responsive pedagogy. This reveals the communication process explanation, taken literally and read narrowly, as an implicitly cultural determinist position in which cultural difference is seen as necessarily leading to trouble and conflict and cultural similarity is seen (implicitly at least) as necessarily leading to rapport and the absence of conflict.

The perceived labor market explanation can account for the school success of immigrant minority students in school. It does not account for the success of domestic minority students, whether the conditions of that success involve culturally responsive pedagogy or not. Yet instances of school success by domestic minority students and their teachers do occur. Even though, in the majority of cases, domestic minority students do not show high rates of school success, enough exceptions to that general pattern can be found so as to raise serious questions about the adequacy of the perceived labor market explanation as it has been articulated presently.

The perceived labor market argument has two chief weaknesses, in my judgment. First and fundamentally, if taken literally and read narrowly it is an economic determinist argument. It appears to presume a strictly functionalist social theory in the manner of Comte and Durkheim or of the later writings of Marx or of Althusser—an organic or mechanical view of society in which there are tight and invariant causal connections across subsystems so that the general social structure drives the actions, perceptions, and sentiments of particular actors in local scenes of action. In such a view there is no room for human agency. Such a social theory, when applied to education, implies that neither the domestic minority students nor their teachers can do anything positive together educationally.

The second major weakness in the labor market explanation is less fundamental, yet also serious. This has to do with the empirical validity of the work. The very comprehensiveness of the causal argument, for all that it satisfies one theoretically, makes the argument very shaky on empirical grounds. Causal linkages across system levels are asserted in the models that Ogbu has published, but those causal relationships are merely asserted, not demonstrated directly. Where empirical quantitative evidence bears on the assertions it is entirely correlational, and no amount of correlational evidence can demonstrate cause. Where empirical ethnographic evidence is presented, as in the case studies of high-achieving immigrant minority students, causal relationships are also not shown. Moreover, these case studies cannot tell us how immigrant minority students might fare in less culturally alien school environments than the ones they usually encounter in the United States. Perhaps the immigrant minority students would do even better than they do already if they were educated in a more culturally responsive learning environment.

It seems necessary to consider the nature of school success or failure from points of view not directly covered by either of the alternative explanations as I have presented them in summary fashion. To speak of school success or failure is to speak of learning or not learning what is deliberately taught there.[1] Learning is ubiquitous in human experience throughout the life cycle, and humans are very good at it. They are also good at fostering learning through deliberate instruction (Poirier and Hussey 1982). Yet in schools, deliberately taught learning seems to be a problem. It is differently distributed along lines of class, race, ethnicity, and language background.

Students in school, like other humans, learn constantly. When we say they are "not learning" what we mean is that they are not learning what school authorities, teachers, and administrators intend for them to learn as the result of intentional instruction (Gearing and Sangree 1979). Learning what is deliberately taught can be seen as a form of political assent. Not learning can be seen as a form of political resistance.

Assent to the exercise of authority involves trust that its exercise will be benign. This involves a leap of faith—trust in the legitimacy of the authority and in the good intentions of those exercising it, trust that one's own identity will be maintained positively in relation to the authority, and trust that one's own interests will be advanced by compliance with the exercise of authority. In taking such a leap of faith one faces risk. If there is no risk, trust is unnecessary. (I should note here that I do not mean in this discussion to imply that the existential choices to be made are necessarily considered in reflective awareness. They may well be made intuitively. But however apprehended, a sense of trust entails a sense of risk.)

In pedagogy it is essential that the teacher and students establish and maintain trust in each other at the edge of risk (Howard van Ness, personal communication). To learn is to entertain risk, since learning involves moving just past the level of competence, what is already mastered, to the nearest region of incompetence, what has not yet been mastered. As learning takes place, the leading edge of the region of incompetence is continually moving. A useful analogy is that of riding a surfboard—in learning, one must lean forward into a constantly shifting relationship with the crest of the wave. In teacher/learner interaction, the learner places himself or herself at the edge of incompetence and is drawn slightly beyond it with the assistance of the teacher and/or other students. Vygotsky (1978:84–91) refers to this as the "zone of proximal development"—that region within which the learner can function with the assistance of another more competent partner. As the learner's bottom threshhold of competence rises (that level at which the learner can function unassisted) so does the top threshold (the level beyond which the student cannot function effectively even with the aid of a teacher).

---

[1] Admittedly it is also important to school success that students learn, or at least appear to comply with, what is nondeliberately taught (i.e., the "hidden curriculum"). Yet what seems to me crucial to school success is that students appear to comply with what school staff think they are trying to teach (i.e., the manifest curriculum of academic and social skills and knowledge).

Thus the zone of proximal development can be thought of as constantly moving upward. However, as new learning takes place with a teacher, the student again engages risk because the student reenters the zone within which he cannot function successfully alone. If the teacher is not trustworthy the student cannot count on effective assistance from the teacher; there is high risk of being revealed (to self and to others) as incompetent. Risk is also involved for the teacher. If the teacher engages a student with the genuine intention to foster the student's learning and the student then fails to learn what the teacher intended, the teacher is revealed, at best, as less than consummately competent pedagogically.

Risk is exciting, yet dangerous. Both for the student and for the teacher, risk in the form of a potential threat to positive social identity seems inherent in the process of learning. Consequently the legitimacy of the school and its teachers, affirmed at the existential level as trust by individual students, is essential if deliberate instruction is to succeed in its aims. School success must be earned by the school staff as well as the students in a process of political rhetoric by which the subordinates in the institution are persuaded to assent to the authority of the superordinates.

Legitimacy, trust, and interest are phenomena that are both institutional and existential. As institutional phenomena, they are located in the social structure and in patterns of role relationships that recur over long time spans and are differentially allocated according to access to monetary capital and cultural capital. But legitimacy, trust, and interest are also existential and emergent phenomena that are continually negotiated within the intimate circumstances and short time scale of everyday encounters between individual teachers, students, and parents. The institutional legitimacy of the school is affirmed existentially as trust in face-to-face encounters between school staff and students and their parents.[2]

Labor market inequity, as perceived by members of a domestic minority community, and conflictual teacher/student interaction that derives in part from culturally differing communicative styles can both be seen as impediments to the trust that constitutes an existential foundation for school legitimacy. It is appropriate therefore to look outside the school, into the local community and the broader social order, as well as inside the school, within classroom interaction, to identify the roots of educational failure or success, trust or mistrust, assent or dissent.

---

[2] The distinction between institutional and existential aspects of legitimacy, and the distinction and connection between the long and short-term patterns by which we can see connections between general history and social order and specific, concrete history and social order, is made in an essay on social theory by Giddens (1984). A related notion is found in the approach to intellectual history taken by Foucault (1979), and in the literary theory of Bakhtin (1981).

I want now to amend the previous discussion of the communication process explanation. We can apply the notion of resistance—withholding of assent—to the progressive development of conflict that occurs between teachers and some domestic minority students. In considering relationships between minority group cultures and student resistance in intercultural learning environments, we can make an important and useful distinction. This is the distinction between cultural boundaries and cultural borders.

Cultural boundaries can be thought of as behavioral evidence of culturally differing standards of appropriateness—for example, two subculturally differing ways of pronouncing final consonants. Boundaries—the manifest presence of cultural difference—are politically neutral phenomena; no difference in rights and obligations accrues to persons who act in either of the culturally differing ways. In situations of intergroup conflict, however, cultural boundaries can be treated as cultural borders; that is, the features of culture difference are no longer politically neutral phenomena. Rights and obligations are allocated differently, depending on whether a person is revealed as possessing one kind of cultural knowledge rather than another.[3]

Different groups with different interests at stake can treat the existence of behaviorally similar items politically as opportunities for cultural boundary work or border work. This was dramatically apparent in my own early research on ethnic and racial cultural differences in communication style in the United States (Erickson 1975; Erickson and Shultz 1982). In detailed analysis of filmed interviews between college counselors or job interviewers and students or job applicants, it was apparent that sometimes subtle cultural differences in communication style made a big difference for rapport and understanding, and sometimes the cultural differences did not seem to impede rapport and understanding. In the absence of special positive motivation to communicate, cultural difference did seem to make interaction difficult. But this was not always true, and it varied from occasion to occasion for the same individual. Distinguishing between cultural boundaries and borders enables one to consider cultural difference as significant in intergroup relations without falling into the trap of a cultural determinist argument. As Bekker and I have noted:

> Cultural difference can be thought of as a risk factor in the school experience of students and teachers; it need not cause trouble but it usually provides opportunities for trouble.... Those opportunities can serve as resources for escalating conflict that might already exist for

---

[3] The distinction between cultural borders and boundaries was made initially by Barth (1969), and has been elaborated in terms of its implications for education by McDermott and Gospodinoff (1979) and by Erickson and Bekker (1986).

other reasons, such as conflict between social classes, genders, or races (Erickson and Bekker 1986:175, 177)

To understand this rather abstract argument more fully let us turn to an instance of classroom research by Piestrup (1973). She studied desegregated first grade classrooms in which predominantly working-class black children were taught with predominantly middle-class white children. We will first look at a single point in time in the school year: a moment in a reading lesson. Then we will consider what Piestrup reports as patterns of resistance that developed across the course of the whole year.

We can consider an example from Piestrup's study of working-class black and middle-class white children and their teachers (Piestrup 1973:96-97). In this example of a first grade reading lesson, all the children are black. (*CC* in the transcript means *children reading aloud in chorus*):

1	**T:**	All right, class, read that and remember your endings.
2	**CC:**	"What did Little Duck see?" (final *t* of "what" deleted)
3	**T:**	What. (emphasis on final *t*)
4	**CC:**	What (final *t* deleted, as in turn 2)
5	**T:**	I still don't hear this sad little "*t.*"
6	**CC:**	"What did—What did—What—(final *t*'s deleted)
7	**T:**	What.
8	**T&CC:**	"What did Little Duck see?" (final *t* spoken)
9	**T:**	OK, very good.

By saying "What" (line 3) with special emphasis on the final /t/ the teacher has adopted a midcourse correction in order to emphasize and correct a particular detail of oral performance. In so doing the teacher departed from the aim of the initial question, which focused on the general content of the utterance being read. Fostering standard English pronunciation in reading aloud is one pedagogical aim, while fostering comprehension of the text being read is another pedagogical aim. What indeed was it that Little Duck saw? We don't know. If the transcription were to continue we could see whether or not the comprehension point got lost entirely as the teacher went on after having sidetracked the students for their nonstandard pronunciation style.

The teacher's emphasis on the final /t/ is not necessary in terms of the aim of teaching comprehension. We can infer that this is not just a matter of simple miscommunication—the teacher not understanding the children's answers. We can assume that he or she could hear the children saying "wha" (in turns 2 and 4) as standing for "what," with the final /t/ pronounced. Rather, we can see this as a deliberate lesson in pronunciation (in turn 1 the teacher said "...and remember your endings"). This was to make a special point of the cultural communication style of the black children and to do so in a negative way.

The cultural border work—making cultural communication style a negative phenomenon in the classroom—seems to have stimulated student resistance that was manifested linguistically. In some of the classrooms the teacher was white, in others the teacher was black. Piestrup monitored the speech style of the working-class black children across the whole school year. In those classrooms in which the teacher, whether black or white, negatively sanctioned the children's use of black English vernacular, by the end of the year the children spoke a more exaggerated form of that dialect that they had done at the beginning of the year. The opposite was true in the classrooms in which the teacher, whether black or white, did not negatively sanction the black English vernacular spoken by the black students. In those classrooms by the end of the year the black children were speaking in the classroom in ways that more closely approximated standard English than did their ways of speaking at the beginning of the year. Consider the implications of this. The culturally distinctive oral performance of working-class black children was initially present in both kinds of classrooms. In the latter kind of classroom the speech style of the students did not become an occasion for stigma and resistance. In the former kind of classroom, however, the use of black English vernacular became an occasion for stigmatizing border work by the teachers and for resistance by the children. As that happened, and as the year progressed, the speech style of the children became more and more different from that of the teacher. This meant that cultural difference was increasing in a situation of cross-cultural contact. This is an instance of a more general phenomenon—progressive cultural differentiation across time as a means of symbolic distancing between competing groups that are subsystems of a larger system. That phenomenon has been called *complementary schismogenesis* by Bateson (1975:107-127), who sees it as a basic process of culture change.[4]

By amending the sociolinguistic communication process explanation for school failure and considering a case of a reading lesson, we can see that cultural difference can, for a variety of reasons, be an initial source of trouble

---

[4] Piestrup's is a single study, to be sure, and some could argue that too much weight should not rest on it in the line of explanation set forth here. But the phenomenon Piestrup reports has been found more generally. The phenomenon is increasing speech style differentiation between speakers across time in situations of conflict. This has been reported in shorter and longer time spans than the single school year studied by Piestrup. Giles and Powesland (1975) showed that social class and regional dialect styles diverged across half-hour conversations in which conflict was experimentally induced. Reporting naturalistic research, Labov (1963) has shown how, across a generation, certain features of the dialect of islanders from Martha's Vineyard have become more marked. Thus the speech of the islanders has become progressively and more distinct from that of tourists who visit the island in the summer.

between teachers and students. But apparently the story does not stop there. What may have begun as simple misinterpretation of intent and literal meaning can develop across time into entrenched, emotionally intense conflict between teacher and student. The cycle can repeat from year to year during elementary school (see McDermott and Gospodinoff 1979).

Teachers and students in such regressive relationships do not bond with each other. Mutual trust is sacrificed. Over time the students become increasingly alienated from school. It is no longer a matter of difference between teacher and student that derives from intergenerationally transmitted communicative traditions. It is also a matter of cultural invention as a medium of resistance in a situation of political conflict. As students grow older and experience repeated failure and repeated negative encounters with teachers, they develop oppositional cultural patterns as a symbol of their disaffiliation with what they experience (not necessarily within full reflective awareness) as an illegitimate and oppressive system. The more alienated the students become, the less they persist in doing schoolwork. Thus they fall farther and farther behind in academic achievement. The student becomes either actively resistant—seen as salient and incorrigible—or passively resistant—fading into the woodwork as an anonymous well-behaved, low-achieving student.

Bekker and I further observed:

> Why would it be a punishable offense for a young black man in an urban American high school to wear a black leather coat in the school hallway?...If a principal can suspend an adolescent for wearing a leather coat, some kind of interactional process of evaluation is happening in which judgments of social identity change in negative directions. If students are dressing in such ways then perhaps the problem is not just a matter of cultural patterns that do not fit. Rather it would seem that struggle is going on—struggle that is mutually constructed by teachers and students who, as conflict escalates over time and their forbearance for one another runs out, become locked in regressive social relationships to which all parties in the local social contribute, as in pathological interaction systems in families. McDermott and Tylbor (1983) use the term *collusion* when describing, this cycle of progressively intense conflict (Erickson and Bekker 1986:177)

Some of Ogbu's recent research suggests that by the time American black students are of high school age, cultural differentiation through resistance has developed to the point that a sharp distinction is made between "acting black" and "acting white." The political definition of school instruction as legitimate or illegitimate is caught up in this symbolic opposition.

Ogbu has noted this phenomenon, citing DeVos (1982) on the development of oppositional identity by domestic minority students. Ogbu observes that

> minority students who adopt the school style in communication, interaction, or learning may be accused of "acting white." Even more serious a problem is that castelike minority students may define academic effort or success as part of the white cultural frame of reference or white way of behavior (1987:268)

Ogbu refers here to research of Signithia Fordham (Fordham and Ogbu 1986). Her findings were reported on National Public Radio ("All Things Considered," 12 June 1987). Phyllis Crockett, an NPR reporter, interviewed two high-achieving black adolescents from the study:

Reporter: Black (high school) students who spend reasonable amounts of time studying and who speak Standard English can be accused by their peers of acting white....This student, we'll call him Eric, attends an inner-city school in Washington, D.C.

Eric: People are afraid to show that they can speak grammatically correct English. When I do, my friends in my neighborhood will say "You nerd!" or "Talk English! Talk to us like we talk to you."

Reporter: High school students, like this student we'll call Paula, who take college prep courses, often are called "oreos"—like the cookie, black on the outside, white on the inside.

Paula: I've been *per se* called an oreo because black as I am and bright, everybody thinks I'm too proper and talk white...and people tend to *tease* me.

Notice that Eric's and Paula' peers focus on their speech style as a badge of group identity. Two points are especially relevant here—the subtlety of the cultural judgments involved and the process of oppositional identity maintenance that is revealed. As evidenced by their recorded speech while addressing the NPR reporter, Eric and Paula do not, in fact, speak fully Standard English. Their grammar is standard but in pronunciation, in voice pitch and stress patterns, and in word choice (i.e., Paula's interpolation of a "fancy" term, *per se*), Eric's and Paula's speech is characteristic of nonstandard black English. Thus Eric's and Paula's peers are making a big issue of slight divergence from a cultural norm. Fine nuances of cultural performance are being attended to as salient, not large cultural differences such as those between immigrant students and American students. These are secondary cultural differences, according to Ogbu's taxonomy (1982). The cultural differences are small, but they are not trivial as Ogbu has claimed

(1987) because they are not being treated as trivial by the actors themselves. On the contrary, Eric's and Paula's friends seem to be treating such cultural differences as a powerful political symbol.

The peers of the high-achieving students use strong sanctions to enforce a stringent cultural standard that symbolizes group membership. This is border maintenance work. It is significant that the students do not invoke the inequity of the labor market. They do not say, "You can't get a job in white America." Rather, their message is much more indirect. Their immediate focus is on the maintenance of oppositional identity within everyday life in school.

In the example of Eric and Paula, the vehemence of the exercise of sanctions and the focus on subtle features of cultural distinctiveness recall the earlier classroom example in which the teacher made a big issue of a final consonant ("What did Little Duck see?"). The first grade teacher was forcing working-class black children to speak Standard English. In mirror image, Eric's and Paula's working-class black adolescent friends are forcing them to speak nonstandard English. Identity definition is involved in both cases. It is the voice and locus of authority and definition that has changed; from the teacher's voice as an individual institutional officer doing border work on white culture to the students' voices doing collective and institutionally illegitimate border work on black culture.[5] In both examples culturally patterned speech performance becomes a symbolic medium within which a student is forced to takes sides between "us" and "them."

The situation reported for American black students is reminiscent of the resistance to school achievement among working-class English high school males reported by Willis (1977). It is also reminiscent of a speculation by Scollon and Scollon (1981) that many Native American school students in Koyukon Athabascan villages of the Alaskan interior associate the acquisition of literacy with betrayal of ethnic identity. Since the students see so many members of their communities as nonliterate (including their parents), to learn to read and write fluently would seem metaphorically to be leaving the community and to be no longer Koyukon.

To summarize, consistent patterns of refusal to learn in school can be seen as a form of resistance to a stigmatized ethnic or social class identity that is being assigned by the school. Students can refuse to accept that negative identity by refusing to learn. Yet the sensitivity and salience of stigmatized ethnic identity among teenagers who are members of domestic minority groups (and of working-class identity more generally) is not a phenomenon that derives exclusively from within a school. Students' school experiences may contribute to their need to resist acceptance of a stigmatized identity, but

---

[5] On the significance of the collective nature of the students's actions, see Everhart 1983:186–187.

the sources of such an identity lie in part outside the school in the conditions of access to the labor market and in the general assumptions of nonstigmatized members of society regarding the members of stigmatized groups.

This is why, within the perspective of resistance theory, both the communication process and the labor market explanations of school failure can be seen as complementary. Influences from outside the immediate school experience of students and teachers, including labor market opportunity as perceived by parents and other members of the minority community, are clearly important to consider, especially among older students for whom issues of future employment become more and more salient. But it is also important to consider the immediate school experience of students and teachers, including the culturally differing communication styles of students and teachers, especially as young children encounter school initially in the early grades and as they continue through high school. Perception of the labor market and cultural style difference both appear to be involved in the development by domestic minority students of oppositional identity in school.

I have argued that both the perceived labor market explanation and the communication process explanation when read literally have serious limitations. Each can be seen as at least implicitly determinist, leaving little room for human agency. Each has trouble accounting for certain kinds of school success. It is therefore appropriate to attach a coda considering some of the reasons why school success might happen with populations of students for whom such success seems demographically unlikely. Let us say that we wanted to try to transform school struggle from working at failure to something more productive. Where then might we look to start?

CODA

If education can be no more than an epiphenomenon tied directly to the requirements of an economy, then little can be done within education itself. It is a totally determined institution. However, if schools (and people) are not passive mirrors of an economy, but instead are active agents in the processes of reproduction and contestation of dominant social relations, then understanding what they do and acting upon them becomes of no small moment. For if schools are part of a "contested terrain,"...then the hard and continuous day-to-day struggle at the level of curriculum and teaching practice is part of these larger conflicts as well. The key is linking these day-to-day struggles within the school to other action for a more progressive society in that wider arena. (Apple and Weis 1983:22)

As an educator I cannot accept the premise that there is nothing we can do to improve the educational situation of domestic minority students in the United States. I am not simply willing to wait for a revolution in the general society. As Apple and Weis have pointed out, there are progressive choices people can make in their own immediate circumstances while they also work for social change in the wider society. The task is not only to analyze the structural conditions by which inequity is reproduced in society but to search out every possible site in which the struggle for progressive transformation can take place.

Schools are one of the arenas in which people can work to change the existing distributions of power and knowledge in our society. When school practice is conducted according to the existing conventional wisdom, minority students—especially domestic minority students—usually do not fare well. The conventional wisdom involves assumptions that are part of the cultural hegemony of established classes in society. Hegemony refers to the ubiquitous and taken-for-granted status of a dominant culture within a culturally plural and class-stratified society such as the United States. Because of the ubiquity of the dominant culture and of the institutional arrangements that are consonant with its assumptions, it is not necessary for dominant groups to use overt means, that is, naked force, to maintain their position of advantage. Rather as members of the society, dominant and subordinate alike, act routinely in concert with the cultural assumptions and interests of the dominant group, existing power relationships can be maintained, as it were, by an invisible hand. This is the essential element in Gramsci's notion of hegemony (Bluci-Glucksmann 1982); through influence, leadership, and by consent from the masses themselves, domination comes to appear as reasonable.[6]

Hegemonic practices are routine actions and unexamined beliefs that are consonant with the cultural system of meaning and ontology within which it makes sense to take certain actions, entirely without malevolent intent, that nonetheless systematically limit the life chances of members of stigmatized groups. Were it not for the regularity of hegemonic practices, resistance by the stigmatized would not be necessary. Were it not for the capacity of the established to regard hegemonic practices as reasonable and just, resistance could be more overt. Resistance could be informed by an explicit social analysis that unmasks the practices as oppressive. Yet currently neither the oppressors nor the oppressed face squarely the character of their situation, and resistance is often inchoate just as oppression is not deliberately intended.[7]

---

[6] Considered in this light, Gramsci looks like an anthropologist. He can be seen as presenting a cultural analysis of the plausibility of domination.

[7] For further discussion, see Giroux 1983.

Hegemonic practices are not only ramified throughout the general society and in the local community outside the school; they are also alive and well inside the classroom. They permeate and frame the school experience of students who are members of stigmatized social groups. These practices are enacted by particular social actors. Domination and alienation of the oppressed does not simply happen by the anonymous workings of social structural forces. People do it. It is the result of choice (not necessarily deliberate) to cooperate with the reigning ideologic definitions of what minority students are, what curriculum is, what good teaching is.

Yet if hegemonic practices are the result of human choice, they are not inevitable. Particular individuals can scrutinize the options enjoined by the conventional wisdom of practice. They can decide which aspects of that conventional wisdom to adopt and which to reject, creating learning environments that not only do not stigmatize minority students, but stimulate them to achieve.

Reconsider what Piestrup's teacher did in the reading lesson. She insisted that the children pronounce the final /t/ in the word "what," while reading the sentence, "What did Little Duck see?" This can be seen as an instance of hegemonic practice (James Collins, personal communication). What makes it so is that the teacher's exercise of a particular pedagogical option at a certain point in the lesson is consonant with a widely held theory or philosophy of reading instruction. According to one well-established view of good reading teaching, drill on isolated subskills, such as recognition and pronunciation of a final /t/, and mastery of that subskill must necessarily precede moving on to mastering the so-called higher order skills of comprehension.

According to another well-established view, the "whole language" or "language experience" approach comprehension of larger semantic units in written discourse takes precedence over drill on isolated subskills. The teacher in this example was not, we can infer, deliberately choosing to make salient in a negative way the culturally patterned pronunciation the children have learned in their homes. Rather, the teacher was acting on a strongly supported belief about good reading teaching. Yet entailed in the choice of one pedagogical strategy rather than another is the opportunity to make a culture trait negatively salient or not. If the teacher had emphasized the sense of the text, focusing on what in fact Little Duck had seen, the children's pronunciation style would not have become visible in the lesson interaction as a stigmatizing badge of racial and social class identity.

We could simply write off the reading lesson example as one in which the teacher produced contradiction and cognitive confusion by beginning one way and then going off on another instructional tack. But I think the example shows more than that, since the new option that was followed—pronunciation correction—made salient the children's home cultural style and negatively evaluated that style. Thus we would not just want to say to this teacher, "Be consistent." We would want the teacher to learn to reflect on his or her practice and say, "What are the consequences of my being consistent in following one pedagogical aim or another?" From the point of view of culturally responsive pedagogy as informed by resistance theory, the teacher could conclude that to choose to fight and temporarily win a small battle over the pronunciation of a final consonant is to risk losing the war, by setting off a long-term process of schismogenetic cultural conflict. The threat to trust inherent in engaging in the pronunciation battle may simply not be worth it in the long run.[8]

In the cultural politics of pedagogy in the early grades one route to maintaining trust and earning the learner's assent to learn is to adapt instruction in the direction of the students' home cultural communication style. We saw this in adaptation to Hawaiian conversational turn-taking patterns, and we considered a hypothetical strategy for avoiding needless conflict over black American children's pronunciation while reading aloud.

Culturally responsive pedagogy is not the only route to establishing and maintaining trust and legitimacy between teacher and students, however. If children and their parents believe very strongly in the legitimacy of school staff and in the content and aims of a school program, as in the case of a black Muslim school (or in the case of some immigrant minority students and their parents as they encounter an arbitrary American public school), then even if the cultural style of classroom interaction is very discontinuous with that of the children's early childhood experience, they may well learn the new cultural styles without setting off a chain reaction of resistance and cultural schismogenesis. The same could hold for the models of "direct instruction" currently mooted. If instructional patterns are very clear and consistent (unlike the reading lesson about Little Duck), the teacher believes strongly in what he or she is doing, and children and parents can recognize the teacher's unambivalently authoritative style as a sincere attempt to foster minority children's learning, then the children may trust the teacher and assent to learn, even though the interaction style of instruction violates the minority community's norms regarding appropriate communication style.

To conclude, the politics of legitimacy, trust, and assent seem to be the most fundamental factors in school success. For cultural minority students, whether immigrant or domestic, the role of culture and of cultural difference varies in relation to school success. In some exceptional circumstances, because of high motivation to succeed in school cultural difference does not seem to prevent students from persisting and achieving. A much more

---

[8] We could argue that such pronunciation battles always makes bad sense in reading instruction—indeed, that reading aloud itself is unnecessary in reading lessons—but these are matters beyond the scope of this article.

prevalent pattern, I have argued, is for cultural differences to make a negative difference, (1) because they contribute to miscommunication in the early grades and (2) because those initial problems of miscommunication escalate into student distrust and resistance in later grades. Moreover, it is important to note that for typical public schools (as distinct from special schools or alternative programs), it appears that in dealing with the majority of domestic minority students, school personnel cannot count on being perceived as highly legitimate, nor can they count on high motivation to learn when they try to teach in learning environments that are culturally alien to the students. Rather, if the ordinary public school is to be perceived as legitimate, the school must earn that perception by its local minority community. This involves a profound shift in the direction of daily practice and its symbolism, away from hegemonic practice and toward transformative practice. In the absence of special effort by the school, the deep distrust of its legitimacy that increases among students as they grow older and the resources for resisting by developing oppositional identity that the school provides (in the cultural hegemony that inheres in its routine ways of doing daily business) pose serious threats to the school's perceived legitimacy. On the other hand, it appears that immigrant minority students may tend to be likely to trust the legitimacy of the school as it currently exists and to hope to benefit by participating in the American labor market.

Culturally responsive pedagogy is one kind of special effort by the school that can reduce miscommunication by teachers and students, foster trust, and prevent the genesis of conflict that moves rapidly beyond intercultural misunderstanding to bitter struggles of negative identity exchange between some students and their teachers. In the light of the preceding discussion, culturally responsive pedagogy seems most appropriate and important in the early grades. It may be especially important for domestic minority students and less important for first generation immigrant minority students. It is only one piece in a large puzzle, yet it provides a positive option for educators who wish, through critically reflective practice, to improve the chances for learning by their students and to improve their own work life as well. Culturally responsive pedagogy is not a total solution. It can, however, be seen as part of a total solution that also includes work to transform the general society within which schooling takes place.

REFERENCES

Apple, Michael W., and Lois Weis
    1983   Ideology and Practice in Schooling: A Political and Conceptual Introduction. *In* Ideology and Practice in Schooling. M. Apple and L. Weis, eds. Pp. 3–34. Philadelphia: Temple University Press.

Au, Kathryn H., and Jana Mason
  1981   Social Organizational Factors in Learning to Read: The Balance of Rights Hypothesis. Reading Research Quarterly 17(1):115–152.
Bakhtin, Mikhail M.
  1981   *The Dialogic Imagination*, Michael Holquist, ed. Austin, TX: University of Texas Press.
Baratz, Joan, and Steven Baratz
  1970   Early Childhood Intervention: The Social Science Base of Institutional Racism. Harvard Educational Review 40(1)29–50.
Barnhardt, Carol
  1982   "Tuning-in": Athabaskan Teachers and Athabaskan Students. *In* Cross-Cultural Issues in Alaskan Education, vol. 2. Fairbanks: University of Alaska, Center for Cross-Cultural Studies.
Barth, Frederik
  1969   *Ethnic Groups and Boundaries: The Social Organization of Culture Difference.* Boston: Little, Brown & Co.
Bateson, Gregory
  1975   Steps to an Ecology of Mind. New York: Ballantine Books.
Bereiter, Carl, and Siegfried Engelmann
  1966   Teaching Disadvantaged Children in the Preschool. Englewood Cliffs, NJ: Prentice-Hall.
Bluci-Glucksmann, Christine
  1982   Hegemony and Consent: A Political Strategy. *In* Approaches to Gramsci. A. S. Sasson, ed. Pp. 116–126. London: Writers and Readers Cooperative Society.
Deutsch, Martin, et al.
  1967   The Disadvantaged Child. New York: Basic Books.
DeVos, George A.
  1982   Adaptive Strategies in U.S. Minorities. *In* Minority Mental Health. E. E. Jones and S. J. Korchin, eds. Pp. 74–117. New York: Praeger.
Erickson, Frederick D.
  1975   Gatekeeping and the Melting Pot: Interaction in Counseling Encounters. Harvard Educational Review 45(1):44–70.
Erickson, Frederick D., and Gary J. Bekker
  1986   On Anthropology. *In* The Contributions of the Social Sciences to Educational Policy and Practice: 1965–1985. Berkeley: McCutchan.
Erickson, Frederick D., and Gerald Mohatt
  1982   Cultural Organization of Participation Structures in Two Classrooms of Indian Students. *In* Doing the Ethnography of Schooling: Educational Anthropology in Action. George D. Spindler, ed. Pp. 132–175. New York: Holt, Rinehart & Winston.
Erickson, Frederick D., and Jeffrey Shultz
  1982   The Counselor as Gatekeeper: Social Interaction in Interviews. New York: Academic Press.
Everhart, Robert B.
  1983   Classroom Management, Student Opposition, and the Labor Process. *In*

Ideology and Practice in Schooling. M. Apple and L. Weis, eds. Pp. 169–192. Philadelphia: Temple University Press.

Fordham, Signithia, and John U. Ogbu
 1986   Back Students' School Success: Coping with the "Burden of Acting White." Urban Review 18(3):176–206.

Foucault, Michel
 1979   *Discipline and Punish: The Birth of the Prison.* New York: Random House (Vintage Books)

Gearing, Fred, and Lucinda Sangree
 1979   Toward a Cultural Theory of Education and Schooling. The Hague: Mouton.

Gibson, Margaret A.
 1987b   Punjabi Immigrants in an American High School. *In* Interpretive Ethnography of Education: At Home and Abroad. G. Spindler and L. Spindler, eds. Pp. 281–310. Hillsdale, NJ: Erlbaum.

Giddens, Anthony
 1984   *The Constitution of Society: Outline of the Theory of Structuration.* Berkeley and Los Angeles, CA: University of California Press.

Giles, Howard and Powesland, F.
 1975   *Speech Style and Social Evaluation.* London: Academic Press.

Giroux, H.
 1983   Theories of Reproduction and Resistance in the New Sociology of Education: A Critical Analysis. Harvard Educational Review 53(3)257–293.

Gumperz, John J.
 1972   The Speech Community. *In* Language and Social Context. P. P. Giglioli, ed. Pp. 219–231. Harmondsworth, Middlesex, England: Penguin Education.

Hess, Robert, and Virginia Shipman
 1965   Early Experience and the Socialization of Cognitive Modes in Children. Child Development 36:869–886.

Heath, Shirley Brice
 1983   Ways with Words: Language, Life, and Work in Communities and Classrooms. Cambridge: Cambridge University Press

Hymes, Dell H.
 1972   Introduction. *In* Functions of Language in the Classroom. Courtney B. Cazden, Vera P. John, and Dell Hymes, eds. New York: Teachers College Press.
 1974   On Ways of Speaking. *In* Exploration in the Ethnography of Speaking. P. Bauman and J. Sherzer, eds. New York: Cambridge University Press.

Jordan, Cathie
 1985   Translating Culture: From Ethnographic Information to Educational Program. Anthropology and Education Quarterly 16(2):105–123.

Labov, W.
 1963   The Social Motivation of a Sound Change. *Word 19;* 273–309. (Also published in W. Labov, *Sociolinguistic Patterns.* Philadelphia, PA: University of Pennsylvania Press, 1972, pp. 1–42)

McDermott, Raymond P., and Kenneth Gospodinoff
 1979   Social Contexts for Ethnic Borders and School Failure. *In* Nonverbal Behavior. A. Wolfgang, ed. New York: Academic Press.

McDermott, Raymond P., and Henry Tylbor
   1983   On the Necessity of Collusion in Conversation. Text 3(3):277–297.
Mehan, Hugh
   1978   Structuring School Structure. Harvard Educational Review 48(1):32–64.
   1980   The Competent Student. Anthropology and Education Quarterly
          11(3):131–152.
   1987   Language and Schooling. *In* Interpretive Ethnography of Education: At
          Home and Abroad. G. Spindler and L. Spindler, eds. Pp. 109–136. Hillsdale,
          NJ: Erlbaum.
Michaels, Sarah, and James Collins
   1984   Oral Discourse Styles: Classroom Interaction and the Acquisition of Liter-
          acy. *In* Coherence in Spoken and Written Discourse. D. Tannen, ed. Pp.
          219–244. Norwood, NJ: Ablex.
Ogbu, John U.
   1974   The Next Generation: An Ethnography of Education in an Urban Neighbor-
          hood. New York: Academic Press.
   1978a Minority Education and Caste: The American System in Cross-Cultural
          Perspective. New York: Academic Press.
   1978b Origins of Human Competence: A Cultural-Ecological Perspective. Child
          Development 52:413–429.
   1987   Variability in Minority Responses to Schooling: Nonimmigrants vs. Immi-
          grants. *In* Interpretive Ethnography of Education at Home and Abroad. G.
          Spindler and L. Spindler, eds. Pp. 255–278. Hillsdale, NJ: Erlbaum.
Philips, Susan U.
   1983   The Invisible Culture: Communication in Classroom and Community on
          the Warm Springs Indian Reservation. New York: Longman.
Piestrup, Ann
   1973   Black Dialect Interference and Accommodation of Reading Instruction in
          First Grade (Monograph No. 4). Berkeley: Language Behavior Research
          Laboratory.
Poirer, Frank, and L. Kaye Hussey
   1982   Nonhuman Primate Learning: The Importance of Learning from an
          Evolutionary Perspective. Anthropology and Education Quarterly
          13(2):133–148.
Scollon, Ronald, and Suzanne Scollon
   1981   Narrative, Literacy, and Face in Interethnic Communication. Norwood, NJ:
          Ablex.
Valentine, Charles A.
   1968   Culture and Poverty: Critique and Counterproposals. Chicago: University
          of Chicago Press.
Vygotsky, Lev S.
   1978   Mind in Society: The Development of Higher Psychological Processes. M.
          Cole, V. John-Steiner, S. Scribner, and E. Souberman, eds. Pp. 84–91.
          Cambridge: Harvard University Press.
Willis, Paul E.
   1977   Learning to Labour. Westmead, England: Saxon House.

4

Explaining School Failure, Producing School Success: Two Cases

Lynn A. Vogt, Cathie Jordan, and Roland G. Tharp

SCHOOL FAILURE AND CULTURAL INCOMPATIBILITY

Why do schools fail to effectively educate the children of some minority groups? The question can be approached in different ways and on different levels of analysis. Answers on these several levels can all be correct—that is, informative and helpful to understanding. What kind of answer is most *useful*, however, depends on why one is asking the question. One reason for asking is in order to inform attempts to rectify the situation—to produce improved school achievement for groups that ordinarily experience underachievement.

If one addresses the question, "Why school failure?" or "Why do schools fail?" with a view to remedying the situation, then a useful model is that of cultural difference or cultural compatibility/incompatibility. This is the model that is the basis for the work discussed in this chapter.

The logic of the argument has been laid out by Jordan and Tharp (1984) and is paraphrased below:

1. It is possible to specify major proximate causes for academic un-
    derachievement in terms of relatively narrow-range mismatches or
    incompatibilities between the natal culture of the children and the
    culture of the school *at points that are critical for school success.* The

incompatibilities that are educationally significant for a particular group
are limited in number and in scope.
2.   If these specific incompatibilities are rectified for a particular population, producing particular, specifiable educational practices that are
more compatible with the child's natal culture, and if improved educational achievement results, then the hypotheses concerning these incompatibilities as cause or explanation for school failure gain support
and credibility.
3.   If features that are culturally compatible and educationally effective for
one group prove *not* to operate in the same way for another cultural
population, then the contention that culturally specific compatabilities
do in fact contribute to educational effectiveness receives further
support. Conversely, the contention that a lack of compatibility is a
significant part of the explanation for school failure is also supported.

In this chapter, the school failure issue will be addressed in the case of native
Hawaiian children and in the case of Navajo children.

EDUCATION IN HAWAII AND THE EDUCATION OF NATIVE HAWAIIAN CHILDREN

Hawaii has a centralized, statewide public school system, controlled by a
state Board of Education and a State Superintendent. This apparatus is
responsible for the public school education of the many cultural groups of the
state. The faculty and administrative bureaucracy of the educational system
are composed largely of people of Japanese ancestry, who participate in the
Hawaii version of Japanese culture. The student population served by the
schools includes Japanese, Chinese, Filipino, Samoan, native Hawaiian, and
haole (Northern European ancestry) children. Except for the lack of any
significant local control over the schools, the educational apparatus operates
much like that of any mainland state.

Working with this varied population, the Hawaii school system has
produced varied results. Among the major groups just mentioned, the schools
generally have a good record with Japanese, Chinese, and *haole* children, and
a relatively poor one with Filipinos, native Hawaiians, and Samoans.

Some native Hawaiian children, notably those from more middle-class,
acculturated families, do very well in traditionally run public school
classrooms. However, the majority do not. Partially in response to this state
of affairs, about twenty years ago a study of modern Hawaiian culture and
behavior was carried out. Part of this five-year work involved study of the
socialization of Hawaiian children at home and examination of the lives of
the same children in school. By the early 1970s, as a result of home and

school ethnography, it was possible to specify major sources of conflict in school for Hawaiian children (Gallimore, Boggs and Jordan 1974).

However, knowing what kinds of school practices were incompatible and resulted in problems did not, by itself, automatically tell one what kinds of school practices would be compatible and effective. This called for a more painstaking examination of classrooms serving Hawaiian children than had previously been done, along with a reexamination of the ethnographic data on children in the home.

The opportunity for this next phase of work was provided by the founding of the Kamehameha Elementary Education Program (KEEP). KEEP (which later became part of the Center for Development of Early Education) is a privately funded, multidisciplinary, educational research and development effort charged with remedying Hawaiian academic underachievement by changing educational practice. After several years of work, KEEP developed a K–3 language arts program that was culturally compatible for Hawaiian children and that, both in lab school and public schools, produced significant gains in reading achievement levels for educationally at-risk Hawaiian children. We will now look at the development and some of the characteristics of that program.

Early Efforts at KEEP

KEEP's lab school provided a setting in which it was possible to study closely Hawaiian children in school and to try out adaptations of classroom practices. The hypothesis first tested was not based on cultural factors but on the knowledge that Hawaiian students had normal potential for school success but were often seen by school personnel as unmotivated and hard to manage in the school setting. This was thought by many educators to be the reason for the children's underachievement. Was this the case? If educationally at-risk Hawaiian children could be persuaded to work diligently at school tasks, and if teachers would systematically deliver basic skills curricula in efficient and timely ways, would academic success follow? It was decided to test this idea. Initially, the focus was on reading/language arts.

Teachers were trained in positive reinforcement, and their use of these techniques was consistently monitored and relayed back to them (Sloat et al. 1977). A phonics-oriented basal reading system that was in common use in the public schools was selected. The scope and sequence of the basic skills of the program were converted to criterion-referenced objectives and tests, and progress through the curriculum was systematically delivered and monitored (Crowell 1976). After three years of this treatment, students at the lab school were on task more, and covered more content, but with no significant improvement in standardized test performance, and no significant difference from matched groups in the public schools. In sum, motivation, industriousness, and content coverage did not result in school success (Crowell 1977; Gallimore et al. 1982).

Successful Adaptations

In the next phase of work, changes were made in *instructional practice, classroom organization,* and *motivation management.* Comprehension took the place of phonics as the basic reading emphasis (Au 1979). Concomitant changes in the way instruction was delivered evolved. The classroom was organized into a system of teacher-independent centers with heterogeneous working groups, instead of traditional seatwork alone at individual desks (O'Neal and Bogert 1978). The strong emphasis on very high rates of teacher praise was relaxed, with teachers instead being encouraged to learn how to use, inside the classroom, some of the information that was available to them about the home culture of Hawaiian children. Success in standardized tests of reading followed, with the students scoring at or above grade-level norms (Gallimore et al. 1982; Klein 1981).

This success of the new program was attributed to the changes in instructional practice, classroom organization, and motivation management. All of these changes involved the selection of educational practices based, in part, on their cultural compatibility for Hawaiian children. This match between practice and culture will be illustrated for each area of change.

Instructional practice. With the unsuccessful early program, students were systematically instructed in phonics, with an emphasis on identifying letters and the sounds represented by them, and then learning rules for applying these sound-symbol relationships to decode new words. The process of instruction was didactic, and while the students passed the objective tests for the curriculum, the results seemed to hold little meaning for them, and they scored in the lowest quartile on standardized reading tests. With the successful comprehension program, students were engaged in the task of understanding stories by relating the ideas and story content to their personal experiences or background knowledge. Instruction took place in the context of highly interactive discussions between teacher and students, in which, after the students read (usually silently) each small segment of text, they talked about the meaning of the events in the story and related them to their own lives, at the end putting all the smaller "chunks" of text together and discussing the overall meaning or pattern. Word identification skills were not taught in isolation, but were always presented in the context of sentences, emphasizing meaning over sounding-out.

This emphasis on comprehension, focusing on *meaning* over decontextualized skills drill, may very well be a better means of teaching reading for all children, but is especially so for Hawaiian students. For Hawaiian children, learning at home is nearly always bound in an immediately meaningful context, usually involving joint participation accompanied by demonstration of a more competent model (Jordan 1977).

In addition, analysis of reading lessons revealed that the comprehension focus, with its emphasis on teacher responsiveness to children's talk, generated a spontaneous change in interaction style and sociolinguistic participation structures (Au 1980; Au and Jordan 1981). This new style has been compared to a linguistic event in the Hawaiian community called "talk-story," and is characterized by overlapping speech, voluntary turn-taking, co-narration and joint construction of a story. It was as if the change in instructional focus and the openness of teachers to greater variety in student contributions to the lessons opened the door for the students to contribute in a speech style that was linguistically familiar to them. When this happened, again because of the new emphasis on teacher responsiveness, on working jointly toward the common goal of story comprehension, and on the content, rather than the form, of student contribution, teachers were able to adapt their own participation style to accommodate the natural style of the children.

An example of the evolution of one such adaptation is that teachers began to call on the reading group as a whole rather than nominating individual students; that is, they allowed the voluntary participation characteristic of Hawaiian teaching-learning interactions. When asked about this change, teachers explained that the students were so eager to participate in the comprehension lessons that they began answering before the teachers finished asking the questions. In dropping the "one person at a time" rule from the traditional school-culture script, teachers adapted to the students' own participation formats. This and other spontaneous adaptations to Hawaiian participation structures were later formalized and made a part of the developing language arts program and teacher training routine.

Classroom organization. The second area of change involved the organization of the classroom. Previously, independent work was done at individual desks, and one of the hardest teacher rules to enforce was, "Do your own work." Because of a pattern of multiple caretakers and companion groups in the home culture, Hawaiian children are accustomed to helping one another, and to being helped more often by peers or siblings than by adults (Gallimore, Boggs and Jordan 1974). In school this manifests itself in high rates of peer interaction, frequent scanning for other children's errors, and offering and soliciting peer help (Jordan 1977, 1984). Teachers tend to think of this not as assistance or modeling, but as cheating. Hence, in the old classroom organization, much of a teacher's time and energy was spent attending to students at homeroom seats, praising those working alone in an effort to cue all students to do so. Under this system, the students became adept in avoiding trouble with the teacher while still behaving like Hawaiian helpers. For instance, while the teacher turned to write on the board, a skilled student could leave his seat, consult with a peer, and get back into his seat again, all before the teacher turned back to face the class.

Dramatic changes occurred with the center organization. In this organization, while the teacher meets with each small homogeneous reading group, the rest of the class works in small groups at "learning centers" located throughout the classroom. The students rotate to new centers with different heterogeneous groupings of children every 20 to 25 minutes. At these centers they work on a variety of language arts tasks designed to provide practice on objectives tailored to the instructional level of whichever reading group a child is in. Since the groups at the centers are made up of children from different reading levels, higher level students often have had prior experience with the tasks assigned to lower level students. Children are allowed to assist each other within the center, and even at times to go to other centers to seek help.

This center system provided a situation in which the students' natural inclination for interaction and assistance could be put into practice without causing disruption, without sacrificing on-task behavior, and without consuming teacher time and energy to regulate it. It was as if what had been needed to promote willing on-task behavior was for the teacher to step back and let the students behave in their accustomed manner. Industriousness, as it turned out, did not require external motivation systems and extreme praise rates or teacher attention. It required school adaptation to the children's culturally based skills and inclinations.

Motivation management. The adaptations that were developed in the behavior management and motivation routines were, in part, a result of this new center organization system. As we mentioned earlier, KEEP teachers had been thoroughly trained in the use of verbal positive reinforcement to get and maintain student attention. With the traditional classroom organization system and the phonics-based curriculum, high praise rates were crucial to on-task behavior, because on-task behavior had to be maintained in contexts that were in many ways culturally incompatible. Thus, teachers were struggling to encourage productive *on*-task behavior in circumstances the natural parameters of which tended to elicit *off*-task behavior. What was eventually learned was that industriousness of Hawaiian students could be achieved more effectively with culturally compatible instruction and classroom organization systems, along with culturally appropriate forms and rates of positive reinforcement. Under the new system, high amounts of teacher attention and praise were unnecessary, and in some circumstances, undesirable.

The use of praise as a reinforcer for desired behavior was found to be more effective when delivered in more culturally compatible ways. For example, in the early unsuccessful program, teachers were trained to utter direct, specific praise stating the desired behavior being observed by the teacher, and naming students who were exhibiting that behavior: "Very good. Lisa and Keoni are sitting quietly and looking up here." Ethnographic work indicated that indirect praise, and praise to a group ("Good. Table 3 is ready.") are more effective than direct praise that spotlights one child. Even then, praise is only one part of building effective relationships between teachers and Hawaiian students.

The work of John D'Amato, a KEEP anthropologist, has contributed greatly to our understanding in this area. He argues that the themes of warmth or solidarity, and toughness or autonomy, form the point and counterpoint in Hawaiian children's interactions. To gain a place in the peer group, a Hawaiian child must show warmth and also prove toughness. Teachers are evaluated by Hawaiian school children in the same framework that the children use with one another. To succeed with the children, teachers must also show warmth and toughness. Praise and the smile should be the touchstone of relationships; but the smile should also "show teeth," that is, it should be balanced with firmness (D'Amato 1986).

KEEP teachers are taught when and how to ignore, to take a "no-nonsense" stand, and to praise, all in ways that are effective with Hawaiian children.

THE KEEP-ROUGH ROCK PROJECT

In spite of the fact that the success of the new program seemed to be attributable in part to its cultural compatibility, some felt that the program was simply good solid educational practice that would work equally well with any other population. This debate generated a collaborative project between the Center and Rough Rock Demonstration School in the heart of the Navajo Reservation. (For a more complete description of the Rough Rock Project, see Jordan, Tharp, and Vogt 1985.)

During the fall semester of 1983, Cathie Jordan, KEEP anthropologist, and Lynn Vogt, KEEP research teacher, lived in the Rough Rock community and worked in a 3rd-grade class at the school. Vogt taught the KEEP reading program, and Jordan organized and ran the research effort. The project involved intensive collaboration with one 3rd-grade teacher, Afton Sells, and her aide, Juanita Estell, and some involvement with the rest of the faculty and staff. All of the faculty except the librarian were Navajo and members of the Rough Rock community.

The purpose of the project was to find out if the KEEP language arts program, developed for Hawaiian children, would work in the same ways and be as effective with children from another culture. Since the team was only at Rough Rock for one semester, it was not possible to focus on reading achievement scores as meaningful indicators of program effects; instead, the focus was on processual issues, on how the program operated for Navajo children. Changes were necessary in all three areas: motivation management, classroom organization, and instructional practice.

Motivation Management

Vogt had not realized how solidly the Hawaiian experience had permeated her behavior management routines, but she soon found out. On the first day of school, she greeted the Navajo students with heavy doses of praise, both to reinforce desired behavior and to cue other students. Things went reasonably well. On the second day of school one boy came into the room shouting, slammed a book onto a desk, and then proceeded to disrupt other students. Vogt responded with a warning followed by a desist statement (specifically telling him to stop the disruptive behavior). In Hawaii, this is a common routine, and quick handling of the first challenge from a student is important to signal the nice-but-tough nature of the teacher.

However, from the moment of the warning, it was evident that this wasn't going to work the same way in Rough Rock. The direct desist resulted in a stand-off and a dramatic confrontation between teacher and student that almost paralyzed both the student concerned and the rest of the class. The immediate crisis was resolved by Vogt backing off from her demands for compliance, and allowing the student to drop out of classroom activity for some time while he recovered his composure, and then to gradually work his way back into the classroom routine on his own initiative and at his own pace.

We learned that both extremes of the "tough-nice" repertoire that was so effective with Hawaiian children would be ineffective with Navajo children. Praise was appropriate to promote good positive relationships, but it was most effective when handled more subtly than with Hawaiian children, and it was seldom very effective for cueing desired behavior. Misbehavior was more easily controlled by ignoring or lowering one's eyes and giving a short, stern lecture to the whole group of students, only indirectly referring to the offense, while speaking of honorable behavior standards, a procedure sure to bring disaster in a Hawaiian classroom.

When management routines were adapted to be more compatible with Navajo culture, the classroom began to function smoothly, and installation of other features of the KEEP program could be addressed.

Classroom Organization

The KEEP center system was installed. The students quickly complied with the formal requirements of the system, and worked diligently at the tasks assigned in centers. However, they virtually ignored each other, neither seeking nor offering assistance, even when it was desperately needed. This contrasted sharply with the behavior of Hawaiian children in centers. It was also somewhat curious, because there were many instances of sibling caretaking and mutual helping in the community, conditions that were thought to be precursors of peer cooperation in centers in Hawaii. However, at Rough Rock this did not result in assistance or cooperation at centers. What was culturally compatible and educationally effective for Hawaiian children was not for Navajo youngsters.

Since the centers are not directly overseen by the teacher, there is a danger that if a child is having trouble with the task, he will not have resources to steer him right unless he relies on his centermates. This can be especially problematic for low-achieving students because it results in loss of time and of opportunity to get feedback when it is most effective. If interaction and assistance could not be promoted, a different system of organization would be needed to assure high rates of meaningful and successful practice.

As it turned out, there were several issues involved. One was that there is a separation of the sexes in Navajo culture, both in roles and for purposes of interaction, a separation that begins to take effect around the age of eight, the age of the students in our class. Boys are admonished not to "play with" their sisters, and girls with brothers. In a small community this means almost everyone, since it extends to clan relations. By puberty this is extremely important, and by adulthood male and female roles are clearly defined and separate.

At KEEP, 4–5 students of mixed sex and ability produce the maximum peer interaction and assistance at a center. At Rough Rock, this combination effectively annihilated interaction. After experimenting with a number of conditions, our early analysis suggested that Navajo children would help and interact in groups of 2–3 students of the same sex, working on the same task. (For a more detailed discussion, see Jordan, Tharp, and Vogt 1985.)

Instructional Practice

Before going to Rough Rock, Vogt worried that the students wouldn't talk to her in the reading lesson, that she wouldn't know the sociolinguistic rules that would elicit verbal interaction in this culture. Surprisingly, this was not the case. The technique of directing questions to the group to avoid spotlighting an individual student seemed to signal that responding was safe for Navajo students, as it did for Hawaiian students, especially when Vogt learned to temper her expressions of enthusiasm when the children contributed. However, there were several differences in the way the comprehension lesson developed.

One of these was that while the general KEEP comprehension strategy of relating text to personal experiences of the student was effective with Navajo students, they seemed uncomfortable with chopping a story into small segments, discussing each segment separately, and putting the pieces together at the end. They preferred to read and discuss the stories as complete units, rather than in an event-by-event, linear way.

A related issue in the attempt to adapt the reading lessons resulted from a challenge offered by the Navajo teacher, Afton Sells. She suggested that it might be possible to represent whole story plots in a circular-pattern visual display, as opposed to the linear way Vogt had been diagramming plots on the chalkboard. After much discussion and planning, the events of one rather complex story were arranged somewhat like a flower, with petals around a circle stating the central problem. When Vogt struggled to explain the story in terms of this complex symbol, one of the students suggested that the story events could also be represented as a spiral, coming up from the central problem. It was startling to learn that while it was a challenge for Vogt to alter her linear, sequential view of the story, this third grader was not only able to comprehend the model Vogt presented, but could offer a second way to show the story as a circular whole.

This preference for having a complete picture before attempting to analyze, perform, or attempt understanding was manifest in a number of other instances with the students and the Navajo teachers and aides. It presents a challenge to educators trained to break down problems to be taught in a series of discrete steps. In holistic thought, the pieces derive their meaning from the pattern of the whole; in linear thought, the whole is revealed through the unfolding of the sections (Jordan, Tharp and Vogt 1985; White et al. 1989). While the literature provides many instances that imply the holistic nature of thought processes among American Indians (e.g., Cazden and John 1971; John 1972; Philips 1972), the KEEP-Rough Rock collaboration only began to scratch the surface as to how this would change approaches to reading comprehension. What is perfectly clear is that the work should be done if the educational system is to effectively serve these students.

Rough Rock Demonstration School was founded as the nation's first bilingual/bicultural community-controlled school for American Indian students. The school has focused on providing instruction that includes Navajo content and language. While most of the teachers are Navajo, and many were raised in the Rough Rock community, they have tended to deliver instruction, organize their classrooms, and interact with students in ways not much different from majority-culture teachers running traditional mainstream classrooms. In fact, many teachers reported to us that even though they had memories of discomfort and unhappiness with their school experience, they tended to behave as their teachers had. The idea of working to make their school bicultural in terms of educational *process,* in addition to content, was a new one for them. The KEEP experience suggested that school success at Rough Rock would be enhanced if process issues were included when working to improve their educational program.

CONCLUSIONS

Let us sum up the implications of these examples for the question of how to explain school performance. The argument is as follows: (1) The KEEP program, which has been developed for native Hawaiian children and in response to data about them, is educationally effective for them, both in terms of process, such as engagement with academic tasks, and outcomes (e.g., achievement scores). (2) Many program elements that are effective for native Hawaiian children have been found *not* to be culturally compatible or effective for Navajo children. (3) There is good reason to believe that it is possible to change these incompatible program elements so that they are more compatible for Navajo children and will function more effectively to produce the desired educational processes and results. (4) Therefore, there is reason to believe that the educationally effective Hawaiian program is, to an extent, culturally specific, and that its specific cultural compatibility contributes to its educational effectiveness. (5) Cultural compatibility is a credible explanation for school success while, conversely, (6) cultural incompatibility is one credible explanation for school failure. At least, we must admit it as a strong contributor to useful explanations in the case of some minority populations and the schools that serve them. Certainly, if one wants to change schools in ways that will change school failure, then it is an explanation that demands to be taken into account.

AFTERWORD—1991

In the four years since this chapter was written, a number of changes have occurred at KEEP and at the Center for Development of Early Education. While the Hawaiian reading program described in the chapter continues to be disseminated in several schools, most of the research support for the program has been withdrawn, and the program itself has changed significantly. One change has been a gradual erosion of the effort to ensure the culturally compatible nature of the program. The original program proved effective for educationally at-risk native Hawaiian children in lab school classrooms, in pilot testing in public school classrooms, and in initial small-scale dissemination into the public schools. Whether the evolved program in any of its forms will be equally effective in the context of a much larger scale dissemination effort is still to be seen.

REFERENCES

Au, Kathryn Hu-pei
  1979   Using the Experience-Text-Relationship Method with Minority Children. The Reading Teacher 32(6):677–679.
  1980   Participation Structures in a Reading Lesson with Hawaiian Children: Analysis of a Culturally Appropriate Instructional Event. Anthropology and Education Quarterly 11(2):91–115.
Au, Kathryn Hu-pei, and Cathie Jordan
  1981   Teaching Reading to Hawaiian Children: Finding a Culturally Appropriate Solution. *In* Culture in the Bilingual Classroom: Studies in Classroom Ethnography. Henry T. Trueba, Grace Pung Guthrie, and Kathryn H. Au, eds. Pp. 139–152. Rowley, MA: Newberry House.
Cazden, Courtney B., and Vera P. John
  1971   Learning in American Indian Children. *In* Anthropological Perspectives on Education. Murray L. Wax, Stanley Diamond, and Fred O. Gearing, eds. Pp. 252–271. New York: Basic Books, Inc.
Crowell, Doris
  1976   The Use of Minimum Objectives in Curriculum Research and Development, 1975–1976 (Technical Report No. 45). Honolulu: Kamehameha Schools, Kamehameha Early Education Program.
  1977   Results of the Minimum Objective System, 1975–1976 (Technical Report No. 77). Honolulu: Kamehameha Schools, Kamehameha Early Education Program.
D'Amato, John
  1986   "We cool, tha's why": A Study of Personhood and Place in a Class of Hawaiian Second Graders. Doctoral dissertation, University of Hawaii.
Gallimore, Ronald, Joan Boggs, and Cathie Jordan
  1974   Culture, Behavior and Education: A Study of Hawaiian-Americans. Beverly Hills, California: Sage Publications.
Gallimore, Ronald, et al.
  1982   Analysis of Reading Achievement Test Results for the Kamehameha Early Education Project: 1972–1979 (Technical Report No. 95). Honolulu: Kamehameha Schools, Kamehameha Early Education Program.
John, Vera P.
  1972   Styles of Learning—Styles of Teaching: Reflections on the Education of Navajo Children. *In* Functions of Language in the Classroom. Courtney B.

Cazden, Vera P. John, and Dell Hymes, eds. Pp. 331–343. New York: Teachers College Press.

Jordan, Cathie
1977 Maternal Teaching, Peer Teaching and School Adaption in an Urban Hawaiian Population (Technical Report No. 67). Honolulu: Kamehameha Schools, Kamehameha Early Education Program.
1984 Cultural Compatibility and the Education of Ethnic Minority Children. Educational Research Quarterly 8(4):59–71.

Jordan, Cathie, and Roland G. Tharp
1984 Level of Analysis and the Specification of Sources of Academic Underachievement for Minority Cultural Groups: Evidence from the Hawaiian Case (Working Paper). Honolulu: Kamehameha Schools, Center for Development of Early Education. (Revised version of a paper presented at the Annual Meetings of the American Anthropological Association, November 1983.)

Jordan, Cathie, Roland G. Tharp, and Lynn Vogt
1985 Compatibility of Classroom and Culture: General Principles, with Navajo and Hawaiian Instances (Working Paper). Honolulu: Kamehameha Schools, Center for Development of Early Education.

Klein, Thomas
1981 Results of the Reading Program. Educational Perspectives 20(1):8–10.

O'Neal, Karen, and Karen Y. Bogert
1978 Classroom Organization for the Language Arts Teacher: A System For Meeting Learner Needs Through the Use of Work Areas and Small Group Instruction (Technical Report No. 78). Honolulu: Kamehameha Schools, Kamehameha Early Education Program.

Philips, Susan U.
1972 Participant Structures and Communicative Competence: Warm Springs Indian Children in Community and Classroom. In Functions of Language in the Classroom. Courtney B. Cazden, Vera P. John, and Dell Hymes, eds. Pp. 370–394. New York: Teachers College Press.

Sloat, Kim C.M., Junko Tanaka-Matsumi, Mele Ah Ho, and Sarah Sueoka
1977 Training Teachers to Use Positive Reinforcement Through Guided Practice in the Classroom (Technical Report No. 68). Honolulu: Kamehameha Schools, Kamehameha Early Education Program.

White, Sheida, Roland G. Tharp, Cathie Jordan, and Lynn A. Vogt
1989 Cultural Patterns of Cognition Reflected in the Questioning Stlyes of Anglo and Navajo Teachers. In Thinking: The Third International Conference. Donald Topping, Victor Kobayashi, and Doris C. Crowell, eds. Pp. 79–91. Hillsdale, NJ: Erlbaum Associates.

5

Change as the Goal of Educational Research

Luis C. Moll and Stephen Diaz

For several years we have conducted research in home, school, and community settings in San Diego. Our work, in general terms, has proceeded as follows: We have analyzed problematic educational situations, usually characterized by children failing. But we did not stop there. Utilizing what we have called the participants' cultural resources (e.g., the children's and adults' bilingualism) information about the children or about their communities, and guided by our theoretical perspective (discussed below), we reorganized instruction in ways that we could claim were more advantageous for teachers and students. The key point here is that the goal in our studies was to produce instructional *change,* to manipulate instructional procedures to improve the conditions for learning. It is our contention that existing classroom practices not only underestimate and constrain what children display intellectually, but help distort explanations of school performance. It is also our contention that the strategic application of cultural resources in instruction is one important way of obtaining change in academic performance and of demonstrating that there is nothing about the children's language, culture, or intellectual capacities that should handicap their schooling (Diaz, Moll and Mehan 1986; Laboratory of Comparative Human Cognition 1986).

In what follows we present two case studies that have shaped the views mentioned above. In particular, we highlight the adult's social mediations in creating varied circumstances for children to learn. We then describe our recent research, which tries to combine what we have learned from the case studies by forming after-school, community-based settings within which to conduct educational research while staying in close contact with community realities. Here we highlight mediations of a different type: the strategic connections we can create between schools and communities to promote educational change.

TWO CASE STUDY EXAMPLES

The research we report below has been influenced by the work of educational anthropologists, in particular the so-called "microethnographers" who have examined in great detail the interactional dynamics of various educational situations (e.g., Erickson 1982; McDermott 1976; Mehan 1979). Central to our research is the study of what Erickson (1982) calls "immediate environments of learning", namely, the analysis of how instructional contexts are socially constituted by adults and children. We have supplemented what we have learned from these "microanalyses" with ideas about learning and development borrowed from sociohistorical psychologists (e.g., Olson 1986; Scribner and Cole 1981; Vygotsky 1978; Wertsch 1985). These researchers also emphasize the critical role of social interactions in learning.

Vygotsky (1978), for instance, wrote that the forms of cooperation between child and adult were the central element of the education process. His famous concept of the zone of proximal development refers to the importance of these forms of cooperation. He stressed how one gets a qualitatively different perspective of children's abilities by contrasting what they do when working alone to what they can perform when working in collaboration with others. And he suggested that for instruction to be effective it must lead students; in our interpretation, it must be aimed not only at weaknesses manifested in individual assessments, but at strengths that are displayed most readily in collaborative activities.

In this section we present two case studies, one on reading and one on writing. These studies have been presented elsewhere, therefore we refer the reader to other sources for details omitted here (Diaz, Moll and Mehan 1986; Moll 1986; Moll and Diaz 1985, 1987; Trueba, Moll, Diaz and Diaz 1982). We use the case studies here to highlight what we consider a major problem in the schooling of the working-class Latino students, indeed in the schooling of working-class children in general: the practice of reducing or "watering down" the curriculum to match perceived or identified weaknesses in the students. This practice is best understood when considered within a more general framework or model for organizing instruction that seems quite pervasive. Heath (1986:150), for example, has called it a tendency to assume the existence of a single developmental model for learning. She writes, "The school expects children to follow a single developmental model in acquiring uses of language," a model that assumes "a linear progression for learning in which earlier stages will not normally be repeated, and behaviors characteristic of later stages will not precede or appear in the place of those behaviors judged as simpler or more fundamental than others." For the children presented in these case studies, this model meant being stuck in the lower levels of the curriculum.

Although student characteristics certainly matter, when the same children are shown to succeed under modified instruction arrangements it becomes clear that the problems these working-class children face in school must be viewed primarily as a consequence of institutional arrangements that constrain children *and* teachers by not capitalizing fully on their talents, resources, and skills. As we have written elsewhere (Diaz et al. 1986; Moll 1986), this conclusion is pedagogically optimistic because it suggests that just as academic failure is socially organized, academic success can be socially arranged.

The reading case study reported herein took place in an elementary school within a Latino working-class community in San Diego. All of the children in the study were labeled limited-English speakers, especially the ones in the lower reading groups. We also conducted the writing study in a predominantly Latino community in San Diego. The students were in junior high school, and those who participated in the work described here were limited-English speakers. In both cases the students were doing poorly academically. In the elementary school, they were reading approximately three grades below grade level; in the junior high school they were doing poorly in writing as measured by districtwide tests.

Reading

The research took place in a bilingual program that featured an instructional model in which children received academic instruction solely in Spanish and then moved to the classroom next door to receive instruction in English. So, the children spent part of the day in one classroom and part of the day in the other, providing us with the opportunity to observe the same children in two distinct yet related sociolinguistic environments for learning. Other relevant factors were: the teacher in the Spanish-language classroom was female, bilingual and Mexican-American; the teacher in the English-language classroom was male, monolingual, and Anglo-American. The first part of the study took place in third-grade classrooms, and the second part in fourth-grade classrooms. All of the children were considered limited English speakers, but all of them were judged by the school, using language assessment instruments as well as teacher opinions, to be sufficiently fluent in English to benefit from instruction in that language.

Our first study, patterned after Mehan (1979), revealed how the focus of instruction and the instructional procedures varied according to ability grouping. In brief, the teachers organized lessons in both classrooms according to a hierarchy of reading skills reminiscent of Heath's (1986) claim of a single developmental model. They assumed that decoding must precede comprehension of text and that advanced forms of comprehension (what we have called "text-free") could not be taught until simpler, text-bound skills were mastered. Consequently, instruction in Spanish ranged from an emphasis on decoding and simple, text-bound comprehension questions for the "lower" reading group, to more difficult but still text-bound comprehension questions for the "middle" group, to a more advanced text-free comprehension focus with the "high" group. This instructional bias, a skills-based approach ranging from simple to complex, characterized both classrooms, but it was particularly problematic in the English-language classroom. Here the emphasis, regardless of ability grouping, was on decoding. Even students who were among the better readers in Spanish were treated in English as low-level readers. We could not find any resemblance within the English language reading lessons of comprehension questions characteristic of the advanced group's lessons in Spanish. We have suggested that because the children decoded in English with an obvious Spanish accent, as second-language readers are bound to do, and because accurate pronunciation is the best index of good decoding, the student never quite sounded right to an English monolingual teacher; therefore, he did something that within context seems quite reasonable to us—he organized plenty of decoding practice to get the students ready for more advanced reading.

We should be clear that we are not interested at all in blaming the teachers. We believe that the "model of learning" implicit in these classrooms, as well as other organizational constraints, helped misguide the teachers into treating their classrooms as self-contained environments: the teachers were unable to relate what was going on in Spanish reading, especially with the high group in Spanish, where the children were obviously competent readers, with reading in English. Put another way, there was no transfer from Spanish to English reading, a goal of most bilingual education programs, because the organization of instruction was such as to make reading in English dissimilar from reading in Spanish. Comprehension, the key to reading, did not enter in any important way into English reading lessons. You cannot transfer what you are not allowed to display.

Our "intervention," therefore, consisted of creating instructional conditions in which the children could fully display their reading abilities regardless of language. For the sake of brevity we will summarize our procedures into four steps.

First, we asked the regular English language teacher to teach a lesson with the children classified as the low reading group. We knew from our observations in the Spanish-language classroom that these children read with differing ability, but they could all read in Spanish with comprehension.

"Reading" in English. The lesson began with a brief discussion about the topic of the story, as the teacher attempted to establish the context for the story. The teacher then told the children that they would take turns reading aloud. In the transcript we present below (from Moll and Diaz 1985), note that the children were unfamiliar with some relatively simple English words and that they also mispronounced some words (e.g., "said" as [seyd]).

1.	**Teacher:**	Let's start reading the first page. We are going to meet a lot of new people in this book. (Two of the girls have their hands up)
2.	**Delfina:**	Can I read first?
3.	**T:**	I am going to let Sylvia read first, she has her hand up. (Sylvia starts reading).
4.	**Sylvia:**	"'You can't guess where we are going,' said David."
5.	**T:**	OK, just a minute, please, Carla, we need you to follow with us. (Carla was not looking at her book).
6.	**Carla:**	OK.
7.	**T:**	Delfina, we need you to follow right along. (Addressing Sylvia) Would you start all over again?
8.	**S.**	OK, I'll start over again." 'You can't guess...'"
9.	**T:**	(Interrupting) OK, what is this? (Points at a word in the text)
10.	**S:**	Can't?
11.	**T:**	Can't. What does that mean? (Pause)
12.	**C:**	Uhmmm...
13.	**T:**	OK, Carla, if I say you can guess or you can't guess.
14.	**D:**	(Raising her hand) Oh! Can't is like no...
15.	**C:**	Don't do that.
16.	**T:**	Uh, yeah, uh huh. Read the sentence, the whole sentence again and let's see what it says...
17.	**S:**	"'You can't guess where we are going,' sayed David Lee."
18.	**T:**	Good.
19.	**S:**	"It's going to be a ..." (Looks at teacher)
20.	**C:**	Surprise.
21.	**T:**	Surprise.
22.	**S:**	Surprise "'I like surprises,' sayed Isabel. 'You bet. I'll bet you can't guess where we are all going,' sayed David." (The other girls raise their hands to read next.)

This excerpt illustrates the deliberate, slow pace of lessons with students in the low reading groups, including the frequent interruptions to help with pronunciation or define words. The children display similar difficulties when they are required to report verbally what they have understood from the reading; they were tentative in their speech, and their answers were fragmentary, as in the next transcript when the teacher asked them why the children in the story thought that one of the girls, Isabel, was lost in the fire station.

1. **D:**   Because, the boys and girls, um, looked... (Sylvia raises her hand)
2. **T:**   Sylvia
3. **S:**   Uh, because the boys and girls, uh (pauses, laughs) the... um...
4. **D:**   Had to go home.
5. **S:**   Because the boys and girls go...
6. **T:**   Mhm...
7. **S**   ...out in the first place and the girls not say "I am here."

Even to an experienced observer, or an experienced teacher, as was the case here, it would be reasonable to conclude that these children could not read at this level. It seemed evident that in the present reading context the children could not do more.

Some Bilingual Counterevidence. Was this conclusion accurate? We turned to Vygotsky's ideas for assistance. Recall the premise of his concept of a zone of proximal development: children differ in their abilities in ways that cannot be assessed solely by techniques that analyze independent performance. Based on our observations of the children in Spanish, we developed a bilingual corollary: children differ in their abilities in ways that cannot be assessed solely by techniques that analyze performance in one language. To apply this corollary, immediately after the lesson was over one of the authors sat with the children and asked comprehension questions in *Spanish* about what the children had just finished reading in *English*. Compare Sylvia's answer to a probe very similar to the one we quoted above: How did the boys know that the girl was lost?

1. **S:**   Porque él, ella, ellos le, le gritaban y, y, la buscaban por donde todo el edificio donde viven los bomberos y ella no contestaba. (Because he, her, they would, would shout for her, and, and, they searched everywhere in the building where the firemen live and she wouldn't answer.)

She later elaborates:

2. **S:**   Porque David dijo que ya se tenían que ir. Entonces dijeron, "Quién falta?" No falta nadie, entonces dijeron, "Isabel." Entonces empezaron a buscar y no la encontraban y decían, "Está perdida ella, señor." El bombero dijo, "No, no, no puede estar perdida." Pues andaban buscándola y llegaron al troque y el senor dijo que allí estaba Isabel. (Because David said that they had to leave. Then they said. "Who's missing?" No one's missing, then they

said, "Isabel." Then they started to search and they couldn't find her and they said. "She's lost, sir." The fireman said, "no, no she can't be lost." So they were looking for her and they got to the truck and the man said that there was Isabel.)

It is obvious from the transcript that Sylvia understood easily the story that she read in English, a conclusion one is unlikely to reach observing her in the English reading lessons. Our analysis showed that oral language and decoding difficulties in English notwithstanding, the students could understand much more about what they were reading in English than they could display solely in that language. How could we reorganize the instructional procedures to take advantage of their Spanish reading competence to advance their English reading? In other words, how could we develop a bilingual zone of proximal development for *English* reading?

Bilingual Communication and English Reading. On the basis of the first "experiment," we asked the teacher to provide us with textbooks at grade level. We knew from the observations in the Spanish-language classroom that the children could understand more complex text, and we wanted to try matching that level of reading in their second language. Next, we asked the students to concentrate primarily on understanding what they were reading; in our terms, we made comprehension the higher order goal of the reading lessons. Finally, we decided that the students and we, the teachers, could switch to Spanish as needed, *in situ*, to clarify the meaning of the text. We labeled this strategy providing children with "bilingual communicative support" in comprehending English text.

We started the lessons by reading the story to the students, removing all potential decoding constraints from the students concentrating on comprehension. After the reading, we sought to clarify the meaning of the text, by finding out how much the students understood and by clarifying aspects of the text. By the third lesson, the students were able, with our bilingual assistance, to answer comprehension questions required of English monolingual readers at grade level. We should also mention that by the third lesson we no longer read to the students, we had transferred the responsibility for decoding to them (for examples, see Moll and Diaz 1985). It was not the case that the children had turned into competent English readers with minimum assistance; that is not our claim. Our claim is that reading and communicative resources can be strategically combined or mixed to provide the children with the support necessary to participate profitably in reading lessons. This point, we believe, has to do with the social organization of instruction and how it interacts with the children's and teachers' characteristics. We showed that the level of the lessons need not be reduced to accommodate the children's English language constraints, and that there are reasonable and credible ways to fruitfully relate lessons across languages for the benefit of the children. In our specific case, we took advantage of the children's Spanish language and literacy skills to facilitate their performance in English. Transfer, when it occurs, is always socially arranged.

Writing

The goal of this study was to document how writing was used in home and community settings and to explore ways of using this information to improve the teaching of writing. As such, we conducted this case study in collaboration with 12 teachers from three junior high schools. In contrast to the reading study, we did not intervene directly in instruction; rather, we created a research site within the community under study in which we met with the teachers every two weeks for three hours or so to discuss changes in their teaching of writing. More specifically, we met to discuss the latest research information and how this information could be used by the teachers to change or improve how they were teaching writing.

We realized quickly that very few of the students, especially the limited-English proficient students, were doing any extended writing. Most classroom writing was in response to teachers' questions or to worksheets. There seemed to be a similar reduction to what we described in the reading study: The students were assumed not to possess the necessary English skills to participate in essay or expository writing; therefore, teachers adjusted lessons to the students' low levels of English oral skills. Other relevant factors that helped frame the study included the following: We found little writing in the homes studied, and most of the writing that did occur was very functional (e.g., a shopping list, a telephone message, and so on). However, most of the literacy-related events in the home occurred in response to the students' homework assignments; so, in short, when writing occurred it had something to do with homework. We should add that all of the parents stated that they valued education highly and that they considered good writing to be part of being well schooled. Further, all of the parents were eager to discuss with us problems and issues having to do with living in that community. These issues ranged from immigration problems to gangs and drugs. Regarding the teachers, only one had been trained in the teaching of writing, and she believed that the methods that she learned did not apply readily to the student population she was teaching.

Therefore, regardless of differences in the two case studies, we were facing a similar phenomenon: how to maximize the use of available resources to overcome reductionist instructional practices. In contrast to the reading study, however, the disconfirming information was not available in the classroom next door; no such asset was present. We needed to turn to community-based information for help.

Communicating Meaning. We started our interventions by using state-of-the-art information (e.g., Graves 1983) in helping teachers to teach writing as communication. We then asked them to select a topic for writing from among the community issues our field studies were identifying as important. We wanted to change not only the process of writing but the *motive* for writing: It was to become an activity to communicate with someone else about something that mattered. The teachers were reluctant to use community-related issues in their lessons. Some expressed concern that the principal or the parents could complain. However, the one teacher who was willing to try to met with instant success in getting her students to write. She got them to produce sufficient text so that it gave her plenty of opportunities to teach, where few existed before.

Using this teacher as a model, we encouraged the others to experiment with their teaching, keep a journal of their activities, and bring it to our sessions for discussion. After the teachers had had some practice and some success, we asked them to think of ways of using homework as a way to extend their writing lessons—that is, as a way of helping the students and themselves increase their knowledge base for writing. Having overcome their initial reluctance, the teachers agreed to implement a series of writing activities in which community information collected through homework assignments would be used to produce and revise written text. The teachers asked the students to write about an issue of significance to them or their community (e.g., societal bilingualism or cheating). They then helped the students create a questionnaire through which they could collect others' opinions about the topic; the students interviewed parents, peers, siblings, neighbors, and adults in the school. The next step included the teachers helping the students compile this information in ways that could be used to revise their articles. An *unedited* example from one student's writing will suffice to make the point.

> First, in my school, I asked students and aduls. If they are bilinguals, some people are bilingual and someones are not in my school. Some them tall me they are bilinguals, somea____ they're not bilinguals about the 50%. Seconly, in my community some people is don't inersting about to be bilingual becaue they think, they don't need other language because they are in America and in America only speak English. Thrith, I don't feel so good, because I think they are a little dum people because they think to be a bilingual person is a waste them time. Also, I think the people who's don't interesting to be them selfs bilingual arre going to the wrong way because the prsons who speatwo language or more have the opportunity to know other culture and language. Finally, in my family they think to be a bilingual is to important because they learn other culture and language. And we

speak spanish and we speak Enghlish because we live in U.S.A. but like in different countries is important to know other languages for we can talk with other persons. (Diaz, Moll, and Mehan 1986:218)

Obviously, the student's writing could stand improvement. But that would be to miss the point. Grammatical mistakes aside, the teacher was able to organize the lesson in ways that minimized the constraining influence of the student's lack of fluency in his second language, while maximizing the use of skills the student did possess in getting him to write for communication. Whether students were fluent or not in English, they participated in comparable, demanding intellectual activities; the goal of writing for communication remained invariant, ways of achieving the goal varied depending on the characteristics of the students and the resources available for teaching. (For additional results, see Trueba et al. 1982.)

These and other studies that have analyzed in detail the "immediate environment of learning" provided us with a good understanding of the interactional mechanisms of teaching and learning; these same studies convinced us how much the ways we routinely organize instruction limit children's thinking. We have also shown, however, that this does not have to be so; even relatively minor changes in the social context of learning can produce important changes in performance. How we are going about creating conditions for change as part of a general research strategy is what we describe next.

INSTRUCTIONAL EXPERIMENTATION IN COMMUNITY CONTEXT

A direct result of our previous research, a logical and necessary progression of it from our perspective, has been the development of community-based research sites. We think of these settings as educational "laboratories." As with any laboratory, they are places especially designed to address specific issues in a reduced, manageable way. At these settings we continue our research on reading, writing, and more recently, on computer communications, an important new addition to our work, as we shall explain (Diaz 1987; Moll 1987). As is now becoming known about laboratories, however, these are not isolated from the world at large (Latour 1983). In our case, we try to link them strategically to different social institutions and practices. In line with the laboratory metaphor, we have called studies that we conduct at these settings "ethnographic experiments." As we implement our instructional studies, we try to retain important classroom or school characteristics while exploring ethnographically the nature of the community and what resources may be available to improve instruction. That is, these settings are intended as permanent locations that allow us to study dynamically and continuously schooling in the context of the community. And in the ethnographic spirit, we try to relate, through a computer network among researchers, teachers, and students, our community and instructional findings to work being conducted in a similar mode in other cities.

For example, at both the San Diego and Tucson sites we meet with 15 to 20 students at least twice a week for approximately two hours. These students are usually working-class Latinos in the bottom 20th percentile of their class, and they represent the type of linguistic diversity common in the schools. On a typical day the students participate in reading lessons, do writing and editing, try our software, and communicate through the computer with students locally and internationally. Reading, writing, and the use of computers are conceptualized as related activities in carrying out broader research projects. Recently, for example, the students in Tucson and San Diego conducted research on murals, a common sight within each community. At each site the children analyzed murals and learned about their purpose, why they were painted, how they were assembled, their messages, and so forth. The students shared in writing all of the data collected with their peers in the other city as well as prepared newsletters to report their work. This arrangement allows us, as part of the same system, to conduct research on reading, writing, and the use of computers, and on how to take advantage of what their respective communities have to offer.

Beyond being sites for instructional research, however, these sites enable us to establish new relationships with key social institutions and players. For example, both undergraduate and graduate students do research at the sites or in the communities. We also use the university's computing resources in facilitating the networking activities. In both instances, through the work, we are establishing a new connection between the local schools and communities and the universities. Similarly the local school districts have contributed to the sites, installing a new telephone line for our use, providing us with access to local schools, or providing funds to remunerate teachers who work with us during after-school hours. We are now planning on increasing the participation of parents; similar research in New York has combined literacy courses for parents with computer-mediated activities for the children (Pedraza, personal communication, January 1987).

CONCLUSION

We think that these community-based, educational laboratories provide us with a leverage point in the study of educational practice (cf. Latour 1983). Our work is simultaneously instructional and analytical of the community; it entails a microanalysis of instruction, so essential to understanding that those events we call lessons are always social constructions, and an analysis of the role of extracurricular factors in this social accomplishment. In this sense we see our approach not so much as dissolving but as mediating the interactive and structural explanations being examined in this volume. Our analysis does not neglect either the inside or the outside of schools; it is in this interplay that our settings function. While we study instruction and change we analyze the social factors that make our settings possible or impossible, relevant or irrelevant, successful or unsuccessful.

The key to understanding school performance is not in the study of mental aptitude or attitude toward schooling; it is in understanding the dynamics of material, local settings. To succeed in school one does not need a special culture; we know now, thanks to ethnographic work, that success and failure is in the social organization of schooling, in the organization of the experience itself. No amount of inquiry into attitudes toward schooling would have revealed the social entrapment of students in the two case studies we reviewed, or the social moves necessary to overcome the status quo. Why and how students succeed or fail, we would argue, are inseparable questions whose answers must be found in the social manipulations that produce educational change.

REFERENCES

Diaz, Stephen
    1987   Bilingual Bicultural Computer Experts: Traditional Literacy through Computer Literacy. Unpublished manuscript.
Diaz, Stephen, Luis C. Moll, and Hugh Mehan
    1986   Sociocultural Resources in Instruction: A Context-Specific Approach. *In* Beyond Language: Social and Cultural Factors in Schooling Language Minority Students. Pp. 186–230. Los Angeles: Evaluation, Dissemination and Assessment Center, California State University.
Erickson, Frederick D.
    1982   Taught Cognitive Learning in its Immediate Environments: A Neglected Topic in the Anthropology of Education. Anthroplogy and Education Quarterly 13(2):149–180.
Graves, Donald
    1983   Writing: Teachers and Children at Work. Exeter, NH: Heinemann Educational Books
Heath, Shirley Brice
    1986   Sociocultural Contexts of Language Development. *In* Beyond Language: Social and Cultural Factors in Schooling Language Minority Students. Pp. 143–185. Los Angeles: Evaluation, Dissemination and Assessment Center, California State University.

Laboratory of Comparative Human Cognition
1986   Contributions of Cross-Cultural Research to Educational Practice. American Psychologist 41(10):1049–1058.
Latour, Bruno
1983   Give Me a Laboratory and I Will Raise the World. In Science Observed. D. Knorr-Cetiona, ed. Pp. 141–170. Beverly Hills: Sage.
McDermott, Raymond P.
1976   Kids Make Sense: An Ethnographic Account of the Interactional Management of success and Failure in One First-Grade Classroom. Unpublished doctoral dissertation, Stanford University.
Mehan, Hugh
1979   Learning Lessons: Social organization in the classroom. Cambridge: Harvard University Press.
Moll, Luis C.
1986   Writing as Communication: Creating Strategic Learning Environments for Students. Theory into Practice 25(2): 103–108.
1987   Literacy Learning: A Community-Based Approach. In Literacy Learning through Family, Community, and School Interaction. Steven Silvern, ed. Chicago: JAI Press.
Moll, Luis C., and Rosa Diaz
1987   Teaching Writing as Communication: The Use of Ethnographic Findings in Classroom Practice. In Literacy and Schooling. David Bloome, ed. Pp. 193–221. Norwood, NJ. Ablex.
Moll, Luis C., and Stephen Diaz
1985   Ethnographic Pedagogy: Promoting Effective Bilingual Instruction. In Advances in Bilingual Education Research, Eugene Garcia and Raymond V. Padilla, eds. Pp. 127–149. Tucson: University of Arizona Press.
Olson, D.
1986   Intelligence and Literacy: The Relationship Between Intelligence and the Technologies of Representation and Communication. In Practical Intelligence. Robert Sternberg and Robert Wagner, eds. Pp. 338–360. New York: Cambridge University Press.
Scribner, Sylvia, and Michael Cole
1981   Psychology of Literacy. Cambridge: Harvard University Press.
Trueba, Henry T., Luis C. Moll, Stephen Diaz, and Rosa Diaz
1982   Improving the Functional Writing of Bilingual Secondary Students. Contract No. 400-81-0023. Washington, D.C.: National Institute of Education.
Vygotsky, Lev. S.
1978   Mind in Society: The Development of Higher Psychological Processes. M. Cole, V. John-Steiner, S. Scribner, and E. Souberman, eds. Cambridge: Harvard University Press.
Wertsch, James V.
1985   Vygotsky and the Social Formation of Mind. Cambridge: Harvard University Press.

Part III

Societal Forces and Minority Responses

6

Frameworks—Variability in Minority School Performance: A Problem in Search of an Explanation

John U. Ogbu

TYPES OF ANTHROPOLOGICAL STUDY
OF MINORITY EDUCATION

I have learned from experience that sometimes unnecessary disagreements arise about why minority children do poorly in school because we fail to distinguish between different types and objectives of anthropological study of minority education. Since this volume is about two different views on the causes of low school performance of minority children, and since readers have different interests and orientations, I will begin my chapter by discussing different research approaches in educational anthropology, at least as I see them; and I will do this somewhat historically.

Although some ethnographic research was conducted earlier, systematic anthropological study of minority education began mainly in mid-1960s. As I pointed out in a recent review of the field of educational anthropology (Ogbu 1985), the stimulus for a systematic ethnography was, in part, the need to respond to conventional educational research. Anthropological criticisms of that research paradigm have been presented in detail by McDermott and Hood (1982), Roberts (1976), Spindler (1982), Valentine (1968), and Wax and Wax (1971). I do not intend to repeat them here.

During the initial stage, anthropologists tried to refute the prevailing notion that minority and poor children were failing in school because they were "culturally deprived." This was done through careful ethnographic studies showing that minority and poor children were neither culturally deprived nor deprived of stimulating learning environments, and that they came from cultures that were different but as viable as the white middle-class culture. Anthropologists then suggested an alternative hypothesis for the academic difficulties of minority and poor children, namely, that the difficulties were probably due to "cultural discontinuities" or "culture conflicts" (Burger 1968; Philips 1972, 1983). There were and still are excellent case studies documenting cultural differences of the minorities in general as well as in specific domains of culture, including cognition, communication, interaction, teaching and learning, socialization, and so on.

My own contribution in this initial period was not really within the framework of the cultural discontinuities hypothesis. Rather, in my research in Stockton, California (Ogbu 1974), I noted the importance of a minority community's experiences in the postschool opportunity structure of how minority community members' perceptions of dismal future opportunities influenced their perceptions of and responses to schooling.

Having established that cultural/language differences between the dominant group and the schools, on the one hand, and the minorities, on the other, existed, and that the difficulties in social adjustment and academic performance experienced by minority children might be due to such cultural/language differences, anthropological research developed into a second stage. This stage is characterized by divergent approaches or styles that have different objectives. Four approaches can be identified and grouped into two types for the purpose of this essay. I will designate as A, or "improvement research," two research approaches, namely, microethnography and intervention ethnographic studies. I will call studies in Group B "explanatory research," consisting of comparative analysis of ethnographic studies and comparative ethnographic research in minority education.

I have described the microethnographic approach and the rationale behind it elsewhere (Ogbu 1981). Its practitioners basically accept the assumption that minority children's social adjustment and academic performance difficulties are due to cultural and language differences. The focus of the study is process, how the assumed cultural/language differences interact with teaching and learning to cause the problems experienced by the minorities. Depending on the background of the investigator, the specific cultural domain considered important in the study of the process—the study of how minority children fail—may be cognitive style, communication style, motivational style, classroom social organization and social relations, interaction style, and, nowadays, "literacy" and "writing" styles. As I noted some years ago (1981a), these are among the best studies of classroom processes that lead to minority children's school failure. But I have also argued that they cannot provide a general explanation of the school success or failure of minority children because they focus only on minority groups who do poorly in school; they do not study other minority groups who do well in school although they, too, possess different cognitive styles, communication styles, interaction styles, teaching and learning styles, and so on. Nor do the microethnographies explore and explain intragroup variability—why, for instance, some black, some Chicano, and some Indian or Native Hawaiian children do well in the same schools and classrooms where their ethnic peers do not, even though they, too, possess the same cognitive style, communication style, and learning style.

Closely associated with microethnography is "applied ethnography," • typified by two case studies in this volume (Moll and Diaz; Vogt, Jordan, and Tharp). In my understanding, these studies are not designed to "explain" why minority children succeed or fail in school. Instead, they are "intervention" studies, as Moll and Diaz repeatedly characterize their case study. Intervention ethnography or ethnographic research in search of "cultural solutions" or "cultural compatibility" is not and cannot be about *why* • minority children succeed or fail in school; the orientation is toward discovering "what works" and, perhaps, "what works best for whom?"—for minority students, for teachers of minority students, etc. Regardless of whether the focus is on problems of cognition, communication, interaction or social organization and relations, teaching and learning styles, literacy or writing, the logic of applied ethnography is not and cannot be an explanation, and certainly not a general explanation of minority children's school success or failure. One reason is that, like microethnography, intervention ethnography generally excludes minorities who are successful in spite of their cultural and language differences.

What I have discussed thus far are improvement studies, not explanatory research, which I take up next. Explanatory research is not explicitly about discovering cultural solutions to educational problems of minority children, and although it includes the study of process, that process extends beyond the classroom and even beyond the school. It is multilevel.

Explanatory research begins with a comparative analysis of available studies, including microethnographic studies and intervention studies, of the school experiences of minority groups in the United States and elsewhere. Such an analysis tends to show that both successful and unsuccessful minorities often face cultural/language difference barriers as well as barriers in employment and other domains in adult life. It is this observation of *variability* in the school performance of culturally different and language minorities that points to the need for comparative ethnographic research. In the latter kind of study the immediate goal is to explain why different minorities adjust and perform differently in school in spite of cultural and language differences. The comparative study is also concerned with determining why and how the problems created by cultural and language differences seem to persist among some minority groups but not among others. The long-range goal is to provide knowledge for better and more effective educational policy as well as for preventive and remedial efforts.

It is important not to confuse explanatory research with improvement research, and not to evaluate the former by the criteria of the latter, as some have mistakenly done (Trueba 1986). I myself have not been engaged in improvement studies; rather, I have been conducting comparative studies of minority education in the United States and elsewhere in order to understand and explain why some minority groups are less successful than others in social adjustment and academic performance in school.

CROSS-CULTURAL EVIDENCE OF VARIABILITY IN MINORITY SCHOOL PERFORMANCE

What evidence do we have that there are differences in the social adjustment and school performance of minority groups who face cultural, language, and other barriers in school and who also face social and economic barriers in the wider society? Evidence for the variability exists for minority groups in the United States and for minority groups in other societies. In the United States evidence comes from local studies (Gibson 1983, this volume; Matute-Bianchi 1986; Ogbu 1974; Suarez-Orozco 1986, this volume; Varlede 1987). For example, in my research in Stockton, California (Ogbu 1974, 1977), I found that in the 1930s both Asian-American students (Chinese and Japanese) and Mexican-American students were experiencing difficulties in school because of limited proficiency in the English language. However, a study by the local school district in 1947 (Stockton Unified School District 1948) showed that the language problems had almost disappeared among the Asian Americans but persisted among Mexican Americans. Furthermore, Asian-American students were doing so well that at this time their representation at the junior college level (grades 13 and 14) had risen to almost 250% of their expected rate. In contrast, less than five percent of the Mexican Americans in the seventh and eighth grades made it to the junior college. Local blacks did not do much better. In my own ethnographic study I found that Chinese, Filipino, and Japanese students in the late 1960s and early 1970s did considerably better than blacks and Mexican Americans in the same schools (Ogbu 1974, 1977).

At the national level, Coleman (1966) reports that Asian-American students do better than blacks, Mexican Americans, Native Americans and Puerto Ricans in reading, verbal ability, and math tests. As reported in the *New York Times* (Slade 1982), Asian-American students did better than other language and cultural minorities on the SAT administered by the Educational Testing Service in 1980—81. Asian-American students are, of course, not the only language and cultural minorities doing well in school. A comparative study of various Hispanic groups in the United States reveals some variability, too. As Suarez-Orosco (this volume) summarizes the situation, Hispanics of Central and South American origins, as well as those of Cuban origin, tend to do better in school than Mexican-American and mainland Puerto Rican students. Matute-Bianchi (1986) found in her ethnographic study of Japanese, Mexican-American and Mexicano high school students in Wattsonville, California, that many of the Hispanic students who were doing well were born in Mexico. Similarly, the results of a recent comparative study of Hispanic high school dropouts and graduates in a southwestern city found that students who were born in Mexico were less likely to drop out than those born in the United States (Varlede 1987).

The variability in minority school performance also exists in other countries. In Britain, for example, East Asian students do considerably better than West Indian students, even though the former are less fluent in English than the West Indians (Ogbu 1978; Tomlinson 1982). In New Zealand the native Maori language and cultural minority group performs less well in school than immigrant Polynesians who share similar language and culture (Penfold, personal communication).

My conclusion is that some minority groups do well in school even though they do not share the language and cultural backgrounds of the dominant group that are reflected in school features and practices. This conclusion is reinforced by two other observations from the comparative studies. One is that in some instances the minority groups who are doing well in school are the ones who differ more from the dominant group in language and culture. For example, as already noted, some studies indicate that students from Mexico appear to be more successful than native-born Chicano students (Fernandez and Nielsen 1984; Matute-Bianchi 1986; Varlede 1987; Woolard 1982). In Britain the more different East Asians do better than West Indians (Ogbu 1978). The second reinforcing observation is that a minority group that does poorly in school in its own country of origin or has an involuntary minority status appears to do much better when its members emigrate to another country, where its culture and language are even more different that the culture and language of the dominant group of the host society. A good example of this is the case of Japanese outcastes. In Japan itself, Buraku students continue to do poorly in school when compared with the dominant Ippan students. But in the United States the Buraku do as well as other Japanese Americans (DeVos 1973; Ito 1967; Shimahara 1983). A similar contrast exists for Koreans in Japan, where they are an involuntary minority group, and in the United States, where they are voluntary immigrants (DeVos 1984; Lee 1984; Rohlen 1981).

The challenge for educational anthropology is to explain the variability in the school performance: Why are some minorities successful in school even though they face barriers in culture, language, and postschool opportunities faced by the minorities that are not successful? It is one thing to conduct research designed to discover "cultural solutions" or other remedies for the school failure for some minorities; it is quite another thing to conduct research in order to account for the variability in the school performance. I do not as yet have a satisfactory explanation for the variability. However, I will indicate below my current thinking on the subject, based on my comparative work.

EMERGING EXPLANATION

The question that my studies and those of my students and colleagues have been addressing can be phrased as follows: Why do some minorities successfully cross cultural boundaries and/or opportunity barriers and do well in school? Why do some minorities not succeed in crossing cultural boundaries and/or opportunity barriers and, therefore, do not perform as well in school?

By comparing the schooling of minority children from different cultural backgrounds it is evident that all minority children encounter social adjustment and academic learning problems, at least initially. For some minority groups these tend to diminish over time, so that they eventually learn more or less successfully. For some other minority groups the problems tend to persist and may even increase in magnitude and seriousness. By comparing different minorities it appears that the primary problem in the academic performance of minority children does not lie in the mere fact that children possess a different language, dialect, or communication style; it is not that they possess a different cognitive style or a different style of interaction; it is not even that the children face barriers in future adult opportunity structure. While cultural, language, and opportunity barriers are very important for all minorities, the main factor differentiating the more successful from the less successful minorities appears to be the nature of the history, subordination, and exploitation of the minorities, *and* the nature of the minorities' own instrumental and expressive responses to their treatment, which enter into the process of their schooling. In other words, school performance is not due only to what is done to or for the minorities; it is also due to the fact that the nature of the minorities' interpretations and responses makes them more or less accomplices to their own school success or failure. There are thus three sources contributing to the school failure of the minorities who are not doing well in school, namely, society, school, and community. Because I want to explain the variability in the school performance of minority groups, I will emphasize the minority groups' or communities' contributions to school success or failure and *why* minority groups differ in their contributions. However, first I will discuss how society at large and the schools contribute to the problem of school performance.

SOCIETAL AND SCHOOL CONTRIBUTIONS TO THE PROBLEM

Societal Forces

What are the societal forces and how do they affect minority school performance? One mechanism is the historical practice of denying minorities access to desirable jobs and positions in adult life that require good education and where education pays off. This was the case in the United States for generations of black Americans, even though Americans espoused the ideology of equality of opportunity and even though American schooling has always been structured on the commonsense idea of preparing young people in marketable skills and offering them credentials for labor force entry, remuneration, and promotion on the job. The minorities were denied equal opportunity through a *job ceiling* (Ogbu 1978). Thus, minority individuals who qualified educationally were denied the opportunity to use their education meaningfully and were not rewarded with jobs and wages commensurate with their training and ability. The history of black American employment experience is the most fully documented and well known. But other minorities in the United States and elsewhere have also experienced a job ceiling (Ogbu 1978). Consider the case of the minorities against AT&T, which was settled by the Equal Employment Opportunity Commission in 1974. It was found that the giant company "saved" about $362 million a year by not paying black, Hispanic, and women employees what they would have earned had they been white males (DeWare 1978; Wallace 1976). By denying the minorities opportunity to gain entry into the labor force and to advance according to their educational qualification and ability, and by denying them adequate rewards for their education in terms of wages, American society discouraged the minorities from investing time and effort into pursuit of education and into maximizing their educational accomplishments. Since this discouragement went on for many generations, the effects have probably been cumulative and relatively enduring. Furthermore, the experience has probably discouraged the minorities from developing a strong tradition of academic achievement.

Another related societal factor is the practice of denying minorities equal access to good education. In the past, black Americans, for example, were given inferior education by formal statutes in the South and by informal practices in the North. Their inferior education was characterized by inadequately trained and overworked teachers, by different and inferior curriculum, inadequate funding, facilities, and services, and in the case of

Southern blacks, by a shorter school year. Although formal aspects of the inferior education have been legally abolished, recent court trials of desegregation cases reveal that some informal practices still remain. Inferior education ensures that the minorities do not qualify as whites do for desirable jobs and other positions in adult life that require good education and where education pays off. More important, by giving the minorities inferior education, it is certain that minority children cannot learn as much or test as well academically as white children who have superior education. Since the practice of providing inferior education for the minorities lasted for many generations, it is not farfetched to suggest that it probably resulted in the evolution of a tradition of inferior academic performance among the minorities.

School and Classroom Forces

Schools contribute to the academic problems of minority children intentionally and unintentionally because they operate according to the norms of American society and according to the norms of the communities in which they exist. Those who doubt that the form and process of schooling are determined in large part by societal interests and directives should study current debates in education and current changes in American education.

Comparative and historical research shows that there have always been factors within the schools and classrooms operating against minority children's adjustment and academic performance. This is true even where schools are integrated so that minority and white children have available to them the same staff, facilities, curriculum, and services. Among the subtle mechanisms that have been found in such a situation is the lowered expectation of teachers and administrators. Another mechanism with increasing significance is the labeling of minority children as having educational "handicaps." Because of this, a disproportionate number of minority children are channeled into special education, which is inferior education. Then, too, there are problems arising from cultural differences between minority students and school personnel. The failure of school personnel to understand and respect minority children's culturally learned behaviors often results in conflicts that obstruct children's adjustment and learning. Note, however, that I am not saying that it is only school personnel who have an obligation to understand and accommodate cultural differences; minority children also have an obligation to understand and accommodate school culture. It is a two-way thing.

The evidence that this treatment by society at large and by the schools affects how the minorities perceive and respond to schooling is found in the autobiographies of many minority individuals, in interviews with minority parents and students, and in public discussions of educational, employment, and other problems facing the minorities. I will show later in this chapter how the minorities respond to this treatment and how their responses enter into their school experiences. Here I want to point out that the treatment of the minorities that elicits responses affecting their schooling encompasses more than the instrumental treatment described above. Equally important are the denigration of the minorities and their culture and the dominant group's expressive exploitation of the minorities (DeVos 1967, 1984; Ogbu 1987). Generally, dominant group members, such as white Americans, ascribe to themselves the proper moral values, cultural norms, good manners, good and correct speech, and good and correct posture (Haynes 1985). They see in the minorities the opposite qualities. The beliefs of dominant group members in the *collective inferiority* of the minorities and their culture enable the former to exploit the minorities expressively: They project onto the minorities undesirable traits, segregate them residentially and socially, and, in some cases, prohibit intermarriage to avoid contamination; they use the minorities as scapegoats in times of political and economic crisis (see *Governor's Task Force*, State of California 1982). These treatments affect how the minorities perceive and respond to schooling and other institutions controlled by the dominant group. However, all minorities do not perceive the treatment alike or respond alike, and the treatment does not affect the schooling of all minorities to the same degree. Why not?

MINORITY RESPONSES AND VARIABILITY IN SCHOOL ADJUSTMENT AND PERFORMANCE

The complex and interlocking forces that affect social adjustment and academic performance of minority children are not limited to those of the wider society, the school, and the classroom; they also include those emanating from the minority communities themselves. The community forces, as I designate the latter, thus constitute the third force in the school adjustment and performance problems. It is largely in consideration of differences in the community forces and their influence that we begin to understand the variability in the school performance. And a prerequisite for understanding the differences in the community forces and their influence is to recognize that there are different types of minority status whose distinctive features have different implications for schooling. What are the minority types and their distinctive features?

Types of Minorities

I have identified three types of minorities in cross-cultural studies. One is *autonomous minorities*. These are people who are minorities primarily in a numerical sense. They may possess a distinctive ethnic, religious, linguistic, or cultural identity. However, although they are not entirely free from prejudice and discrimination, they are not socially, economically, and politically subordinated. Autonomous minorities do not experience disproportionate and persistent problems in learning to read and to compute, partly because they usually have a cultural frame of reference that demonstrates and encourages school success. This type of minority is typically represented in the United States by Jews and Mormons. They will not be considered further in this chapter.

Immigrant minorities are the second type. These are people who have moved more or less voluntarily to the United States because they believe that this would lead to greater economic well-being, better overall opportunities, and/or greater political freedom. Although the immigrants often experience difficulties due to language and cultural differences, they do not experience lingering disproportionate school failure. The Chinese in Stockton, California (Ogbu 1974), and Punjabi Indians in Valleyside, California (Gibson, this volume), are representative examples.

Castelike or *involuntary minorities* are people who were *originally brought into United States society involuntarily* through slavery, conquest, or colonization. Thereafter, these minorities were relegated to menial positions and denied true assimilation into mainstream society. American Indians, black Americans, and Native Hawaiians are examples. In the case of Mexican Americans, those who later immigrated from Mexico were assigned the status of the original conquered group in the southwestern United States, with whom they came to share a sense of peoplehood or collective identity. The Burakumin in Japan and the Maori in New Zealand are examples outside the United States. It is castelike or involuntary minorities that usually experience more difficulties with social adjustment and school performance.

My classification of minority groups is heuristic; it is not intended to stereotype the minorities, just as it is not stereotyping them to classify them as linguistic and nonlinguistic minorities. Furthermore, while I recognize individual differences within a given minority group, my work is not about individual differences. However, when I refer to or describe the distinctive features of a minority group I do not thereby deny that there are individual and subgroup differences within that minority group (Ogbu 1989). It is necessary to emphasize this point in view of my subsequent discussion.

Distinctive Features

Immigrant minorities and involuntary minorities may differ from the dominant group in culture, language, and social or collective identity, as well as in folk theories of getting ahead. However, *the quality of the differences* in these matters between the immigrants and the dominant group on the one hand and between the involuntary minorities and the dominant group on the other is different. This qualitative difference affects how minority children perceive and respond to schooling.

Cultural Differences. I have suggested elsewhere (Ogbu 1982) that the immigrants are characterized by *primary cultural differences* in relation to the dominant group in society, while involuntary or castelike minorities are characterized by *secondary cultural differences.* Primary cultural differences are differences that existed *before* two populations came in contact, such as before the immigrants came to the United States. For example, Punjabi Indians in Valleyside, California (Gibson, this volume), spoke Punjabi, practiced Sikh, Hindu, or Moslem religion, had arranged marriages, and males wore turbans before they came to the United States, where they continue these beliefs and practices to some extent. The Punjabis also brought with them their own way of raising children. For example, they differ from white people in Valleyside in the way they train their children to make dicisions and to manage their money (Gibson 1983). However, in spite of these differences, Punjabi immigrants are by and large successful in school. What can be said in summary is that most studies of primary cultural differences emphasize *differences in content,* and that *the differences existed prior to emigration* of the minorities to the United States or, in the case of non-Western peoples, prior to their entry into Western-type schools.

Secondary cultural differences are those differences that arise *after* two populations have come in continuous contact or *after* members of a given population have begun to participate in an institution controlled by another population, such as the schools. In other words, secondary cultural differences develop as *a response to a contact situation,* especially a contact situation involving the domination of one group by another.

Although at the beginning of the contact the minorities and dominant group may be characterized by primary cultural differences, a new type of cultural difference begins to emerge after this initial phase, particularly as the minorities begin to respond or adapt to their treatment by the dominant group.

An example of a contact situation encouraging secondary cultural differences is the case of black Americans. During slavery white Americans used legal and extralegal means to discourage blacks from acquiring literacy and associated beliefs and benefits. After slavery whites also created barriers for blacks in employment and other areas of life, which effectively denied them adequate social and economic benefits of whatever education whites made available to them. Under this circumstances, black Americans, like other involuntary minorities, developed new or "secondary" cultural ways of coping, perceiving, and feeling in regard to their relationship with white

Americans and their place in the United States society. That is, they made new adaptations, some of which involved a reinterpretation of aspects of their primary cultural differences or the differences that blacks brought from Africa.

There are specific features of secondary cultural differences that should be noted because they play an important role in the school experience of minority children and in the attempt by educational anthropologists to explain the behavior of these children. One of these features is *style*. The descriptions of the cultural differences faced by involuntary minority children usually stress differences in style, not differences in content, as in the case of the immigrants. The cultural differences of involuntary minorities have been described in regard to differences in cognitive style (Ramirez and Castenada 1974; Shade 1982), communication style (Gumperz 1981; Kochman 1982; Philips 1972, 1983), interaction style (Erickson and Mohatt 1982) and learning style; Boykin 1986; Philips 1976, 1983).

The significance of style also lies in the fact that it is related to another feature, namely, *cultural inversion*. Cultural inversion is the tendency for members of one population, in this case involuntary minorities, to regard certain forms of behaviors, certain events, symbols, and meanings as not appropriate for them because they are characteristic of members of another population (e.g., white Americans); at the same time, the minorities claim other (often the opposite) forms of behaviors, events, symbols, and meanings as appropriate for them because these are not characteristic of white Americans. Thus, what the minorities consider appropriate or even legitimate behaviors or attitudes for themselves are defined in opposition to the practices and preferences of white Americans.

Minorities use cultural inversion sometimes to repudiate negative stereotypes or derogatory images projected onto them by the whites. Sometimes they use it as a strategy to manipulate whites or to get even with whites, or, as Holt put it in the case of black Americans, "to turn the table against Whites" (1972:154).

Cultural inversion usually results in the *coexistence of two opposing cultural frames of reference* or ideal ways, orienting behavior, one considered by the minorities as appropriate for themselves and the other as appropriate for white Americans. As will be indicated later, there are social (including peer) and psychological pressures on minorities not to act according to white cultural frame of reference.

Social or Collective Identity. Another feature that differentiates immigrant minorities from involuntary minorities is the type of social or collective identity they assume vis-à-vis their perceptions of the social identity of the dominant group. From comparisons of the two types of minorities it appears that immigrants perceive their social identity as *primarily different* from the social identity of white Americans. At least during the first generation, the immigrants tend to retain the sense of peoplehood that they had prior to emigration.

Involuntary minorities, on the other hand, appear to *develop a new sense of social identity in opposition* to the social identity of the dominant group *after they have become subordinated,* and they do so in reaction to the way that dominant-group members treat them in social, political, economic, and psychological domains. The treatment by the dominant group may include deliberate exclusion of the minorities from true assimilation, or the reverse, namely, forced assimilation (Castile and Kushner 1981; DeVos 1967, 1984; Spicer 1966, 1971). Involuntary minorities also develop oppositional social identity because they perceive and experience their treatment or "oppression" by the dominant group as collective and enduring. Furthermore, these minorities *know* that they cannot easily escape from their birth-ascribed membership in a subordinate and disparaged group by "passing" or by returning to "a homeland" (DeVos 1984; Green 1981). The oppositional social identity combines with their new cultural coping mechanisms discussed above to give a different meaning to "crossing cultural/language boundaries" than it has for the immigrants.

Folk Theory of Making It and "Survival Strategies." Immigrant and involuntary minorities differ in their "theories" of how one gets ahead in the United States. However, before discussing the differences, I will clarify the role of schooling in getting ahead in general in contemporary United States and other urban industrial societies. The clarification is necessary because those who are making educational policies or involved in intervention research and programs often ignore the fact that people, be they white Americans or minorities, go to school and work hard to succeed when they perceive and experience or anticipate significant economic and other benefits of education.

The United States society, like other societies, structures schools to prepare citizens to support the existing economic system as workers producers and consumers, and to teach them to believe in the system. It also structures the schools to train the citizens to support other institutions. American schools try to accomplish their task of recruiting people into the labor force by (1) teaching young people the beliefs, values, and attitudes that support the economic system; (2) teaching them some practical skills, like reading and computing, which make the system work; (3) enhancing the development of personal attributes compatible with the habits required at the workplace; and (4) credentialing young people to enter the work force. However, for the schools to succeed in educating children of a given segment of American society, school credentials must play a positive role in the people's folk theory of getting ahead. An example of such a positive role can be found in the case of the white middle class. Their folk theory asserts that one gets a good job that pays well by getting a good education. And they implicitly or explicitly base their education on the idea of preparation for goods jobs that pay well. Since white middle-class Americans have traditionally obtained jobs and earned wages commensurate with their school credentials, they have usually not only perceived schooling from this point of view, but have also responded by investing the time and effort necessary to do well in school.

What happens when people, such as the minorities, face barriers that prevent them from getting ahead in the United States according to the prevailing folk theory of success (i.e., through education)? The two minority types differ in their responses to the situation. Initially the immigrants tend to accept the dominant group's folk theory of getting ahead (Gibson, this volume; Suarez-Orozco, this volume; Ogbu 1978), to believe that in the United States they, too, can get ahead through hard work, school success, and individual ability. Their perceptions of opportunity structure in the United States seem to contrast sharply with their perceptions of the opportunity structure "back home" in their countries of origin (Suarez-Orozco, this volume). When the immigrants encounter discrimination they tend to rationalize it by saying that it is because they are "guests" in the country (Gibson, this volume), because they do not speak the language, or because they do not have an American education. Furthermore, at least cognitively, the immigrants have some options: they can return to their homeland or reemigrate to another country where they can benefit more from their American education (Ogbu 1983; Sung, 1967).

Involuntary minorities do not have the option of returning to a homeland or reemigration; nor do they feel that white Americans have a right to discriminate against them in jobs and wages because they, too, are citizens. Furthermore, they know from generations of experience that the barriers facing them in opportunity structure are not temporary. For these reasons involuntary minorities tend to develop a different version of the folk theory of getting ahead, which may emphasize other strategies likely to be in competition with schooling (Ogbu 1974, 1983).

The situation is however, paradoxical, for when questioned directly, involuntary minorities often respond, like white Americans and like immigrants, that to get ahead one needs a good education. But other evidence suggests that the involuntary minorities do not really believe that they have an equal chance with white Americans to get ahead through education. They tend to reject or attack the criteria by which academic achievement is measured and also the use of educational qualifications or measures as a criterion for employment in some situations. They do not work hard enough in school to get the education that will help them get ahead. They employ a variety of techniques, often through "collective struggle," to remove, reduce, or circumvent the barriers in opportunity structure. Moreover, the minorities have developed a variety of "survival strategies" to compensate for apparent lack of equal opportunity for equal and fair competition in mainstream economic and other institutions.

Degree of Trusting Relations. Although immigrant minorities encounter and resent discrimination in the larger society and in the schools (Gibson 1983, this volume), they do not perceive such treatment as institutionalized or permanent. And their response can best be described as an accommodation. Some immigrants even dismiss the discriminatory treatment as due to white American ignorance of their culture and background (Gibson, this volume). The reason for the accommodation response is that many immigrant minorities came to the United States partly because they perceived the opportunity structure in the United States to be better than the opportunity structure in their own homeland and partly because they wanted to give their children the opportunity to get an American education. Thus, Suarez-Orozco (1986, this volume) reports that many Central and South American parents interviewed in San Francisco "explicitly stated that they made great sacrifices to come to the United States so that their children could get an education and become somebody." For a similar expression by other immigrants, see Ogbu (1983) and Wong (1972). Furthermore, the immigrants frequently find their relationship with American public schools and school personnel much more to their liking than their previous relationship with schools in their homeland. They speak favorably of the fact that in the United States the schools give children textbooks and other supplies (Suarez-Orozco 1986).

In contrast, there is a deep distrust that runs through the relationship between the public schools and the involuntary minorities. In the case of black Americans, for example, one finds many episodes throughout their history that seem to have left them with the feeling that white people and the institutions they control cannot be trusted (Ogbu 1985). The public schools, particularly in the inner city, are therefore not generally trusted to give black children the "right education." This distrust arises from perceptions of past and current treatment of blacks by the schools as discriminatory.

In summary, immigrant minorities differ from involuntary minorities in origins of minority status, in the nature of cultural differences between them and the dominant group, in social identity vis-à-vis white American social identity, in folk theory of getting ahead, and in degree of trusting relations with white Americans and the institutions the latter control. I will discuss in the next section how these differences enter into the process of minority schooling and cause different problems for the immigrants and for involuntary minorities.

EXPLAINING THE VARIABILITY OR DIFFERENCES IN PROPORTION AND PERSISTENCE

The Immigrants

The primary cultural differences of the immigrants initially cause problems in school both in interpersonal/intergroup relations and in academic teaching and learning. But the nature of the problems is affected by the nature of primary cultural differences, especially the *differences in content and absence of oppositional quality.* For example, minority children may come to school with different assumptions about getting ahead or about interpersonal/intergroup relations. Thus, Central and South American immigrants enter the public schools from cultural backgrounds that stress getting ahead on the basis of whom you know or because of your name, rather than on the basis of individual training and ability (Suarez-Orozco, this volume). Punjabi Indians enter the public schools from a cultural background that teaches children to defer to adult authority, in contrast to the school expectation that children should defend their ideas even when those ideas are in conflict with those adults, including the teacher. The Punjabi also face problems of gender relations in school. Their culture teaches them to avoid eye contract with members of the opposite sex. But in the classroom they are expected to look directly at teachers and classmates of the opposite sex when addressing them or being addressed in order to be considered polite (Gibson 1983). In some cases immigrant minority children and children from non-Western societies come to school lacking certain concepts that are essential for learning mathematics and other subjects because the concepts do not exist in their own cultures. This problem is more fully documented for non-Western children attending Western-type schools in their own societies (Gay and Cole 1967; Lancy 1983). The children may also bring to school a style of learning that is quite different from the one emphasized by the public schools. For example, the Chinese have a traditional style of learning that emphasizes external forms and rote memorization rather than observation, analysis, and comprehension (Ogbu 1983b). Of course, a major barrier facing immigrant minority children in school is lack of fluency in the English language, the medium of instruction. In some cases the non-English-speaking children, such as the Chinese, come with a language that is structurally and in other important respects different from the English language. Because of these language, cultural, and opportunity structure barriers, the immigrants initially experience difficulties in social adjustment and academic learning. But eventually they appear to adjust and learn more or less successfully or, put differently, the immigrants succeed in crossing cultural/language boundaries to do relatively well in school. Why do they succeed in crossing cultural/language boundaries?

The extent to which the immigrants succeed in crossing cultural/language boundaries and in learning successfully in school depends in part on what schools do to help them. But it also depends on their own perceptions of and responses to the cultural and language differences facing them. In this regard there are features of the primary cultural differences and of the immigrant minority status that aid immigrant minority children, so that they eventually overcome the initial problems, adjust socially, and learn more or less successfully.

One facilitating factor is that the cultural differences developed *before* the immigrants came to the United States and did not arise as a part of their boundary-maintaining mechanisms in opposition to equivalent features in the culture of the dominant group and the schools they control. For this reason, the immigrants see the *cultural differences as barriers to be overcome* in order to achieve their long-range goals of future employment and *not as markers of identity to be maintained*. They therefore do not perceive or interpret learning the cultural features of the school required for social adjustment and academic performance as threatening to their own culture, language, and identity, but rather as an additive learning, that is, as acquiring another language (standard English) and aspects of the dominant group culture that will help them succeed in school and later in the labor market. Immigrant minorities thus adopt what Gibson (1983) calls a strategy of "accommodation without assimilation." That is, while they may not give up their cultural beliefs and practices, they are willing and actually strive to play the classroom game by the rules and try to overcome all kinds of difficulties in school because they believe so strongly that there will be a payoff later. Furthermore, because the immigrants perceive cultural and language differences as barriers to be overcome, they do not expect the schools to teach them in their own culture and language. Rather, they usually go to school expecting and willing to learn the school culture and language, although they do not necessarily do so without difficulties. Finally, immigrant minorities are able to cross cultural boundaries because primary cultural differences and the problems they cause for students are usually specific in nature and can thus be identified through careful ethnographic research. This specificity and identifiability make it possible to develop appropriate educational policies, programs, and practices to eliminate them or reduce their adverse impacts.

In addition, the fact that the immigrants came to the United States with the belief that this would lead to greater economic well-being and better overall opportunities influences how they respond to schooling. As we have seen, the immigrants tend to adopt the folk theory of success of the dominant group, and they also tend to have favorable perceptions and interpretations of opportunity structure in the United States. Still another factor facilitating the success of the immigrants is their dual frame of reference in regard to the opportunity structure. The immigrants often compare themselves with the standard of their home country or with their peers "back home" or in the immigrants' neighborhood. When they make such a comparison they usually find plenty of evidence that they have made significant improvements in their lives and/or that there are good prospects for their children *because of better opportunities in their new country.* Thus, the promise of wealth, opportunity, and political freedom that motivated emigration continues to influence the immigrants' adaptive strategies in their host society, including their schooling strategies.

Finally, the immigrants' interpretations of and responses to their relationship with the schools also facilitate their academic success. The relationship between the schools and the minority communities may raise similar educational problems for the immigrants and involuntary minorities. But the two types of minorities may interpret and respond to these problems differently. For example, both may be channeled into suggested and/or inferior schools. In such schools the immigrants may still do well academically, whereas the involuntary minorities may not. Three factors seem to work in favor of the immigrants. One is that many immigrants regard the public schools as offering an education far superior to what was available in their homeland, so that even when they attend an inferior school in the United States they may not recognize it as inferior. Their frame of reference in evaluating their education is the quality of education in their homeland, not the quality of education in the white suburbs. Second, some immigrants believe that they are treated better in the public schools than they were or would be treated by the schools of their country of origin. In ethnographic studies, immigrant minorities often express both surprise and appreciation for the fact that they do not have to pay school fees to attend the public schools and that they receive textbooks and school supplies free (Suarez-Orozco 1986, this volume). Third, even when the immigrants recognize, experience, and resent prejudice and discrimination in the public schools, as in the case of the Punjabis in Valleyside, California (Gibson 1983, this volume), they appear to respond in ways that do not discourage them from doing well in school. They rationalize the prejudice and discrimination against them by saying that as guests in a foreign land, they have no choice but to tolerate prejudice and discrimination. Punjabi parents impress this attitude on their children and place the responsibility for doing well in school on the children themselves.

In summary, the immigrants overcome their initial problems, adjust socially, and do well academically because the primary cultural differences make it easy for them to overcome the cultural/language discontinuities they encounter in school. That is, even though they have their own language, cultural frame of reference, and social identity, the differences existed before they came to the United States; they did not arise in opposition to the language, cultural frame of reference, and social identity of white Americans who control the public schools. Because of this the immigrants do not equate learning English and other aspects of the culture of the whites essential for school success with learning a cultural frame of reference that threatens their own language, culture, and identity. Furthermore, their ability to overcome the initial problems is also due to the instrumental expectations that motivated their emigration to the United States and their trusting or accommodative relationship with the public schools.

As a consequence of these perceptions, responses, or adaptations, the immigrant community, family, and children adopt schooling strategies that enhance academic success and promote social adjustment. What are some of the strategies? At the community and family levels children are encouraged and/or guided to develop good academic work habits and perseverance; parents and other members of the community, sometimes through gossip and related techniques, communicate to children nonambivalent instrumental messages about education, namely, that it is a *sine qua non* for getting ahead in the United States and that it is also a means to overcome or reduce discrimination in employment; parents and community tend to insist that children follow school rules of behavior that enhance academic success. For their part, immigrant minority children seem to respond positively to their parents' training and advice and to parental and community pressures. The children try to develop and maintain serious academic attitudes, value making good grades, respect school authority, follow school rules and standard practices, and invest a good deal of time and effort in their schoolwork. If language problems persist, older children tend to select courses requiring less use of language, and they avoid fields of study that prepare them for jobs where there is a job ceiling or discrimination against their group.

Involuntary Minorities

Involuntary minorities also encounter in the public schools interpersonal/ intergroup and academic learning problems due to cultural/language differences, conflicts, or discontinuities. But they are less able than the immigrants to overcome these problems and therefore tend to experience a greater degree of social adjustment problems and persistent high rates of school failure. There are complex community forces that make it more difficult for involuntary minorities to overcome their initial school problems. One reason they do not overcome their initial difficulties as easily as the immigrants is that they have greater difficulty crossing cultural/language boundaries due to the oppositional nature of their cultural frame of reference and identity. *Thus, unlike the immigrants, involuntary minorities perceive the cultural differences they encounter in school as markers of identity to be maintained, not as barriers to be overcome.* Moreover, involuntary minorities tend to equate school learning with the learning of a white American cultural frame of reference and to equate following the standard practices and related activities of the school that enhance academic success and social adjustment with "acting white." Consequently, learning some aspects of the school curriculum and adopting the school's conventional attitudes and practices appear to be threatening to their language, culture, and identity. Under this circumstance there are both external (i.e., social) and internal (i.e., psychological) pressures against adopting classroom and school conventional communication and other behavioral "styles" or against "acting white."

The social pressures against "acting white" include accusations of "Uncle Tomism" or disloyalty to the minority group and its cause, fear of losing one's friends, and fear of losing one's sense of community. The psychological pressures come about because the minority individual who desires to do well in school may also define the behavior enhancing school success and the success itself as "acting white." Knowing/fearing that striving for academic success and the success itself may result in loss of minority peer affiliation and support, and at the same time being uncertain of white acceptance and support if he or she succeeds in learning to act white, creates a personal conflict for the student.

The social and psychological pressures discourage bright minority students from adopting serious academic attitudes and from investing sufficient time and effort in their schoolwork. The dilemma of involuntary minority students is that they have to choose between "acting white" and "acting minority," as it were.

Many of the conflict situations that microethnographers describe as discontinuities in "style"—cognitive style, communication style, interaction style, etc.—are in our framework, good examples of the oppositional process that discourages crossing cultural boundaries to learn successfully in school.

The reluctance to cross cultural/language boundaries or to "act white" appears to begin at the elementary school level but becomes increasingly manifest as the children pass through junior and senior high schools. Philips's study (1972, 1983) clearly shows that the phenomenon begins early and that it originates in the community. The Indian children she studied learned in the course of their upbringing "the participant structure" of their community, which appears to be not only different but oppositional to that of school and the white people who control it. Similar oppositional behaviors and attitudes have been reported for blacks (Abdul-Jabbar and Knobles 1983; Fordham and Ogbu 1986; Petroni 1970) and for Chicanos (Matute-Bianchi 1986).

Problems of social adjustment and school performance also arise from the instrumental responses of involuntary minorities to economic and related barriers. In contrast to the immigrants, involuntary minorities did not choose to come to the United States motivated by the hope of economic success or political freedom. Nor do they have the comparative reference to conditions or peers "back home" or to a less favorable former status or standards in regard to their present condition in the United States. If they make any comparisons, they are inclined to consider their former state or preminority status period as considerably better than their current state. The main comparative frame of reference they have, though, is that of the dominant white Americans; and when they compare themselves with the whites the minorities often conclude that they are far worse off than they ought to be because of white treatment, and this makes them resentful. They also attribute their poorer conditions to what they perceive as institutionalized discrimination perpetuated against them by the whites and the institutions, like the public schools, controlled by whites.

As noted earlier, because involuntary minorities perceive the barriers against them in opportunity structure as more or less enduring, the tend to evolve a folk theory of getting ahead that stresses other strategies besides schooling. Some of these "survival strategies" are in competition with schooling, and some shape attitudes and endeavors toward schooling. Ethnographic studies show, for instance, that black children tend to divert their efforts into nonacademic activities as they get older and become more aware of their limited future opportunities for mainstream employment and as they become more aware of how some people in the community "make it" without good school credentials or mainstream employment (Bouie 1981; Ogbu 1974).

Finally, the relationship between involuntary minorities and white Americans who control the public schools, characterized by conflict and distrust, contributes to the minorities' social adjustment and academic performance problems. One consequence of the minorities' distrust of white people and the public schools appears to be that they are skeptical that the schools can educate their children as well as they educate white children. Furthermore, due to this distrust, involuntary minorities do not necessarily accept or interpret school rules of behavior and standard practices in the same way that white people and immigrants do. The latter seem to endorse the rules and standard practices as necessary, desirable, and compatible with their own educational goals. Involuntary minorities appear, on the other hand, to interpret the same rules and standard practices as an imposition of the white cultural frame of reference, which does not necessarily meet their real educational needs. To make the situation worse, the schools themselves appear to approach the education of involuntary minorities defensively through strategies of control and paternalism, which divert attention from efforts to educate minority children. I suggest that the distrust of white people and the public schools as well as the skepticism of involuntary minorities about the appropriateness of school rules and standard practices probably make it more difficult for minority parents and community to teach their children effectively to accept, internalize, and follow the school rules and practices that lead to academic success, *and* for their children, especially as they get older, to accept, internalize, and follow the school rules and standard practices (Ogbu 1984).

These factors—difficulty in crossing cultural/language boundaries, folk theory of making it and survival strategies, and distrust of white people and the public schools—shape the schooling strategies of involuntary minorities. Their strategies appear to be less effective than those of the immigrants in promoting good social adjustment and academic performance. Among the strategies of involuntary minority parents and community are the following: active or passive confrontation with the schools; verbal encouragement but nonteaching involvement with children's education/school learning; continual quest for "better education," involving collective struggle; unconsciously teaching children ambivalent attitudes about education and success in adult life or in the opportunity structure; a weak control of children's use of time; a weak socialization of children to develop good academic work habits and perseverance at academic tasks; and a weak sanction of academic instrumental behavior and academic responsibility. On the part of the children, involuntary minority students do not develop or maintain good academic work habits and attitudes; they tend to have a norm of minimum effort, do not work hard, and spend limited time on academic tasks; they avoid taking "hard"/"difficult"/"White" courses; they tend to be satisfied with average grades; although the children may do their homework, they do not routinely study; they do not usually separate academic tasks from other activities; they seem to prefer peer solidarity to schoolwork and easily submit to peer pressures that take them away from their schoolwork; they distrust school authorities with whom they are frequently in conflict; and they have a tendency to resist following school rules and standard practices.

ONTOGENETIC DEVELOPMENT

How do these things—the community forces—get into the minority child so that he or she comes to behave at school in the manner described above? In brief, the initial term of incorporation into American society (voluntary immigration or involuntary incorporation) together with subsequent subordination and exploitation shape the minority group's cultural model of schooling. The latter includes the members' perceptions and interpretations of schooling, degree of reliance on schooling as a strategy for "making it," relationship with "the system" and with the white people who control it, and so on. The cultural model, in turn, shapes the strategies that the minorities adopt toward schooling.

Now, the minority group's adaptations to minority status in the wider society, its cultural model of schooling, and strategies toward schooling form an integral part of the cultural curriculum that a minority child learns in the course of growing up in the community. This curriculum—minority adaptations, cultural model of schooling, and strategies—is taught to the child consciously and unconsciously through culturally patterned processes and techniques by agents responsible for the child's upbringing, including the family, peer groups, religious organizations, the mass media, and role models. As the minority child gets older he or she may actively seek to acquire the adaptations, the cultural model, and educational strategies of the group. Thus, when the minority child comes to school, he or she comes with an emerging knowledge, set of attitudes, and strategies that can promote or discourage social adjustment and academic performance, depending on what the child encounters at school.

CONCLUSION

Both immigrant and involuntary minority children appear to experience difficulties in learning to read and to compute, as well as in social adjustment, at least initially. This has been documented in several studies both in the United States and in other countries. The reason both groups of children experience initial difficulties is that they come from cultures that equip them with cognitive styles, interactional styles, learning styles, and so on that are different from those of the mainstream and the public schools. Furthermore, the contents of the school curriculum may be foreign to immigrant and involuntary minority children alike. However, what seems evident from a close and comparative analysis of available data is that immigrant minority children in the public schools in the United States do not manifest the kinds of attitudes and behaviors commonly found among involuntary minority children in the public schools.

On the basis of comparative analysis I suggest that the real issue in the school adjustment and academic performance of minority children is not whether the children possess a different language or dialect, a different cognitive style, a different style of interaction, a different communication style, or a different style of socialization or upbringing. Rather, the real issues are threefold: first, whether the children come from a segment of society where people have traditionally experienced unequal opportunity to use their education or school credentials in a socially and economically mean- ingful and rewarding manner; second, whether or not the relationship between the minorities and the dominant-group members who control the public schools has encouraged the minorities to perceive and define school learning as an instrument for replacing their cultural identity with the cultural identity of their "oppressors" without full reward or assimilation; and, third, whether or not the relationship between the minorities and the schools generates the trust that encourages the minorities to accept school rules and practices that enhance academic success.

Comparative work leads me to conclude at this point that involuntary minorities have persistent high rates of school failure and social adjustment problems because they have greater difficulty crossing cultural boundaries due to an oppositional cultural frame of reference and oppositional identity; there evolved a folk theory of getting ahead in which schooling competes with and may be adversely affected by other survival strategies; and their distrust of white people and skepticism make it harder for them to accept and follow school rules and standard practices that enhance academic success.

REFERENCES

Abdul-Jabbar, K. and P. Knobles
   1983   Giant Steps: The Autobiography of Kareem Abdul-Jabbar. New York: Bantam Books.
Au, K. H.
   1980   Participant Structure in a Reading Lesson with Hawaiian Children: Analysis of a Culturally Appropriate Instructional Event. Anthropology And Education Quarterly, 11(2):91–115.
Bouie, A.
   1981   Student Perceptions of Behavior and Misbehavior in the School Setting: An Exploratory Study and Discussion. San Francisco: Far West Laboratory For Educational Research and Development.
Boykin, A. W.
   1980   Reading Achievement and the Social Cultural Frame of Reference of Afro American Children. A Paper presented at NIE Roundtable Discussion on Issues In Urban Reading, Nov. 19–20, Washington, D.C.
   1986   The Triple Quandary and the Schooling of Afro-American Children. The School Achievement Of Minority Children: New Perspectives. In U. Neisser, ed. Pp. 57–92. Hillsdale, NJ: Lawrence Erlbaum.
Burger, H. G.
   1968   Ethno-Pedagogy: A Manual In Cultural Sensitivity, With Techniques for Improving Cross-Cultural Teaching By Fitting Ethnic Patterns. Albuquerque, NM: Southwestern Cooperative Educational Laboratory.
California, State of
   1982   Governor's Task Force On Civil Rights: Reports on Racial, Ethnic And Religious Violence In California. Sacramento: Department of Fair Employment & Housing.

Castile, G. P. and G. Kushner, eds.
  1981   Persistent Peoples: Cultural Enclaves In Perspective. Tucson: University of
        Arizona Press.
Coleman, J.S.
  1966   Equality of Educational Opportunity. Washington, DC: U.S. Government
        Printing Office.
DeVos, G.A.
  1967   Essential Elements of Caste: Psychological Determinants in Structural
        Theory. *In* Japan's Invisible Race: Caste In Culture And Personality. G.A.
        DeVos and H. Wagtsuma, eds. Pp. 332–384. Berkeley: University of
        California Press.
  1973   Japan Outcasts: The Problem of the Burakumin. *In* The Fourth World:
        Victims of Group Oppression. [B. Whitaker, ed.] New York: Pp. 307–327
        Schocken Books.
  1984   Ethnic Persistence and Role Degradation: An Illustration From Japan. Paper
        presented at the American-Soviet Symposium on Contemporary Ethnic
        Processes in the USA and USSR. New Orleans, LA, April 14–16.
DeWare, H.
  1978   Affirmative Action Plan at AT & T Is Permitted, The Washington Post, July
        4, pp. A1, A7.
Diaz, S. and L. C. Moll
  1987   Activity Settings for Educational Change. "Explaining the School Perfor-
        mance of Minority Students (eds.) Special Issue, Anthropology and Educa-
        tion Quarterly.
Erickson, F. and J. Mohatt
  1982   Cultural Organization of Participant Structure in Two Classrooms of Indian
        Students. *In* Doing the Ethnography of Schooling: G. C. Spindler, ed.,
        Educational Anthropology in Action. Pp. 132–175 New York: Holt.
Fernandez, R. M. and F. Nielsen
  1984   Bilingualism and Hispanic Scholastic Achievement: Some Baseline Results.
        Unpublished Manuscript. Dept. of Sociology, University of Arizona.
Fordham, S. and J. U. Ogbu
  1986   Black Students' School Success: Coping with the Burden of Acting White."
        The Urban Review 18(3): 176–206.
Gay, J. and M. Cole
  1967   The New Mathematics and an Old Culture: A Study of Learning among the
        Kpelle of Liberia. New York: Holt.
Gibson, M. A.
  1982   Reputation and Respectability: How Competing Cultural Systems Affect
        Students' Performance in School. Anthropology and Education Quarterly
        13(1):3–27.
  1983   Home-School—Community Linkages: A Study of Educational Opportunity
        for Punjabi Youth. Final Report to the National Institute of Education,
        Washington, D.C.
  1987   The School Performance Of Immigrant Minorities: A Comparative View. E.
        In "Explaining the School Performance of Minority Children Jacob and C.
        E. Jordan, eds. Special Issue, of Anthropology and Education Quarterly.

Green, V.
  1981 Blacks in the United States: The Creation of An Enduring People? *In* Persistent Peoples: Cultural Enclaves in Perspective G. P. Castile and G. Kushner eds.: pp. 69–77 Tucson: University of Arizona Press.
Gumperz, J.J.
  1981 Conversational Inferences and Classroom Learning. *In* Ethnographic Approaches to Face-to-Face Interaction. J. Green and C. Wallat, eds. Norwood, NJ: Ablex.
Haynes, R. L.
  1985 Minority Strategies For Success. Unpublished Manuscript, Special Project Berkeley: University of California, Department of Anthropology.
Holt, G. S.
  1972 "Inversion" in the Black Communication. *In* Rappin' and Stylin Out: Communication in Urban Black America T. Kochman, ed. Pp. 152–159. Chicago: University of Illinois Press.
Ito, H.
  1967 Japan's Outcastes in the United States. In Japan's Invisible Race: Caste in Culture and Personality. [G. A. DeVos and H. Wagatsuma, eds.] Berkeley: pp. 200-221. University of California Press.
Kochman, T.
  1982 Black and White Styles in Conflict. Chicago: University of Chicago Press.
Lancy, D.F.
  1983 Cross-Cultural Studies in Cognition and Mathematics. New York: Academic Press
Lee, C. and G. DeVos, eds.
  1981 Koreans in JapanBerkeley: University of California Press.
Lee. Y.
  1984 Koreans in Japan and United States. Unpublished manuscript Evanston, IL: Northwestern University, Department of Anthropology.
Matute-Bianchi, M.E.
  1986 Ethnic Identities and Patterns of School Success and Failure among Mexican-Descent and Japanese-American Students in a California High School: An Ethnographic Analysis. American Journal of Education 95(1):233–255.
McDermott, R.P. and L. Hood
  1982 Institutionalized Psychology and the Ethnography of Schooling. *In* Children In and Out of School: Ethnography and Education. P. Gilmore and D.M. Smith, eds) Pp. 232–249. Arlington, VA: Center for Applied Linguistics.
Ogbu, J. U.
  1974 The Next Generation: An Ethnography of Education in an Urban Neighborhood. New York: Academic Press.
  1977 Racial Stratification and Education: The Case of Stockton, California. ICRD Bulletin 12(3):1–26.
  1978 Minority Education and Caste: The American System in Cross-Cultural Perspective. New York: Academic Press.
  1981 Schooling in the Ghetto: A Cultural-Ecological Perspective on Community and Home Influences. ERIC ED 252 270.

1982   Cultural Discontinuities and Schooling. Anthropology and Education
        Quarterly 13(4):290–307.
1983   Minority Status and Schooling in Plural Societies. Comparative Education
        Review 27(2):168–190.
1984   Understanding Community Forces Affecting Minority Students' Academic
        Effort. Oakland, CA: The Achievement Council. Unpublished Manuscript.
1985   Research Currents: Cultural-Ecological Influences on Minority School
        Learning. Language Arts, 62(8):860–869.
1987   Opportunity Structure, Cultural Boundaries, and Literacy. *In* Language,
        Literacy, and Culture: Issues of Society and Schooling. J. Langer, ed. Pp.
        149-177. Norwood, NJ: Ablex.
1989   The Individual in Collective Adaptation: A Framework for Focusing on
        Academic Underperformance and Dropping Out Among Involuntary Mi-
        norities. *In* Dropouts from Schools: Issues, Dilemmas, and Solutions. L.
        Weis, E. Farrar, and H.G. Petrie, eds. Pp. 181-204. Buffalo: State University
        of New York Press.

Ow, P.
1976   The Chinese and the American Educational System. Unpublished Man-
        uscript, Special Project. Berkeley: University of California, Department of
        Anthropology.

Petroni, F.A.
1970   "Uncle Toms:" White Stereotypes in the Black Movement. Human Organi-
        zation 29(4):260–266.

Philips, S. U.
1972   Participant Structure and Communicative Competence: Warm Springs
        Children in Community and Classroom. *In* Functions of Language in the
        Classroom. C. Cazden, D. Hymes, and W. J. John, eds. Pp. 370–394. New
        York: Teachers College Press.
1976   Commentary: Access to Power and Maintenance of Ethnic Identity as Goals
        of Multicultural Education. Anthropology and Education Quarterly
        7:30–32.
1983   The Invisible Culture: Communication in Classroom and Community on
        the Warm Springs Indian Reservation. New York: Longman.

Ramirez, M. and A. Castenada.
1974   Cultural Democracy, Biocognitive Development and Education. New York:
        Academic Press.

Roberts, J.I.
1976   An Overview of Anthropology and Education. *In* Educational Patterns and
        Cultural Configurations: The Anthropology of Education. J. I. Roberts and
        S. K. Akinsanya, eds. Pp. 1–20. New York: David McKay.

Rohlen, T.
1981   Education: Policies and Prospects. *In* Koreans In Japan: Ethnic Conflicts
        And Accommodation. C. Lee and G. DeVos, eds. Pp. 182–222. Berkeley:
        University of California Press.

Shade, B. J.
1982   Afro-American Patterns of Cognition. Unpublished manuscript. Madison:
        Wisconsin Center for Education Research.

Shimahara, N. K.
  1983 Mobility and Education of Buraku: The Case of a Japanese Minority. Paper
        presented at the Annual Meeting of AAA, Chicago.
Slade, M.
  1982 Aptitude, Intelligence or What? New York Times, Oct. 24.
Spicer, E. H.
  1966 The Process of Cultural Enclavement in Middle America. 36th Congress of
        International de Americanistas, Seville 3:267–279.
  1971 Persistent Cultural Systems: A Comparative Study of Identity Systems That
        Can Adapt to Contrasting Environments. Science, 174:795–800.
Spindler, G.D.
  1982 Introduction. In Doing The Ethnography Of Schools. G.D. Spindler, ed. Pp.
        1–8. New York: Holt.
Stockton Unified School District
  1948 Community Survey: In-School Youth. Unpublished manuscript. Stockton,
        CA: Research Dept., Stockton Unified School District.
Suarez-Orozco, M.M.
  1986 In Pursuit of a Dream: New Hispanic Immigrants In American Inner City
        Schools. Unp. Doct. Dissertation, Dept. of Anthropology, U.C. Berkeley.
  1987 "Becoming Somebody:" Central American Immigrants in U.S. Inner City
        Schools. In Explaining the School Performance of Minority Children. E.
        Jacob and C.E. Jordan, eds. Special Issue, Anthropology and Education
        Quarterly: 287–299.
Sung, B. L.
  1967 Mountain of Gold: The Story of the Chinese in America. New York:
        Macmillan.
Tomlinson, S.
  1982 A Sociology of Special Education. London: Routledge and Kegan Paul.
Trueba, H.T.
  1986 Review of Beyond Language: Social and Cultural Factors in Schooling
        Language Minority Students. Anthropology and Education Quarterly
        17(4):255–259.
U.S. District Court For Northern California
  1979 Larry P. v. Wilson Riles: Opinion. San Francisco: Unpublished Document
        (#C-71-2270RFP)
Valentine, C.A.
  1968 Culture And Poverty: Critique and Counter Proposals. Chicago: University
        of Chicago Press.
Varlede, Sylvia A.
  1987 A Comparative Study of Hispanic High School Dropouts and Graduates:
        Why Do Some Leave School Early and Some Finish? Education and Urban
        Society 19(3):320–329.
Vogt, L. A., C.E. Jordan and R.G. Tharp
  1987 Rectifying the School Performance Of Hawaiian and Navajo Students. In
        Explaining the School Performance Of Minority Children. E. Jacob and
        C.E. Jordan, eds. Special Issue, Anthropology and Education Quarterly.

Wallace, P. A.
1976   Equal Employment Opportunity and the AT&T Case. Cambridge, MA: The MIT Press.

Wax, M. and R. Wax
1971   Great Tradition, Little Tradition, and Formal Education. *In* Anthropological Perspectives on Education. M. L. Wax, S. Diamond, and F. O. Gearing, eds. Pp. 3–18. New York: Basic Books.

Wong, K.
1972   An Investigation of the Reasons for Changing Political Mood in San Francisco Chinatown. Unpublished manuscript. Berkeley: Department of Anthropology, University of California.

Woolard, K.A.
1981   Ethnicity in Education: Some Problems of Language and Identity in Spain and the United States. Unpublished manuscript. Berkeley: Department of Anthropology, University of California.

7

The School Performance of Immigrant Minorities: A Comparative View*

Margaret A. Gibson

Students whose cultural and linguistic backgrounds differ from those of the dominant group in this society do not yet enjoy equal educational opportunities. All minority students face special problems in school. In spite of the barriers, some groups of minority students do comparatively well in school. This article explores some of the factors that both promote and impede success in school for one group of immigrants, the Punjabi Indians. My own data are set within the context of the international and comparative literature on minority school performance. I conclude with some thoughts on why immigrant minorities often meet with greater success in school than nonimmigrant groups and the implications of comparative analysis for the improvement of educational practice.

Immigrant minorities have been found to do well in school in many parts of the world (see Gibson 1987a; Gibson and Ogbu 1991). Here in the United States there is increasing evidence that students of Asian ancestry, both immigrant and U.S.-born, complete more years of education than majority-group agemates (U.S. Bureau of the Census 1984a). Young people of Cuban ancestry also persist in school longer than non-Hispanic white Americans (U.S. Bureau of the Census 1983).

Statistical evidence of immigrant school persistence must be interpreted with care. Many of the more recently arrived immigrants are highly

---

* An earlier version of this chapter was presented at the 84th Annual Meeting of the American Anthropological Association and subsequently published in *Education and Cultural Process* (a special issue of *Anthropology and Education Quarterly*), George D. Spindler, ed. (Gibson 1987a).

educated, affluent professionals, and the fact that their children do well academically may simply provide us with further evidence of how schools help to reproduce class status from one generation to the next. Asian Indians are a case in point. The large majority of all Asian Indians now residing in the United States are "New Wave" immigrants who have arrived in the United States since 1970. As a group they are highly educated. More than half (63.1%) have completed four years of college, and the majority hold managerial, professional, and technical positions. Their income level is also high, in keeping with their educational and occupational backgrounds (U.S. Bureau of the Census 1984a).

Ethnographic research indicates, however, that the general pattern of academic persistence and achievement applies not only to the offspring of well-educated Asian Indian professionals, but also to children of Punjabi Indian agricultural laborers, factory workers, and small-scale orchard farmers. My data come from two years of fieldwork in a California agricultural town and the area's one comprehensive high school. I call the town "Valleyside."

METHODOLOGY

Fieldwork was carried out by a team of researchers, Punjabi and non-Punjabi, male and female, insiders and outsiders to the Valleyside setting.[1] The major research methods were those of participant observation and interviewing, both formal and informal. In addition, we analyzed school performance data for all 2,100 students attending Valleyside High School, grades 9–12. At the time of fieldwork, Punjabi students constituted 11% of the total high school enrollment.

We concentrated our attention on the school performance and experiences of students in their final year at Valleyside High. Research samples included all 44 Punjabi seniors (class of 1981) and 42 white Valleysider seniors, selected by random sample. Interviews with these students, their parents, and their teachers form the heart of the project's data base.

SETTING

Most of the Valleyside Indians, who in 1981 numbered around 6,000 are Punjabi Sikhs. Most have come to this country direct from rural Punjab in

[1] The fieldwork was funded by the National Institute of Education (Grant Number 80-0123). I gratefully acknowledge the support of the Institute and the contributions of fellow research team members Amarjit S. Bal, Gurdip K. Dhillon, and Elizabeth McIntosh.

northwest India, where, prior to emigration, they had lived in small villages of 500 to 2,000 inhabitants. There they were farmers. Their holdings, in most cases, were large enough to provide a basic level of subsistence for their families, but not large enough to improve their status or subdivide further. Many had emigrated to improve opportunities for their children, for whom employment prospects in India were particularly bleak. They had come, too, in hopes that they might improve their own economic situation and because they had relatives already settled in the Valleyside area.

Upon their arrival in this country these Punjabi agriculturists have little choice but to take backbreaking jobs, usually for the minimum wage, in the fruit orchards surrounding Valleyside. In 1981 the median income for Punjabi families with children in their senior year at Valleyside High was barely $15,000 or just half that of white Valleysider families with children in their final year of high school. Income figures in the Punjabi case include the earnings of teenage children, while for the majority group they represent only parents' earnings. One-third of the Punjabi men had been in the United States for less than five years, another third for five to ten years, and the final third for more than ten years. At the time of fieldwork (1980–82) about half of the Punjabi men were working as farm laborers. Another quarter commuted from Valleyside to factory jobs in Sacramento or the San Francisco Bay Area. And the final quarter had become orchard farmers. Most of the latter group had arrived in the United States prior to 1970, often coming alone and only sending for their wives and children after they had established themselves in this country. Many of the more recent arrivals had come with their families. About one-half of the 231 Punjabi students attending Valleyside High had been in the United States less than five years.

Few Punjabi parents spoke English with ease, even those who had been in the United States for many years, and Punjabi was the language of the home. Most of the Punjabi students attending Valleyside High had begun school in America speaking little or no English. A majority of the Punjabi mothers, and quite a few of the fathers, were illiterate or semiliterate. The fathers, as a group, were better educated but less than half had finished secondary school, which in India means ten years.

PUNJABI SCHOOL PERFORMANCE PATTERNS

Analysis of school records for all 231 Punjabi high school students revealed a strong relationship between age on arrival in this country and students' performance in high school. Inspection of school data also indicated a strong relationship between gender and course selection during the final two years of high school. Both of these variables—students' age on arrival and gender—proved to be far more critical determinants on the Punjabi school

Table 7.1.   Track Placement On Entering Ninth Grade, By Ethnic Group*

	Remedial & ESL Track	Average Track	Accelerated Track
Science			
Punjabi	28.6%	71.4%	
Majority Group	28.3	71.7	
Mathematics			
Punjabi	21.4	60.7	17.9%
Majority Group	37.9	39.8	22.3
Social Studies			
Punjabi	35.7	64.3	
Majority Group	11.2	41.1	47.7
English			
Punjabi	25.0	42.9	32.1
Majority Group	11.2	41.1	47.7

*Note: Compiled by the author from school records. The Punjabi sample included all students in the class of 1984 who had entered American schools by second grade (*N* = 425 majority group, 28 Punjabis).

Table 7.2.   Percentage of Valleyside High Students Taking College Prepatory Science and Mathematics Classes*

	Majority Group Total (*N* = 1679)	Punjabi		
		Male (*N* = 27)	Female (*N* = 22)	Total (*N* = 49)
Science				
Physical Sciences	72.0%	66.7%	81.8%	73.5%
Biology 1	52.0	55.6	40.9	48.9
Chemistry	31.0	44.4	13.6	30.6
Biol. 2/Physics	15.0	37.0	9.1	24.5
Mathematics				
Algebra 1	67.0	70.4	63.6	67.3
Geometry	47.0	59.3	36.4	48.9
Algebra 2	26.0	44.4	13.6	30.6
Trig/Math Analysis	10.0	37.0	4.5	22.4

*Note: Compiled by the author from school records. The Punjabi sample included all students in the Classes of 1981–83 who had entered U.S. schools by second grade.

performance patterns than parents' income, education, occupation, or proficiency in English.

Punjabi students who received *all of their education in the United States* did quite well academically. American-educated Punjabis were nearly as likely on entering 9th grade to be placed in college preparatory classes as majority-group classmates classmates (see Table 7.1). More Punjabis were placed into remedial or ESL English; more majority-group students were placed into remedial math. During high school, Punjabis' grades equaled or, in the case of boys, surpassed those of majority peers. The Punjabi boys, moreover, took more upper-level, college preparatory math and science classes than major-ity-group males or females (see Table 7.2).[2] This was in keeping with their aspirations for careers in computer science, engineering, and electronics.

The Punjabi girls, on the other hand, although no less likely than the boys to be placed in college preparatory classes on entering 9th grade, tended to enroll heavily in business classes during their final two years.[3] The gender difference related directly to parents' assumptions about the necessity and desirability of higher education for their daughters. Although most Valleyside Punjabis said their daughters were free to go as far with their education as they wished, they said too that the girls should marry first, and that decisions about higher education and careers should be made in concert with their husbands and in-laws. Parents worried that too much education before marriage would make a girl too independent in her views and behavior, thus tarnishing her reputation and quite possibly jeopardizing arrangements for her marriage.[4] The girls themselves aspired to a four-year college education, but, not expecting that their parents would permit them to go away to college—there was no four-year college in Valleyside—they saw little reason to take the more demanding math and science classes. Most of these girls liked school and did reasonably well academically, but they channeled their energies into vocational classes once all basic academic requirements had been met.

The study revealed a close relationship between English language profi-ciency and the grade that Punjabi students entered American (or English-medium) schools. Those who had begun their education in the United States, although often not as skilled in English as native speakers, even after ten years of schooling, had acquired sufficient proficiency in academic English to pursue the tougher college preparatory classes in high school. This was the case even though most of these students had entered kindergarten or first grade knowing little or no English, and even though they had received little or no special assistance from the school district in learning English. These students managed to learn English and to become competitive academically through what may be characterized as an all-English submersion program, that is, a program that makes "virtually no concessions to the child's language or culture" (Cummins 1984:156).[5]

---

[2] See Gibson (1988) for a fuller discussion of Punjabi school achievement patterns.

[3] I found no similar disparity between the sexes within the majority group.

[4] Such attitudes are characteristic of Indians of rural background. Quite different patterns emerge among the urban middle class. Attitudes appear to be changing in Valleyside, too, as parents come to see that some postsecondary education is necessary if their daughters are to compete successfully for desirable jobs.

[5] The fact that these Punjabi students survived academically in a submersion program does not mean that this is the best approach for Punjabis or for other groups of language minority students. The school district has since instituted ESL classes at the primary, as well as the secondary, level.

In sharp contrast, nearly all of the Punjabi students who had emigrated from India after fourth grade were classified, in high school, as limited-English proficient and placed into the high school's ESL (English-as-a-Second-Language) program. Many of the more recent recent arrivals earned 70 or more high school credits—graduation required 220 credits—through their ESL classes. Most of their other credits came from a combination of general education and vocational classes. Limited-English-proficient students were moved along through the system with little chance to take either solid basics or college preparatory classes.

Even these students, however, persisted in high school through 12th grade. By my estimates, 85% to 90% of all Punjabi students, new and old alike, graduate from high school compared with 70% to 75% of all majority-group students. Following graduation, most Punjabis enroll for further studies at the local community college (80% of the girls and 74% of the boys in my senior sample). More than half of the Punjabi students sampled went on to complete a two-year course of study at Valleyside Community College.

EXPLAINING PUNJABI ACHIEVEMENTS

Valleyside teachers, like their counterparts across the nation, point to a lack of "home support" for schooling as the number one factor impeding school success for American youngsters today (Gallup 1984; Gibson 1983b). Almost as frequently, teachers note students' lack of motivation, poor attitudes, or truancy. Negative peer pressure is another commonly cited variable.

In the Valleyside case, teachers were referring, by and large, not to Punjabi students, but to white Valleysiders. Many of these majority-group students admitted to not working hard in school. Boys in particular invested little time in homework. Many explained that senior year was "kickback time." They had completed all requirements for a high school diploma and they were simply putting in time until graduation. Most saw little need to take the more advanced classes in math, science, or English offered by Valleyside High. Such classes, typically labeled "college preparatory," were not viewed as part of a basic high school education. Students explained, moreover, that they could always take these courses later, at a community college, if they decided to go on for a four-year college degree. Teachers and counselors appeared to support such a strategy. Only one-fifth of the majority-group students took a fourth year of high school English, and fewer still took four years of math or science.

A somewhat different pattern emerged among students who planned to enter directly into a four-year college. College preparatory classes were mandatory for these students, and such courses usually required more homework. Still, these students had time for the many other activities that the typical American teenager feels are necessary to his or her existence. Most held after-school jobs. Most also participated in extracurricular activities at school and maintained an active social life.

The Punjabi students presented a different pattern. Few had after-school jobs. Few participated in extracurricular activities. By the standards of majority-group peers, moreover, these Punjabi students led extremely restricted social lives, girls in particular. Their parents urged them to invest their time in homework and to treat schoolwork as a job. "The main thing is to study," one Punjabi mother explained, "nothing else." Their social life would come later, parents explained, after their studies and after they were married. Three-quarters of the Punjabi boys reported doing an hour or more of homework nearly every day, compared to the white Valleysider males who reported "almost never" doing homework.

High school teachers were aware of these differences.[6] The teachers characterized Punjabi students as highly motivated, hard working, and coming from households where the parents seemed to value education. The Punjabi students were rarely absent from school and created few discipline problems. They were also more likely than majority peers and parents to assume that effort was the key to school success. Accordingly, they seemed less likely than majority peers to shy away from classes they found demanding or that required a great deal of homework. This pattern of academic diligence and persistence is a common one in the literature on immigrants. Common, also, is the belief that effort, not intelligence, is the key to academic success (Gibson 1988:175).

SCHOOL BARRIERS TO PUNJABI SUCCESS

Punjabi students, even those who are American-born or who arrive in this country at an early age, have far from an easy time in school. Most of those whom I sampled had started school knowing little or no English and, prior to high school, had received no special assistance in learning English. In addition, the Punjabi students had to cope both with severe prejudice and with sharp conflicts between home values and those promoted by the school. Valleyside is "redneck" country, and some white residents are extremely hostile toward immigrants who look different, act different, and speak a different language. In school, Punjabi teenagers are told they stink, directly by white students and indirectly by their teachers. They are told to go back to India. They are accused of being illegals. They are physically abused by majority students, who spit at them, refuse to sit by them in class or on

---

[6] See Gibson (1987b) for fuller discussion of how the cultural backgrounds of Punjabi minority and white majority students bear directly on academic performance.

buses, crowd in front of them in line, stick them with pins, throw food at them, and worse. They are labeled troublemakers if they defend themselves. Only a minority of white youths participate actively in the harassment, but the majority either condone their classmates's behavior, or feel powerless to alter the status quo.

In one way or another Punjabi students are told that India and Indian culture are inferior to Western and American ways. They are criticized for their hairstyle, their diet, and their dress. They are faulted because they place family ahead of individual interests, defer to the authority of elders, accept arranged marriages, and believe in group decision making. They are condemned most especially for not joining in majority-dominated school activities and for resisting as best they can the forces for cultural assimilation.

While teachers commend Indian students for their diligence in the classroom, they are perplexed by their parents' reluctance to attend school functions. Some Punjabi parents had never visited the high school, and most came only if a school official called specifically to request a meeting about their child. Teachers seemed to assume that for children to excel academ- ically their parents had to participate directly in school affairs. Few seemed conscious that the Punjabi model of non-intervention worked equally well, perhaps better, at least in the Punjabi context.

Teachers were similarly disturbed about the Punjabi students' reluctance to participate in most nonessential school activities, such as clubs, sports, class picnics, and school dances. To most teachers, participation in such functions was the primary measure of fitting in socially, and fitting in socially was, for many, a primary measure of school success. Thus, as defined by teachers and administrators (and many college admissions officers, as well), success in high school required participation in majority-dominated extracurricular activities. This was the case, even though involvement in these activities often ran counter to values deeply embedded in the Punjabi community.

ACCULTURATION WITHOUT ASSIMILATION

The more the schools pressured Punjabi children to conform to prevailing norms for behavior, the more tightly their parents supervised their behavior and advised against too much social contact with non-Punjabi peers. Punjabi parents defined "becoming Americanized" as forgetting one's roots and adopting the most disparaged traits of the majority group, such as young people making decisions on their own without parental counsel, leaving their families at age 18 to live independently, dating, dancing, and friendship between the sexes.

Punjabi parents constantly admonish their young that they will dishonor themselves, their families, and their community if they adopt the values and behaviors of majority peers. Such warnings, together with community gossip about those whose behavior deviates from Indian village norms, usually suffices to bring wayward adolescents into line. If inappropriate behavior persists, however, the family will likely decide to withdraw the offender from school, first for a period of time and then permanently. A boy is put to work in the peach fields and a girl is kept at home until her marriage can be arranged. The individual who insists on having his or her own way risks being cut off from family and community.

Many Punjabi teenagers themselves criticized those who socialized at school with white classmates. They would say, "He's Anglo, or he thinks he's white. He's not one of us." Valleyside Punjabi tended to stick with their own because, as one student put it, "you don't want to be an outcast from your own people." Punjabi young people, in effect, are forced to choose sides. Few find it possible to mix socially in both worlds.

No such pressure is brought to bear on Punjabi students for accepting the authority of white teachers or doing well in school. Adapting oneself to teachers' expectations, even when such expectations conflict with traditional Indian or Punjabi values, is not viewed as "acting white" (Gibson 1987a). Quite the reverse. Students are encouraged to excel academically and teased when grades or behavior are poor. Parents remind their offspring that they have made great sacrifices for them and that the parents' lives will have been wasted if their children are not successful. Young people are also told that those who do well in school can expect to find better marriage partners, that their accomplishments bring credit to their family, and that they set an example for other younger Punjabis to follow. These are powerful messages.

Punjabi parents have high expectations for their children's achievement. If a child does poorly, however, only rarely do they blame the system or the teachers. "If the child does not wish to study, then what can the teacher do?" parents remark. "Those who wish to learn, will learn" is the general attitude.

Punjabi adolescents, for their part, know firsthand the drudgery of manual labor and the precarious nature of orchard farming in Valleyside. They want a better, more secure future. Almost all Punjabi children have direct contact with adults who have overcome substantial obstacles, and these adults, often, are their role models. Academic achievements, in the Punjabi view, represent what can be done even without parental wealth and education. Parents urge their children to become proficient in these ways of the dominant culture. They take great pride in the fact that their children speak English well and can help them deal with the host society, *providing* they also are maintaining strong roots within the Indian community.

Punjabi students conform to their teachers' expectations to the degree possible, but they are nevertheless no bunch of goody-goodies or pushovers.

Punjabis do not shy away from confrontation when they feel their identity or interests threatened. Boys are instructed, for example, that they must protect the honor of family and community. "Turn the other cheek once, twice," their parents say, "but the third time defend yourself."

In general, however, Valleyside Punjabis choose to minimize the problems they face at school and in the community at large. They point out that prejudice and discrimination exist in every country and that "when you go to another country, you go there knowing that this kind of thing is possible." The situation in Valleyside, moreover, although difficult, is, in the Punjabi view, far better than in Canada or in England. Several parents commented:

> It is nothing here compared to Canada. There is a lot of hatred there. Our people are successful and they hate us.

> The English are prejudiced because they ruled over us and now they feel that they are superior and we are inferior.

> In England, the whites are very prejudiced. If you go to a pub in the evening, you have to go together in a group.... If you are by yourself, they beat you up.

Punjabis noted, too, that U.S. laws provide greater protection to the individual than Indian laws.

Valleyside Punjabis urge their children to ignore racist remarks and to avoid fights. The parents recognize that they are operating from a position of weakness and that they have little power to turn things around. Their response to prejudice stems from this reality as well. But it is also a deliberate and conscious strategy of putting education first. The parents I surveyed stated specifically that a situation of response and counterresponse would only promote greater ill will between groups and would distract their children from their studies. In spite of the prejudice and the pressures to conform to the dominant culture, Punjabis believe that they have the ability both to improve their lot economically, especially if they are well educated, and to maintain essential aspects of their Indian way of life.

Punjabi advocate a strategy of *accommodation and acculturation without assimilation.*[7] Adapt to the formal demands of the classroom—do what you must to get a high school education—but resist the forces for unwanted

---

[7] By *acculturation* I mean a process of culture change and adaptation that results when individuals with different cultures come into contact. Acculturation may be an additive process, or one in which old and new traits are blended. Unlike *assimilation*—the process whereby individuals of one society or ethnic group are incorporated or absorbed culturally into another—accultration need not result in the rejection or replacement of old traits, or the loss of identification with one's former group. I explore the Punjabi strategy of accommodation and acculturation without assimilation more fully in Gibson (1988).

cultural assimilation. "Dress to please the people," Punjabis say, "but eat to please yourself."

DISCUSSION

The comparative literature on immigrant school achievement reveals considerable success on the part of immigrant youths of non-English-speaking and working-class backgrounds in using formal education as an avenue to middle-class occupational status (see Gibson 1987a). On the whole, immigrant students seem more committed than indigenous students—majority as well as minority—to using education as the avenue to upward socioeconomic mobility. Even when their performance in school is poor, the immigrants persist in school. Most appear to believe that if they work hard enough they can succeed in school, regardless of all other obstacles.

Age on arrival and *length of residence* appear also to be closely related to the school performance of linguistic minority immigrant children. Language minority students who arrive in the new country by age 6 or 7 tend to do better academically than those who arrive in the upper elementary and junior high years (Cummings 1984; Dumon 1979; Little et al. 1968; Masemann 1975; Mehrlander 1986). In general, those who receive all of their schooling in the new country gain sufficient proficiency in the dominant language to be competitive in their academic classes.

Not all immigrant groups perform equally well in school. Here in America there are studies showing that in the early part of this century the children of Italian immigrants did significantly less well in school than children of Jewish immigrants from Germany and Russia (Cohen 1970; Ravitch 1974; Tyack 1974). More recently, studies in Britain point to a serious and persistent disparity between the school performance of Asian Indian students and those of Afro-Carribbean origin (Swann Committee Report 1985). Other recent studies indicate that children of Turkish "guest workers" in West Germany and Finnish students in Sweden perform below national norms (Castles 1984; Paulston, 1982; Skutnabb-Kangas 1981). Yet my own research in the American Virgin Islands showed West Indian immigrants to be doing quite well academically, and far better, in the case of boys, than the native Crucian West Indian population (Gibson 1983a). There also is some evidence that children of Turkish and Finish origin in Australia do better in school than their counterparts in Germany and Sweden (Inglis and Manderson n.d.; Troike 1984).

To understand these variations in the school performance of immigrant minorities, we need to look not only at the social structure of the host society and the cultural background of the minority group, but also at the minority group's situation in the host society, including its perceptions of the opportunities available and the historical context of its relationship to the dominant group. When parents and students do not believe there will be a sufficient return for investing their time and energy in schooling, they turn their energies elsewhere. Likewise, if they feel hostility and suspicion toward the school system and those in authority, it is more difficult for students to accept this authority and to seek to become skilled in the ways of the dominant group.

Some minority groups, most frequently those that have been incorporated into the host society against their will and who have experienced long histories of prejudice and discrimination, see schooling as providing an unequal return to minorities (Ogbu 1978). There is ample evidence to substantiate their views. Minorities generally earn less than white Americans with comparable years of schooling and experience a higher rate of unemployment (U.S. Bureau of the Census 1984b).

Objective chances for upward mobility clearly influence minorities' expectations about the value of formal education, but so too do their subjective views regarding their chances to get ahead in society. Many immigrant minorities recognize that white Americans have an edge in the job market, but, for a time at least, they rationalize this by saying, "It's their country. What country doesn't favor its own?" More importantly, perhaps, immigrants see America as a land of opportunity, where even a newcomer with few skills and little formal education can get ahead economically and where employment opportunities are far more open than in countries left behind. Their reference point, at least initially, is not the majority group, but members of their own ethnic group here in this country and back in the country of origin. Even a minimum wage may be far better than wages in the old country.

A similar set of perspectives shapes immigrant attitudes about the American system of education. Schooling, in the eyes of many working-class immigrants, is the primary avenue to higher paying and less physically strenuous jobs for their children. Although their children may have to endure a certain amount of discrimination in school, schooling nonetheless provides the skills and credentials that will open doors to better employment. Immigrants often persist in school longer than majority students, in part as insurance against discrimination. Judged through the comparative lens of the immigrants, moreover, schooling in America is less expensive, more readily available, and, in the view of the Punjabis at least, less discriminatory than in their country of origin.

Ivan Light has commented on the relationship between the immigrants' psychological satisfaction with their new country and their economic achievements (Light 1984). Most immigrants, Light notes, have come to the United States because it offers better opportunities than those available in the country of origin. They tend to view social and economic hardships encountered in this country from a distinctly different perspective than the native-born American population. Until fully adapted to the standard of living in the new homeland, immigrants are more willing to work hard at low-paying jobs and to endure the prejudice and discrimination of the dominant group than members of nonimmigrant minority groups. Light stresses the importance of these and other situational factors in promoting entrepreneurship independently of cultural factors (1984:199). Other social scientists note, too, that explanation for the economic achievements of many immigrant groups lies in the dynamic interplay among cultural, structural (or contextual) and situational variables (see Boissevain and Grotenberg 1986; Bonacich and Modell 1980; Lieberson 1980; Nee and Wong 1985; Turner and Bonacich 1980).

The literature on immigrant economic enclaves is directly relevant to the present analysis because factors that contribute to immigrant socioeconomic achievement seem also to contribute to immigrant academic achievement. Immigrants, in part at least, are willing to play the school game by the rules of the dominant group because, from their perspective, there will be a return from their investment. If adequate jobs are not forthcoming, it may be anticipated that they will adjust their strategies.

Although immigrant minorities encourage their children to invest a great deal of effort in their studies—more than majority group parents, it appears—they also are deeply concerned about conformist pressures in school. Most immigrant minority parents reject the goal of assimilation and, to guard against assimilationist pressures, they may even admonish their offspring to avoid socializing outside of school with white American peers. At the same time, however, they urge their children to adopt what they perceive as good from the majority culture, to abide by school rules, and to learn what they can from their teachers. The learning of English and the acquisition of other academic skills are actively promoted and rewarded.

CONCLUSION

A major question emerging from ethnographic research on minorities within school settings is why some groups, most frequently involuntary minorities (see Ogbu, this volume), appear to equate school learning with loss of their separate cultural and ethnic identities, while immigrant minorities tend to respond quite differently. Immigrants appear to see the acquisition of academic learning and skills in the majority culture as an *additional* set of skills to be drawn upon as appropriate, while involuntary minorities more frequently see school learning as *replacing* their traditional culture. Put another way, some minority groups view school learning and acculturation in a linear fashion leading ultimately to assimilation. Others see school learning and acculturation in a multidimensional fashion whereby new skills and values are incorporated into the old culture, transforming but not replacing it.

These differing school-adaptation patterns, although in need of further substantiation among additional groups and in additional settings, have implications for educational policy and practice.[8] Many minority students, especially involuntary minorities, see cultural conformity as the price required for school success because *this is the model set by the schools themselves.* To encourage students to cross ethnic boundaries within classroom settings, educators would do well consciously and explicitly to foster learning environments where students are given full opportunity to participate in the mainstream of society while also, if they so choose, maintaining their separate cultures and identities. The American system of education has much to gain from the immigrant model.

REFERENCES

Boissevain, Jeremy, and Hanneke Grotenbreg
 1986   Culture, Structure and Ethnic Enterprise: The Surinamese of Amsterdam. Ethnic and Racial Studies 9:1–23.
Bonacich, Edna, and John Modell
 1980   The Economic Basis of Ethnic Solidarity: Small Business in the Japanese American Community. Berkeley: University of California Press.
Castles, Stephen
 1984   Here for Good. London: Pluto Press.
Cohen, David K.
 1970   Immigrants and the Schools. Review of Educational Research 40:13–27.
Cummins, Jim
 1984   Bilingualism and Special Education. Clevedon, Avon: Multilingual Matters.
Dumon, W. A.
 1979   The Situation of Children of Migrants and their Adaptation and Integration in the Host Society, and their Situation in the Country of Origin. International Migration 17:59–75.
Gallup, Alec
 1984   The Gallup Poll of Teachers' Attitudes Toward the Public Schools. Phi Delta Kappa 66:97–107.
Gibson, Margaret A.
 1983a   Home–School–Community Linkages: A Study of Educational Opportunity for Punjabi Youth. Washington, D.C.: National Institute of Education.
 1983b   Ethnicity and Schooling: West Indian Immigrants in the United States Virgin Islands. Ethnic Groups 5:173–198.

---

[8] See Gibson and Ogbu (1991) for comparative case studies of immigrant and involuntary minorities.

1987a   Playing by the Rules. *In* Education and Cultural Process, George D. Spindler, ed. Pp. 274–281. Prospect Heights, IL: Waveland Press.

1987b   Punjabi Immigrants in an American High School. *In* Interpretive Ethnography of Education: At Home and Abroad. George and Louise Spindler, eds. Pp. 281–310. Hillsdale, NJ: Lawrence Erlbaum.

1988   Accommodation without Assimilation: Sikh Immigrants in an American High School. Ithaca, NY: Cornell University Press.

Gibson, Margaret A., and John U. Ogbu, eds.

1991   Minority Status and Schooling: A Comparative Study of Immigrant and Involuntary Minorities. New York: Garland Publishing.

Inglis, Christine, and Lenore Manderson

n.d.   Education and Reproduction among Turkish Families in Sydney. [Unpublished Manuscript]. Sydney: Department of Education, The University of Sydney.

Lieberson, Stanley

1980   A Piece of the Pie: Black and White Immigrants Since 1880. Berkeley: University of California Press.

Light, Ivan H.

1984   Immigrant and Ethnic Enterprise in North America. Ethnic and Racial Studies 7(2):195-216.

Little, A., C. Mabey, and G. Whitaker

1968   The Education of Immigrant Pupils in Inner-London Primary Schools. Race 9:439–452.

Masemann, Vandra

1975   Immigrant Students' Perceptions of Occupational Programs. *In* Education of Immigrant Students. A. Wolfgang, ed. Pp. 107–121. Toronto: Ontario Institute for Studies in Education.

Mehrlander, Ursula

1986   The Second Geration of Migrant Workers in Germany: The Transition from School to Work. *In* Education and the Integration of Ethnic Minorities. Dietmar Rothermund and John Simon, eds. Pp. 12–24. New York: St. Martin's Press.

Nee, Victor, and Herbert Y. Wong

1985   Asian American Socioeconomic Achievement: The Strength of the Family Bond. Sociological Perspectives 28:281–306.

Ogbu, John U.

1978   Minority Education and Caste: The American System in Cross-Cultural Perspective. New York: Academic Press.

Paulston, Christina Bratt

1982   Swedish Research and Debate About Bilingualism. Stockholm: Report to the National Swedish Board of Education.

Ravitch, Diane

1974   The Great School Wars: New York City, 1805–1973. New York: Basic Books.

Skutnabb-Kangas, Tove

1981   Guest Worker or Immigrant—Different Ways of Reproducing an Underclass. Journal of Multilingual and Multicultural Development 2:89–115.

Swann Committee Report
   1985   Education for All. The Report of the Committee of Inquiry into the Education of Children from Ethnic Minority Groups. Cmnd. 9453. London: HMSO.
Troike, Rudolph C.
   1984   SCALP: Social and Cultural Aspects of Language Proficiency. *In* Language Proficiency and Academic Achievement. Charlene Rivera, ed. Pp. 44–54. Clevedon, Avon: Multilingual Matters.
Turner, Jonathan H., and Edna Bonacich
   1980   Toward a Composite Theory of Middleman Minorities. Ethnicity 7:144–158.
Tyack, David B.
   1974   The One Best System: A History of American Urban Education. Cambridge, MA: Harvard University Press.
United States Bureau of the Census
   1983   1980 Census of Population, Volume 1: Characterisitics of the Population, Chapter C: General Social and Economic Characteristics, Part 1: U. S. Summary, PC80-1-C1, Washington, D.C.
   1984a   1980 Census of Population, Volume 1: Characteristics of the Population, Chapter D: Detailed Population Characteristics, Part 1: U.S. Summary, PC80-1-D1-A, Washington, D.C.
   1984b   1980 Census of Population, Volume 2: Subject Reports, Earnings by Occupation and Education, PC80-2-8B, Washington, D.C.

8

"Becoming Somebody": Central American Immigrants in U.S. Inner-City Schools

Marcelo M. Suarez-Orozco

The problems facing Hispanic Americans in schools have gained increasing scholarly attention in the past two decades (Brown, Rosen, Hill, and Olivas 1980; Carter and Segura 1979; Hispanic Policy Development Project [HPDP] 1984; Lefkowitz 1985; Suarez-Orozco 1987a; Walker 1987). Although much research has been done to further our understanding of the issues facing Hispanic Americans in schools, many areas of the problem remain virtually unexplored. One such area that demands proper systematic treatment is related to the differences emerging from a consideration of the educational adaptation of the various Hispanic American groups.

Mexican Americans, mainland Puerto Ricans, Americans of Cuban descent, Americans of South American origin, as well as the recent immigrants from troubled Central American nations are distinct populations. They differ in demography and history, face different issues in schools, and should, therefore, be understood as such (Davis, Haub, and Willette 1983: Suarez-Orozco 1987b). For example, research suggests that Hispanics of Central and South American origin tend to do better in U.S. schools than their Mexican American and mainland Puerto Rican peers (Brown, Rosen, Hill, and Olivas 1980: 101; HPDP 1984: vol. 2, p. 57). According to some measurements, the differences in school functioning among the various Hispanic American subgroups are extraordinary. For example, HPDP reports that whereas 21.15% of Mexican American sophomores dropped out of school in 1982, only 11.4% of Hispanics of Central and South American origin dropped out of school that same year (HPDP 1984: vol. 2, p. 57). Davis, Haub, and Willette similarly conclude that Cuban Americans and more recent immigrants from Central and South America tend to be better educated than Mexican Americans and mainland Puerto Ricans (1983:29). Likewise, Brown, Rosen, Hill and Olivas report that "Puerto Rican and Mexican Americans had much higher non-completion rates [in high school] than the other Hispanic subgroups" (1980:101). I must underscore the fact that further research is needed to explore the different experiences among the various Hispanic American subgroups.

Yet the data already available tend to support Ogbu's contention (Ogbu this volume, 1983: Ogbu and Matute-Bianchi 1986) that overall *immigrant* minorities, such as Hispanics of Central and South American origin in the United States, generally perform better in schools and certainly experience different kinds of problems than *castelike* minorities, such as blacks, Mexican-Americans, and Native Americans.

This chapter explores the specific issues facing recent arrivals from Central America as well as their unique motivational patterns in the context of resettling in the new land. The experiences of these immigrants will be framed in reference to Ogbu's coutural ecological approach to the study of education and minority status in plural societies (Ogbu 1974, 1978, 1981). I must emphasize that due to a number of critical reasons, the Central American case considered here is far from an ideal paradigm of immigrant adaptation to schooling.

We have witnessed in the last several years an impressive and continuous flow of immigrants from war-torn Central America to the United States (LaFeber 1984; Mohn 1983; Suarez-Orozco 1987b). It is difficult to find reliable estimates on the numbers of Central Americans now residing in the United States. Some researchers estimate that between 300,000 and 400,000 Salvadoreans reside in the United States (Diskin 1983:43). The Central American Refugee Committee [CRECEN] estimates that over 500,000 Salvadoreans make the United States their place of residence (CRECEN 1985). CRECEN estimates that as many as 220,000 Guatemalans may be residing in the United States (CRECEN 1985). This is not counting the Nicaraguans who came to the United States in one of several waves.

MIGRATION AND RESETTLEMENT: THE IMMIGRANT ETHIC AND SCHOOLING

The research reported in this and other writings (Suarez-Orozco 1985, 1987a, 1987b) was conducted in two inner-city high schools containing over 600 recent arrivals from Central America. The study consisted of participant observations plus systematic ethnographic interviews with some 50 core informants from El Salvador, Guatemala, and Nicaragua. All immigrants had entered the United States within five years prior to the research. Of the 50, 30 were males aged 14 to 19, and 20 were females aged 14 to 19. Thirty-three of my informants came from El Salvador, 9 from Guatemala and 8 from Nicaragua. All remained enrolled in school during the period of fieldwork.

In addition to work in the classrooms and counseling office, my formal position in one of the school sites as "Bilingual Parent/Community Liaison" put me in regular contact with parents, relatives, and guardians of most immigrant students. Toward the end of the ethnography, I collected, scored, and analyzed over 400 Thematic Apperception stories from the new arrivals.

In these sites teachers reported that, considering the very special problems that immigrant Central Americans face as a legacy of the war they had escaped and the pressures to work in the inner city to help the family (Arroyo and Eth 1985), the new arrivals in my sample were "desirable students," as one informant put it. For example, two bilingual teachers with ample experience in the field confided that they could never go back to teaching "American students" (read U.S. minority), because their immigrant students (mostly Central American and Asian) were so eager to learn, so appreciative, and, above all, so polite that they could not face regular unruly classes in the rough inner-city high school.

A number of my teacher-informants reported early on that these Central American students were well motivated to learn (particularly English). The teachers noted that immigrant students exerted greater effort, studied harder, and often received better grades than other minority students. The teachers reported that my informants were more respectful and "nicer to have around" than either Anglo or other minority students. More objective measures seem to confirm these impressions. For example, in both school sites the Central American students were statistically underrepresented in numbers of school suspensions (Suarez-Orozco, 1987b). Five of the graduating recent arrivals from Central America in my sample (10% of the total sample) were accepted into prestigious American universities.

Many Central American students were learning English at a rapid pace. In fact, many were learning English so fast that in both school sites, teachers privately reported that the counselors systematically kept the immigrants in English as a Second Language (ESL) classes and lower-level bilingual classes longer than required. This was done because of lack of space in the regular English classroom.

A systematic pattern of subtle discrimination was evident as I became more intimate with the teachers, counselors, and staff. The powerless immigrant students were not a priority: They were thus assigned to lower-level classes, classes that in some cases they had successfully completed in their country of origin.

Recent arrivals from Central America were routed to overcrowded, understaffed classes in overcrowded understaffed, poor inner-city schools.

Students found themselves trying to learn a new culture in a new language in the rather poisonous environment that has made the American inner-city school infamous. Drugs were on display for sale all around the schools. In both sites gang and ethnic violence was a common occurrence. Teachers were very much afraid of their students. They systematically complained that they had to operate with far more students than they had been trained to teach.

Despite a school atmosphere of drugs, violence, low expectations, the calculated tracking of minority students to nonacademic subjects (in already nonacademic schools), bitter teachers, the seductive offers by more acculturated peers to join the street culture, and the need to work to help the family, my informants remained in school trying to learn English. I was naturally attracted to these students: Indeed, considering the legacy of economic scarcity and political terror in Central America (Arroyo and Eth 1985; Durham 1979; Suarez-Orozco 1987b), it is most remarkable that *any* of these youngsters should stay in the inner-city schools, trying "to become somebody," seemingly against all odds. Although ten percent of my informants did go on to enroll at major universities, it would be erroneous to imply that all Central American students became model students. Elsewhere (Suarez-Orozco 1987b) I explore in great detail why some younger new arrivals develop specific schooling problems in the inner city. Yet, I maintain, the intellectually challenging question is not to explain why some recent arrivals would leave school to join the labor market, or have learning problems, but why, given their current realities and immediate history, so many should stay in school at all.

A possible way to begin to approach this question is by exploring parental expectations among the new arrivals. Central American parents articulated the notion that a primary factor in the decision to escape to freedom was the welfare of the children. As one mother from Nicaragua put it, "We came here for them," referring to her five children. She added, "so that they may become somebody tomorrow....I am too old, at my age it is too late for me....if anything, it is harder for me here than there [Nicaragua]...." She had decided to leave her small town in rural Nicaragua over a year before our interviews because she was afraid that her oldest son, a 16-year-old, would be drafted to fight the *contras* on the Honduran border.

A dual frame of reference comparing present opportunities in the United States and past realities in the land of fear and economic scarcity emerged among the immigrants to face and interpret current conditions in the inner city. Because in most cases they had escaped their country in search of a better tomorrow and because their parents sacrificed a great deal for the journey north, recent immigrant students thought the advantages in the new land were self-evident and required little elaboration. For them it was very clear: despite ongoing difficulties there were more opportunities to study, more help to do so, better training facilities, and more and better future job opportunities in the United States than back home.

Once this theme was identified, I turned to isolate the emergence of a specific folk system of mobility. Given that there was a collectively held perception among immigrants that more opportunities for advancement existed in the United States than in El Salvador, Guatemala, or Nicaragua, the next issue was to document specific shared beliefs on the nature of how one "makes it" in the new land.

Universally, informants reported that schooling was the single most significant avenue for status mobility. It is important to note that the majority of my parent-informants had been pushed out of school in their native lands (Suarez-Orozco 1987b). Some could not afford the luxury of schooling in remote rural areas of Central America. Others had to face hard physical labor at an early age to contribute to the family's income. The parents were mostly laborers and semiskilled laborers. The current opportunities open to their children in the new land were seen by many parents in contrast to their own experiences in Central America.

The belief in education as a key mode of status mobility in the host country was often constructed in opposition to the conceived system of status mobility in the country of origin. As one Salvadorean informant succinctly put it, "Here [US] is *what* you know, there [El Salvador] is *who* you know."

According to these immigrants, in the United States, schooling, knowledge, and individual effort emerged as the primary avenue for status mobility. On the other hand, in the country of origin, one made it through networks and friends of friends, or through nepotism or *"por apellido"* (because of one's last name) and not because of individual efforts, knowledge or achievements.

To summarize, the fact that my informants left their land for a better tomorrow is of importance for understanding subsequent school adaptation. A dual frame of reference, comparing present and prior (often brutal) realities, emerged as a matrix in which they evaluate and face experiences. In thinking about the meaning of schooling and the future, immigrants often paused and made comparative evaluations between "here" and the "there." And "here" schooling offered many opportunities for advancement. Next I explore how advancement became the idiom to repay parents and those left behind for their sacrifices.

THE PSYCHOSOCIAL CONTEXT OF MOTIVATION

Most of the Central American students I came to know well were keenly aware of the degree of parental sacrifice involved in getting out of the country of origin (Suarez-Orozco 1985, 1987b). Parents often framed sacrifices in reference to the future of the children. Perceptions of parental sacrifice emerged as a key interpersonal concern among the immigrants as captured in their responses to the Thematic Apperception Test (Suarez-Orozco in press).

Although they were greatly appreciative of their new lot in the United States, the immigrants continued to live through the hardships that must be endured in order to survive in a foreign land. Students saw their parents become janitors, maids, busboys, and, in some cases, take two jobs so they could go to school to receive the education the parents themselves never had.

The majority of my informants (64%) had one or more members of their nuclear family still residing in a war-torn Central American nation. Most of my informants (68%) worked about four hours a day, commonly after school, to help their relatives and those left behind with remittances. Some have reported that the recent arrivals from El Salvador alone send between 350 million to 600 million dollars annually in remittances (Pear 1987:8).

Others, particularly young men, had left their entire nuclear family in Central America and were living in the United States with distant relatives or friends. In some of these cases parents had used vital resources to send a youth to the safety of the United States. Among these immigrants, I found a severe sense of responsibility to those left behind. Schooling efforts in the new land were framed in reference to a wish to "rescue" those relatives still in Central America (Suarez-Orozco 1985, 1987b).

Such interpersonal issues put a particular psychological burden to achieve on many of my informants. An intense sense of duty to less fortunate relatives gains center stage in the psychosocial profile of many immigrants. Guilt about one's survival and present opportunities in the new land not shared by those left behind fueled the immigrants' project for a better tomorrow, for themselves, and, most importantly, for their families.

Among many informants, and most particularly among those with close relatives remaining behind, something akin to "survivor guilt" has appeared (Bettelheim 1980:274–314). The syndrome experienced by many of the recent arrivals from Central America is similar in some respects to the guilt described by Bettelheim occurring among some survivors of the Nazi death machine. Betteheim described how survivors in the death camps often shared a belief that one's life was spared because someone else has suffered or died (Bettelheim 1980:274–314).

Many immigrant youths live with the conscious knowledge that they were sent out of Central America, whereas others, including siblings and parents, had to remain. Among many informants, concern over those left behind becomes the focus in a plan to "rescue" others and to alleviate the ongoing hardships of those responsible for sending them to freedom.

PSYCHOCULTURAL CONSIDERATIONS AND ACHIEVEMENT MOTIVATION

Psychological tests, ethnographic interviews, and participant observations allowed a careful consideration of the psychosocial profile of these immigrants. Most informants showed a remarkable sense of duty to the parents and family members for their suffering. This accentuated a wish to achieve, to do well in school, in order to repay parents and relatives, to make their endurance worthwhile by *"llegando a ser alguien"* (becoming somebody). The following case study in some ways provides a paradigm of a successful immigrant's psychocultural motivational dynamics. (For more extensive psychocultural analysis of fifty case studies, see Suarez-Orozco 1988.)

Antonio was a 17-year-old young man from El Salvador. He came to the United States with his mother, a maid, and older sister in 1981. None spoke any English then. His father, a postal worker in San Salvador, stayed behind.

Antonio completed the 9th, 10th, 11th, and 12th grade in the United States.During his senior year he had a cumulative grade point average of 3.75 (out of 4.0 possible points). During his senior year, Antonio was accepted into a very prestigious U.S. university. His father completed the 6th grade and his mother the 7th grade before they both had to work full time to help their respective families. Antonio's sister graduated from high school in El Salvador. In the United States, Juana, his mother worked as a maid, often six days a week. Juana normally left at about 6 A.M. and usually came back after sundown. The work schedule was particularly hard on her during the winter months. Because she did not have access to a car, she had to take public transportation to the different homes she cleaned. And because the homes were usually in upper middle-class neighborhoods (and she lived in the inner city), she often had to take two, at times even three buses, to reach work.

Juana did not allow Antonio to work during the academic year. She noted that they came to the United States so that the children could "become somebody" here. War and a wrecked economy in her native El Salvador had pushed away any fantasies that her children could escape out of the very modest existence she herself had endured. But in the United States things changed. As she concluded, "Antonio now has to dedicate himself to school."

In fact, Juana wanted Antonio to go to the university. She was full of pride when he was accepted: "He'll be the first *universitario* (professional) in the family," she observed with effervescent joy. As many other informants, Antonio was fully aware of why his mother wanted him to study: "She does not want me to lead a life such as the one they had live when they were young. They had to work hard, sacrifice themselves," he said.

Antonio's plan was to become a professional. "I believe the most important thing I can do for my parents is to become a doctor, that would make them happy. I would be the first professional in my family...." Like many other informants, Antonio said that he wanted become a professional in order "to work with my community, to help the Hispanic community as a doctor."

In order to achieve this, Antonio studied hard 4 or 5 hours after school every day. He took his schooling very seriously, spending each one of his summers in the United States going to special summer programs at a local private university to learn more English and science.

Antonio was given the Thematic Apperception Test (TAT) in his native Spanish language in late 1984. The TAT consists of a series of vague drawings that are presented sequentially to the informant. The informant is simply asked to "make up a story" based on what he/she sees on the drawings. The narrative should have a past, a present, and a future. The TAT rests on the logic that presented with vague stimuli, informants will "talk about themselves." They will articulate their latent wishes, fears, dreams, and worries. The TAT has been widely used as an anthropological tool complementing ethnographic participant observations to capture systematically patterned interpersonal concerns in given populations (e.g., Lindzey 1961; Scheper-Hughes 1979; Wagatsuma and De Vos 1984). Representative parts of Antonio's TAT follow.

Card 1 [A boy contemplating a violin]:

[Takes a long look, over 30 seconds] May I begin? This is about a family that lives in a small town outside San Francisco. The family is composed of two brothers, the father and the mother. The family has financial problems, economic problems. They are thinking how to solve these problems. Up to now the children do not know anything about this. But the father and the mother are worried about it. They cannot hide their worry over this problem. During one of the conversations between the mother and the father, one of the boys realizes the nature of the problem. At that point, the child that found out about the problem went to tell his brother. They begin to talk about the problem and about what they will [do] to help.

That same evening one of the brothers is doing his schoolwork. He cannot concentrate on his school work because he is thinking about the economic troubles facing his family.

The two brothers then organize a campaign. They read the want-ads in the paper and they find that there is a job for two kids to deliver newspapers after school. They begin to work after school so that the mother and father do not realize. That way they get together enough money between the two of them to pay their parents' debt.

Analysis: This story captures the interpersonal context of achievement motivation among many Central American informants. The motivation to achieve is most often directly related to a wish to help relieve parental suffering (Suarez-Orozco 1987b). Also note how in the story economic problems emerge as interfering with academic tasks. This was a common issue among my informants, who often noted that the need to work often prevented them from study as much as they would like to.

Card 2 [A farm scene, a young woman is in the foreground with books in her hands, in the background a man is working the land. A woman leans on a tree].

This is about a girl named Maria. She was a country girl, a very beautiful farmer that lived with her mother and brother. Maria's family was a hard working farm family. They cultivated the land. Maria's brother was a hard working man, he worked very hard next to his mother. They had a hard life.

Maria was a studious woman. She looked at her family's future and her own future. One day Maria went to the city. In the city she realized how different life there was from life on her farm. She said, "One day I shall have the commodities city families have." Seeing the difference between the city and her farm, Maria began studying and studying. She studied more and harder than ever. She went to the most prestigious universities of her county, with scholarships and working part-time.

Finally Maria was able to move her family, her mother and brother from the farm to the city. They lived for a long time with Maria. But the family did not really like city life, they went back to the country. Maria was very sad, so she went back to her farm to help them there, to work with them there, to teach there.

Analysis: The hard-working family lived off their work on the land. Maria, a studious character, was concerned about "her family's future." One day she goes to the city and sees how life in the city can be different, *significantly not only for herself but for her sacrificing mother and brother.* There she was witness to the commodities of city life. She saw a difference. As is the case with many immigrant informants, a comparative perception of opportunity leads the *dramatis persona* to further hard work, through study. Studying becomes the way out of a hard existence. The perception of opportunity juxtaposed with a realization of familial sacrifice is the framework in which motivation flourishes. Here is a chance to help change the hard life of one's relatives. Studying prepares Maria to attend "the most prestigious universities" and with the help of available scholarships and part-time work she makes it.

"Finally she was able to move her family" from the farm to the city. Her objective was not mere self-advancement and independence but rather, to help the family out of hard farm work. This is the meaning of success. But there is a conflict between the young professional and her farm relatives. The mother and brother do not really like life in the city. Maria is saddened by their choice to go back. Yet, rather than breaking off with her family and staying in the city, she chooses to go back with them to further help them, "to teach there."

Upon close scrutiny, the structure of the motivational pattern in Antonio's story about Maria and Antonio's own life are, perhaps not surprisingly, isomorphic. Both are witness to the hardships the family must endure to survive. Both are further motivated by a perception of opportunity in a new land. In neither case is the achieving motive rooted in an individualistic wish for self-betterment, or in a wish for becoming independent. Rather, the aim is to help end, through studying, the family's hardships.

Card 6BM [A man in the foreground looks down; a somewhat older looking woman in the background looks out a window]:

Luis was an attorney in the city. He had many offices and was very rich. He lived with his children and spouse in a mansion north of the city. Luis worked well with his coworkers and was a family man. He always took interest in his children and spouse. Nobody knew about Luis's past.

His past was a sad past. Ever since he was a little boy he had to work in the streets: shining shoes, or selling tickets in buses. But he was interested in his studies. Through studying he achieved his law career.

Once Luis became an attorney he forgot his family. He forgot where he came from. He forgot that he had a mother that struggled for him when he was a little boy. One day Luis's mother went to visit him in his office. His mother was very sick, she had a few months to live. She told Luis this because she wanted him to inherit her house. When Luis heard this he became very sad because now he could not do anything for his mother: she would have needed medical attention two years before, and he was not there next to her then, so she was not treated.

Luis could not find the words to beg her to forgive him. But his mother knew that Luis was sorry for what he did. She forgave him.

When Luis's mother died, he went back to the place he once lived with her. Being a very rich man, he founded three schools to help the needy classes in his community.

Analysis: Luis, the high-achieving wealthy attorney, had a dark past. His sad past is not that he had to work shining shoes to become a rich attorney.

Rather, it was that he had committed a serious transgression. Luis violated a law so fundamental it need not be in the books: "He forgot his family. He forgot where he came from. He forgot that he had a mother...."

The consequences of this callous disregard for his mother, who so "struggled" on his behalf when he was a boy, are devastating. The mother will die and there is nothing the powerful attorney can do to prevent this. It is too late; he should have been next to his mother two years earlier when she needed medical attention.

Luis was overcome by sadness. He was so paralyzed that he could not even bring himself to beg her forgiveness. Yet the all-understanding, sacrificing mother forgave him anyway. She "knew that Luis was sorry."

It is psychosocially significant that the story should not end with her death and his sorrow. In fact, his mother's death brings Luis back to his people.

At the end, her death was not in vain. It brings him back to his people *so he can share with them,* as he should have done before the tragedy occurred. It is of symbolic significance that he should choose to honor his mother by donating three *schools* to needy people. School was his way out of poverty, and the schools he donated should do the same for his people. He learned his lessons the hard way: One can not achieve and forget.

Dynamically the story is an exceptional capsule of basic interpersonal themes among many immigrants. The hero makes it with the help of a sacrificing mother who struggles so he can get ahead. Rather than turning to her, he chooses to leave her and his people behind. This is a severe violation that is certain to bring devastating consequences.

Let us underline the emergence of a pattern in which achievements are neither individualistic nor for the sole purpose of independence or self-advancement. Rather, achievements are embedded in a pattern of cooperation and mutual nurturance. One "makes it" with the precious help of significant others, and must turn to them to complete the cycle.

Card 13B [A barefoot boy, sitting down in front of a door]:
    This is about a boy, Rodolfo. He lives in a hamlet outside the city. He is a poor boy, from a very poor family. So he had to work hard from a young age. At five years of age he has to go to work and live a street life.
    His mother is sick. His father left her when he was born. Rodolfo has to work shining shoes and selling candies in the buses. Sometimes he even works at night to earn enough to have a tortilla to eat.
    One day Rodolfo began thinking about the future. Will he be a good man? Or, will he be a bad man? He also thinks about school and the streets and the differences that exist between the two. After thinking

about all this he discovered that there was a great difference between the street and school: That difference is knowledge. Knowing what is good and what is bad.

After meditating about this, Rodolfo told his mother that he was going to do his best to continue in school. He told his sick mother not to worry about anything because he would also work.... He would work for both...and study, no matter how hard it was to do both or how much he would suffer. This is what Rodolfo did. Years passed and he was a model student in his school. After finishing high school he went to the university to study law. He chose law because he thought that it would be the best way to help as many poor children, as he once was, as possible.

Analysis: Little Rodolfo had to work since the age of five to buy food. His poor mother was sick, his father left them. Rodolfo paused to mediate about his future and concluded that there was a fundamental difference between the street and school: knowledge. Knowledge represents a capacity to tell good from bad. Rodolfo thus chooses to go to school over street life. He tells his poor, sick mother not to worry because he will take care of both: He will study and work.

He becomes a model student and chooses a career to help as many poor kids as possible.

The pattern emerging is isomorphic to previous stories: The boy from a poor home has the insight that education is the route out of misery. Through hard work and study he becomes an attorney. Rather than turning away from his people, he both studies and works so his poor sick mother would not "worry." At the end, his achievement is translated into helping "as many" poor kids as possible. The culmination is not some sort of narcissistic self-indulgence, but rather the conversion of success into concrete help for his people.

In summary, among the recent immigrants the emergence of perceptions of opportunity in the new land became intertwined with a severe sense of duty to relatives and other folk (Suarez-Orozco 1987b). Achievement motivation in this case does not follow the pattern found among more individualistic Anglo-Americans described by McClelland and associates (McClelland 1961, 1984). In McClelland's Anglo-American samples, high achievement need was often correlated with high independence need, a pattern contrary to the Central American case. In fact, the Central American case shows high achievement motivation related to a wish for affiliation and mutual nurturance. For example, in a sample of 50 responses to TAT Card One, 36% of the Central American stories were about achievement and nurturance (where the boy achieves to help others or with the help of others). And in fifty responses to Card Two of the TAT, fully 56% of the Central American stories were about achievement coupled with nurturant themes. (For a full analysis of other TAT themes among fifty new arrivals, see Suarez-Orozco 1988).

CONCLUSION

Almost all of the Central American informants stated that in the United States, schooling was the key to a better future for themselves *and* their families. I must emphasize that, as stated earlier, some recent arrivals, particularly younger ones (14- to 16-year-olds in my sample), do become vulnerable to systematic school hostilities and the psychosocial factors derivative of having escaped the culture of terror in Central America. I note it would be an error to think that all Central Americans became model students. Many developed specific problems, which I consider elsewhere (Suarez-Orozco 1988). Having said this, I repeat that the intellectually challenging question remains: Why, given their history and ongoing reality in the inner city, do so many of the Central American youth stay in school at all?

To conclude, a key implication emerging from this ethnographic research is that, obvious as it may seem, not all Hispanic American students share the same problems. As Ogbu (1973, 1983; Ogbu and Matute-Bianchi 1986) has advocated, we need more comprehensive comparative studies exploring the different *kinds* of school problems facing different kinds of minority populations. As my research suggests, immigrants from Central America do not face the same problems in schools as their U.S.-born Hispanic peers.

The Central American students escaped a situation of war and misery. *That* reality overshadowed many of the subsequent hardships and marginality encountered in the new land. For many informants the sacrificing life of family members and the folks "back home" remained a significant point of reference against which to check more current developments. In their eyes, the relative advantages of life in the United States were self-evident. In this context many developed notions in which schooling emerged as the most important avenue to make it in the new land, and, in turn, to help the less-fortunate relatives.

REFERENCES

Arroyo, William, and Spencer Eth
   1985   Children Traumatized by Central American Warfare. *In* Post-Traumatic Stress Disorder in Children. Spencer Eth and Robert S. Pynoos, eds. Pp. 103–120. New York: American Psychiatric Press.

Bettelheim, Bruno
  1980   Surviving and Other Essays. New York: Vintage Books.
Brown, George H., Nan L. Rosen, Susan T. Hill, and Olivas
  1980   The Condition of Education for Hispanic Americans. Washington, D.C.:
          United States Department of Education, National Center for Education
          Statistics.
Carter, Thomas P., and Roberto D. Segura
  1979   Mexican Americans in School: A Decade of Change. New York: College
          Entrance Examination Board.
Central American Refugee Committee (CRECEN)
  1985   CRECEN National Bulletin 1(2):1–8.
Davis, C., Carol Haub, and JoAnne Willette
  1983   Trouble in Our Backyard: Central America and the United States in the
          Eighties. New York: Pantheon Books.
Diskin, Martin, ed.
  1983   Trouble in Our Backyard: Central America in the Eighties. New York:
          Pantheon Books.
Durham, William
  1979   Scarcity and Survival in Central America: Ecological Origins of the Soccer
          War. Stanford: Stanford University Press.
Hispanic Policy Development Project (HPDP)
  1984   "Make Something Happen": Hispanics and Urban High School Reform. 2
          volumes. New York: Hispanic Policy Development.
LaFeber, Walter
  1984   Inevitable Revolutions: The United States in Central America. New York:
          W.W. Norton.
Lefkowitz, Bernard
  1985   Renegotiating Society's Contract with Public Schools: The National Com-
          mission on Secondary Education for Hispanics and the National Board of
          Inquiry into Schools. Carnegie Quarterly 29(4):2–11.
Lindzey, Gardner
  1961   Projective Techniques and Cross-Cultural Research. New York: Appleton-
          Century-Crofts.
McClelland, David C.
  1961   The Achieving Society. Princeton: D. Van Nostrand.
  1984   Motives, Personality and Society: Selected Papers. New York: Praeger.
Mohn, Sid L.
  1983   Central American Refugees: The Search for Appropriate Responses. World
          Refugee Survey. 25th Anniversary Issue: 42–47.
Ogbu, John U.
  1974   The Next Generation: An Ethnography of Education in an Urban Neighbor-
          hood. New York: Academic Press.
  1978   Origins of Human Competence: A Cultural-Ecological Perspective. Child
          Development 52:413–429.
Ogbu, John U., and Maria Matute-Bianchi
  1986   Understanding Sociocultural Factors: Knowledge, Identity, and School
          Adjustment. In Beyond Language: Social and Cultural Factors in Schooling

Language Minority Students. Pp. 73–142. Sacramento: Bilingual Education Office, California State Department of Education, Evaluation, Dissemination and Assessment Center.

Pear, Robert
1987 Salvadoreans Cite Fears on Return. New York Times, Sunday, April 26, pp. 1 and 8.

Scheper-Hughes, Nancy
1979 Saints, Scholars and Schizophrenics: Mental Illness in Rural Ireland. Berkeley: University of California Press.

Suarez-Orozco, Marcelo M.
1985 Opportunity, Family Dynamics and School Achievement: The Sociocultural Context of Motivation among Recent Immigrants from Central America. Paper read at the University of California Symposium on Linguistics, Minorities and Education. Tahoe City, May 30–June 1.
1986 In Pursuit of a Dream: New Hispanic Immigrants in American Inner City Schools. Ph.D. dissertation, Department of Anthropology, University of California, Berkeley.
1987a Towards a Psycho-social Understanding of Hispanic Adaptation to United States Schooling. *In* Success or Failure? Learning and the Language Minority Student. Henry T. Trueba, ed. Pp. 156–168. Cambridge: Newberry House Publishers.
1987b Spaanse Amerikanen: Vergelijkende Beschouwingen en Onderwijsproblemen. Tweede Generatie Immigrantejongeren. Cultuur en Migratie (2):21–49.
1988 In Pursuit of a Dream: The Experience of Central Americans Recently Arrived in the U.S. Stanford: Stanford University Press (in press).

Wagatsuma, Hiroshi, and George A. DeVos
1984 Heritage of Endurance: Family Patterns and Delinquency Formation in Urban Japan. Berkeley: University of California Press.

Walker, Constance L.
1987 Hispanic Achievement: Old Views and New Perspectives. *In* Success or Failure? Learning and the Language Minority Student. Henry T. Trueba, ed. Pp. 15–32. Cambridge: Newberry House.

Part IV

Additional and Alternative Perspectives

9

Building Our House From the Rubbish Tree: Minority-Directed Education

Barbara Harrison

Minority-directed education is not a new idea, and the desire for direction by local communities is not limited to minority group members. The International Declaration of Human Rights adopted by the United Nations in 1946 stated that it is the right of all parents to choose appropriate education for their children, and minority participation and direction of education were major themes of the civil rights movement of the 1960s. Parent participation and direction are also important concerns in white upper-middle-class areas of the United States.

In spite of the emphasis on minority direction in the past, the predominant form of authority is still the large city or district school board where individual parents have little impact on the formation of policy and where minority parents are often represented only on advisory committees. However, minority groups in a wide range of situations have demanded greater control in the education of their children, and there are a number of disparate examples of minority-directed schools in the literature. For example, there are private schools such as that run by Marva Collins and Black Muslim schools (both cases mentioned by Erickson in this volume), the Amish schools described by Hostetler and Huntington (1971), and 24 American Indian groups who have established their own community colleges.

From the cases of minority-directed education where information is available, there seem to be some cases where minorities have chosen to

147

emphasize their own culture in the classroom and other cases where they have chosen to emphasize Western education. The particular groups who have established their own schools and who believe those schools are successful are groups who have had the capacity, power and authority to make choices about the schooling of the children. In other words, they are groups who have a keen sense of empowerment with respect to their children.

The discussion which follows draws ideas and themes from the author's experience in Alaska Native and New Zealand Maori situations. In Alaska, the author spent five years living and working in various education-related roles in predominantly Yup'ik Eskimo communities, and an additional five years as a university faculty member travelling to Native Alaskan villages throughout the state. More recently, the author has lived for four years in New Zealand at Waahi Marae, an important Maori tribal center, and has conducted fieldwork in predominantly Maori primary schools and adult training programs, as well as coordinating the Waahi Community Training Centre and being involved in a range of tribal development projects.

Although these settings are geographically separated by thousands of miles, the educational issues and problems facing the indigenous people in the two settings have much in common (cf. Ogbu 1978). Members of the indigenous communities in both regions have perceived that the power to direct the education of their children was taken from them in the past. Alaska Natives and New Zealand Maori have, in some communities, demanded the right to control their own schools, and, where they have gained that authority, they have established schools under their own direction addressing problems as they themselves define them. These cases demonstrate that minority directed schooling can play a role in confronting both the problems associated with cultural conflict in the classroom and, to a limited extent, problems of economic and social inequality.

Parents in both settings—Alaska and New Zealand—have described their reasons for wanting control of the schools. First, parents defined successful schooling differently from the way it was defined by school personnel. Second, parents believed that each child's identity should be grounded in his or her cultural background, and the types of schooling their children were receiving were destroying rather than supporting the growth of a strong cultural identity. Finally, parents believed that their position in the society as a whole depended on their empowerment in all domains of life—including schooling.

The existing theories which explain variations in minority school achievement are useful, but they are incomplete because they do not take sufficient account of the perceptions of the individuals and groups concerned. The contribution of Erickson, Jordan, and the many others who have examined the effect of cultural differences on classroom communication and organization must be acknowledged because that contribution has been substantial. Their work implies that education for some minority groups can be improved by training teachers in cross-cultural communication and by designing instruction appropriate to particular cultural groups. However, the techniques that have so far been devised cannot yet provide comprehensive solutions in every situation.

Ogbu's work suggests that we must change more than classroom interaction and curriculum; power and economic relationships between members of the dominant society and members of involuntary minority groups must also change if all children are to have the opportunity to succeed in school. But concerned educators must wonder how they can take responsibility for a shift in relationships within a complex society such as we find in the United States today.

The existing theories which explain variations in minority school achievement are useful, but they are incomplete because they do not take sufficient account of the perceptions of parents and other individuals and groups concerned. In the following sections, parental perceptions are described in more detail. Perceptions of successful schooling, the importance placed on cultural identity, and the need that parents see for a significant role in decision making are outlined. Then, the more general issue of benefits of minority direction are discussed, and two cases are described where major restructuring has been undertaken in order to increase opportunities for minority participation in decision making. Recommendations for the empowerment of minorities and for appropriate support are offered. The chapter concludes with a discussion of research needs.

MINORITY DEFINITIONS OF SUCCESSFUL SCHOOLING

In this volume, parent perceptions have been identified by Gibson and Suarez-Orozco as well as by Ogbu as significant factors in minority student achievement, but Moll and Diaz have argued that attitudes of parents toward schooling cannot explain the variations. Attitudes toward schooling will not explain school success or failure unless, as Ogbu explained, the particular economic and social history of a group and the groups' interpretation of that history are also taken into consideration.

Each community has its own particular history as well as its own definition of school success, so each situation must be carefully examined before one becomes a "true believer" in one educational approach or another in a particular setting. As Ogbu noted in this volume:

> While cultural, language, and opportunity barriers are very important
> for all minorities, the main factor differentiating the more successful

from the less successful minorities appears to be the nature of the history, subordination, and exploitation of the minorities, *and* the nature of the minorities' own instrumental and expressive responses to their treatment, which enter into the process of their schooling.

Native Alaskan communities have been affected by and have responded to Euro-American contact in different ways. As a result, each Native Alaskan community has defined school success in a different way. In some communities, parents want their children to maintain traditional language and customs. In others, parents want good positions in a cash economy for their children, and in some communities, parents want both (or even something else again).

In several communities in Alaska where parents were questioned about their concerns, the most important concern of parents was to know that their children were loved and cared for in school.

In New Zealand, many Maori parents consider the maintenance of the Maori language as the most important task of the school. Some religious groups view religious goals as the priority and have established their own schools. In virtually all of these situations, parents say that they want their children to succeed in school. The difficulty arises when the concerns and goals of the parents are different from the concerns and goals of the dominant society educators who ordinarily direct school activities. In response to these differing perceptions, minority parents in widely separated settings have been demanding the right to direct the schools in their own local communities.

IDENTITY, EMPOWERMENT, AND SCHOOLING

Parents in both Alaska Native and New Zealand Maori settings have expressed the belief that the development of a strong cultural identity is essential to their child's achievement in school and in the wider world, but they often feel powerless to bring that development about in the schooling situation. Many believe that parents must be empowered to oversee the schooling process because members of other cultural groups cannot provide an appropriate schooling context for the development of cultural identity in their children.

Taitimu Maipi, Chairman of the Waahi Marae (Maori community center) Committee in Huntly, New Zealand, expressed the historical sense of powerlessness in his local community when he told the following story to a group of visitors in 1986. In 1863, the settler army invaded the Waikato region of New Zealand's North Island, eventually driving the Tainui Maori tribe into a 20-year exile in the King Country. When King Tawhiao finally led his people out of the King Country and back into the Waikato, all he saw in their former territory was destruction. He said to his people: "I will build my house from the rubbish tree." Taitimu continued, "We are the rubbish trees. And, today, the people are still building from the rubbish trees, the trees that were left after the destruction of the wars." One way in which King Tawhiao's descendants want to build is through the control of their local schools.

Both Erickson and Ogbu argue in this volume that involuntary minorities may sometimes develop social identities in opposition to the dominant society. But, I have heard some Alaska Natives and Maori say, "We don't know who we are." One Maori added:

The reason Pacific Islanders do better in school is because they know who they are. If we are going to know who we are, then our culture must be strongly represented in the school. In order for that to happen, we must run our own schools.

During a recent regional conference in New Zealand, a discussion group composed of about 25 Maori men and women representing several government departments (Education, Labour, Justice, Social Welfare, and so on) were asked to address the question: What can we do to improve education standards for Tainui (Maori) people? The opening comments of the participants seemed to make clear connections between the issues of perceived powerlessness, schooling, and identity as follows:

"Return respect and *mana* to the people. Our people need to be empowered."

"Get our own people on the Boards of Trustees. In order to do that, we have to believe that we can do that. We have to stop calling on the Pakeha to fix things for us."

"We need to do it in our own way."

"Restore *tino rangatiratanga*—the self-respect and dignity of our children—through *Taha Maori* (schooling in Maori culture and philosophy)."

"Restore it to children, parents, and elders through the Treaty of Waitangi."

"In order to do this, they must know the *reo* (language) and the *tikanga* (customary ways of behaving) to enhance their learning."

Tino rangatiratanga was translated by one speaker in the group as "dignity and self-respect," but it is also translated as "authority" and "self-determination" in other contexts. Eventually, the group developed a consensus on a mission statement focusing not on specific types of instruction or communication in the classroom but on children's development of a strong sense of identity and empowerment through the return of *tino rangatirantanga* to Tainui Maori children and adults.

When these individuals spoke of culture in the schools, they meant considerably more than communication style and classroom organization. These individuals and many other parents believe that, if their children are to feel strong in their Maori identity, the school curriculum must include Maori language immersion, literacy, values, history, arts, crafts, music, medicine, spirituality, and Maori people as teachers, administrators, and staff. At the same time, parents and school staff members intend that children's academic achievement in English will equal the achievement of other New Zealand children (Harrison 1987).

In the Waikato region of New Zealand, individuals heard from their grandparents accounts of the atrocities committed against their ancestors during the land wars in the 1860s. Maori communities are surrounded by rich farms, attractive homes, and wealth created from land that, only yesterday it seems, belonged to Maori. At the same time, Maori experience high unemployment, low income, over 90% school drop-out rates in some secondary schools, and high rates of ill health. Maori people in this region would scoff if they were told that their problems are due to inferior educational opportunities and lack of opportunity in the labor market or cultural differences in classroom communication and organization. They realize that inferior education, discrimination in the job market, and cultural differences are part of the problem, but they also believe that the return of at least some of their lands and *mana,* establishment of an economic base, and a political system where Maori play significant roles are essential. Political and legal strategies to address these problems have been in process for decades.

The same general beliefs about the nature of school failure and the necessity for maintaining local control of schools are prevalent in Native Alaskan communities. Ray Barnhardt's recent study of the school in the city of St. Mary's in a Yup'ik region of Alaska describes a school where the indigenous culture and academic achievement go hand in hand. The people of St. Mary's chose to establish a city governmental organization so that they could have greater control over the schooling of their children Barnhardt reported that the success in the school (including scores on standardized achievement tests) was the result of that control and the resulting representation of Yup'ik culture in the school (Ray Barnhardt 1990).

There are other Alaskan case studies where local participation and the inclusion of the indigenous culture in school curricula have been successful. In 1984-85, three teachers, two local community members, and the author (then a university faculty member) conducted a case study of the school in Manokotak where community members participated as Rural Education Attendance Area (REAA) board members, local advisory committee members, on the curriculum development committee, in staff selection, in Indian Education and Johnson O'Malley programs, in adult basic education, in all elementary classrooms as certificated teachers and aides, and in extracurricular activities (Harrison 1985,1986). There was a high degree of cooperation between non-Native certified staff and Native school participants. In that case,it appeared that the high level of participation was primarily the result of (1) a 40-year history of willingness of certificated and district-level personnel to work with local people in decision making, (2) a high proportion of Yup'ik individuals from the local community in certificated teaching positions within the school. Although standardized test scores were lower than the scores of urban Alaskan students, community members believed the school was successful in terms of their own goals: A high percentage of community members described a successful school as a school where all participants worked together in a cooperative way.

Howard Van Ness (1982) and Carol Barnhardt (1982) both conducted studies in an Athabaskan region of Alaska in a school where all elementary classrooms were staffed with certificated Native Alaskan teachers.

> This fact alone made the school interesting, but far more intriguing was the fact that schooling in this community appeared to be working. Students were performing well by nearly all traditional standards. Test scores were on or above the national average and were higher than in past years; attendance was good; discipline was not a problem, and students participated eagerly in class activities. (Carol Barnhardt 1982:145)

Although Barnhardt and Van Ness were both cautious in their conclusions, their studies imply that one condition related to the success of the school in that setting was the participation of Native Alaskan people in directing the activities of the school through their positions as certificated teachers.

Another case study by Madsen (1983) described a small village with a Bureau of Indian Affairs (BIA) "contract" school as well as a state-funded elementary school administered through an REAA. Madsen described the "contract" school in that village as the symbol of villagers'

...reaffirmation of their personal, communal, and societal integrity and vitality; it signified a new sociopolitical relationship between themselves and the dominant society. In contrast, they perceived dominant society schooling as symbolizing political control, social domination, and cultural hegemony. (Madsen 1990:44)

In this case, the "contract" school was only in its second year of operation at the time of Madsen's study so no conclusions could be drawn about the long-term success of the venture. However, the study was indicative of the importance placed on empowerment in some Native Alaskan regions.

One other development in Alaska has gained a reputation for success based upon a high level of parent involvement—Headstart. There have been a number of evaluative studies claiming success to one degree or another, and the survival of Headstart for nearly 20 years in Native Alaskan communities—a period which has included severe retrenchment mandated by Republican administrations since 1981—also contributes to Headstart's positive reputation. Parent participation in decision making through local parent advisory committees has been an important element in the Headstart philosophy throughout its history.

BENEFITS OF MINORITY DIRECTION

What advantages has minority direction offered to schooling in New Zealand and Alaska? First and foremost, parents who have gained authority to make decisions about the schooling of their children have achieved a sense of empowerment. The term *empowerment* was something of a "buzzword" a few years ago, but it was never widely used by professional educators or academicians. However, the term struck a responsive chord with Alaska Natives and Maori—and they continue to use it.

Parent participation in decision making has helped to establish trusting relationships—identified by Erickson in this volume as essential to the success of children in school—between school staff, community members, and children. And, when local community members have been at work in classrooms as certified teachers or instructional aides, cultural conflicts and disagreements about the goals of the school have diminished.

As noted in the previous section, parents in different communities have different definitions of successful schooling. Schools directed by local community members have made it possible for each community to see that its own priorities have been reflected in the curriculum, and, when local priorities have been reflected, parents and other community members have been more likely to support the work of the school. Parents who have had authority in schools have been more likely to assume active responsibility for the quality of their children's education.

Participation of local community members has had at least a small impact on the economy of the local community. When they are school employees, local community members have access to middle-class incomes.

Why do parents in some groups need to have this authority while parents in other groups seem not to need it? Ogbu has asserted in this volume that immigrant parents already have a certain amount of choice in regard to the schooling of their children in that they can return to the homeland. And, there are some groups—such as the Jews and Chinese-Americans—who have compartmentalized schooling by establishing ethnic language schools in the late afternoons after their children have completed public school days. This procedure may help to provide choices for parents who are seeking accommodation without assimilation for their children (cf. Gibson this volume). It may be that the parents who need to be empowered in the schooling of their children are those parents who have perceived their past as so oppressive that all power to make choices was taken from them.

EMPOWERING MINORITIES: TWO CASES

Within the past 15 years, the school systems in Alaska and New Zealand have been restructured, ostensibly to provide greater opportunities for community participation in decision making. In Alaska, there have been dramatic increases in the number of Native Alaskan youth who complete secondary school although it is impossible to isolate the effects of the restructuring from effects of other changes that have taken place during the same time period. In New Zealand, the major restructuring has just begun, and the long-term effects are not yet known. However, the cases are presented in order to provide examples of the way in which major changes in school systems can be undertaken in response to demands for the empowerment of local communities. These cases illustrate the potential for change in schooling which may affect local participation in decision-making in large numbers of communities.

Alaska Native Programs

In 1975, Alaska's State-Operated School System with headquarters in Juneau, the state capital, had authority over most rural (primarily Native) schools although the Bureau of Indian Affairs (BIA) was still operating schools in some areas of the state. In 1976, the State-Operated School System was disbanded, and authority was transferred to Rural Education Attendance Areas (REAAs). Authority in each REAA was lodged with a democratically elected board, and, because the rural areas were populated predominantly by Alaska Natives the elected board members were predominantly Alaska Native. Each community within a region was required to have a school committee to advise the regional board on all matters related to the local school. A few years later, the requirement for the advisory school committees was dropped, but most districts had already established local committees and most maintained the committees thereafter.

During the same time period, Alaska's boarding high schools were discontinued, and small high schools were established in nearly 200 villages. In most cases, these high schools were included under the jurisdiction of the REAAs and local school advisory boards.

Also during the late 1970s and early 1980s, the BIA completed its transfer of elementary schools to the state so that additional elementary schools came into the REAA system. In making the transfer, the BIA offered the option of the "contract" school to local communities. Under the "contract" school system, traditional village councils could contract with the BIA to administer their own elementary schools.

Eventually, the "contract" schools were also shifted to the state-funded system, but the villages where "contract" schools had been established were adamant about maintaining local control. Their desire to control their own schools was closely connected to their desire to be recognized as a sovereign political entity, known as the Yupiit Nation. The end result of the political action taken by those villages was the establishment of REAAs specifically to administer what were originally the "contract" schools.

During the 1970s, the Yup'ik Teacher Training Program and the Cross-Cultural Education Development Program were established through the University of Alaska system. These programs provided two-year and four-year field-based teacher training primarily for Alaska Natives, and they made it possible for just over 100 Alaska Natives statewide to enter classrooms as certified teachers.

The overall effect of the structural changes was an increase in opportunity for parents and other local community members to participate in the direction of the village schools at the elementary and secondary levels. The degree of local participation made possible by the changes varied from region to region depending on the particular superintendents and other administrators involved. In some areas, school administrators did everything possible to maintain their own control, while, in other areas, administrators willingly encouraged local people to join the decision-making process. Even though the early years under the restructured system were difficult and there are still conflicting opinions on various issues, the new system is sufficiently successful to make regional and village control of the schools a fact of life in the foreseeable future.

There have been attempts to establish Native direction at the university level, too, although these attempts have encountered overwhelming opposition from on-campus university faculty and administration. When the Alaska Rural Teacher Training Corps was established under the national Teacher Corps, federal regulations required that a consortium including Native people have authority to govern the program. Regional committees or panels were also established. But, when federal funding diminished and the program came under the University of Alaska administrative structure, university administrators ruled that the Board of Regents would have authority to govern. All Native committees and panels within the University of Alaska system are officially advisory now.

New Zealand Maori Programs

In New Zealand, too, major restructuring of the educational system has been underway. One explanation given by the government for the restructuring is that the new system will give greater control to the indigenous Maori people as well as the general population over choices in the schooling of their children.

Maori initiatives and political pressure in the 1970s and early 1980s provided a major stimulus for the restructuring. The establishment of *Te Kohanga Reo,* the early childhood language nests, and the bilingual schools have been seen as one element in the overall action for Maori development which has been underway for the past 15 or 20 years where self-determination and empowerment are major themes.

Te Kohanga Reo programs were initiated in the early 1980s. The language nests are Maori language immersion preschool programs for infants from birth to five years of age. They were initiated in response to the realization that the Maori language was disappearing because children were learning only English, but it was also an attempt to place both the authority and the responsibility for the preschools with local family groups of *whanau.*

The initial establishment began in 1982. The New Zealand government provided a $5,000 establishment grant to each site and a small salary for a *kaiako* or teacher (usually a Maori speaker from the local community), but local communities had to provide the rest of the funding for rent, utilities, materials, teacher aides, etc. One hundred and twelve sites were established in the first year. By the end of the third year when government funding was increased to $18,000 per year per site, there were 315 in existence. By the end of 1989, nearly 700 had been established, and more than half of the entire

Maori preschool population was enrolled. The government has now recognized *Te Kohanga Reo* as sufficiently successful to warrant permanent funding appropriated in the same manner as that for kindergartens and other established early childhood institutions.

The success of *Te Kohanga Reo* influenced the government's decision to decentralize authority throughout the primary and secondary school system in 1989. The successful management at low cost of the language nests by local communities indicated that other schools could be managed in the same way. In 1989, the New Zealand government restructured the national school system so that funding is now administered by locally elected boards of trustees for each primary and secondary school. The board of trustees for each school has prepared a charter or contract with the government which outlines the local community curriculum priorities for that particular school. Although many questions have been raised about the implementation process, Maori parents are optimistic about the new system.

The establishment of *Te Kohanga Reo* in the early 1980s generated parental pressure on the primary schools to provide expanded Maori language teaching to accommodate the children coming from the language nests. Convincing government and school authorities to establish Maori language schools was not an easy task for Maori parents, but, in response to Maori political action, there are now 18 official bilingual schools and 76 bilingual classrooms (units) in other schools. The political action undertaken by one local community and its bilingual school were described in a 1987 report (Harrison 1987). Not surprisingly, there is now pressure on the secondary schools to expand their Maori language units as well as the Maori representation in decision-making processes. Presumably, the 1989 restructuring will provide greater opportunities for parents to determine the place of the Maori language in local school instruction.

Other proposals for Maori-directed institutions have been put forward. Within the Tainui Maori region, proposals exist for endowed colleges within Waikato University and University of Auckland (regional nationally funded universities) and for a Tainui Maori directed two-year postsecondary institution. The major problem in implementing either of these plans is, of course, funding.

The restructuring of the system in New Zealand is, in certain respects, similar to that undertaken in Alaska in 1976 where the intention was to provide for increased parental and community participation in school decision making, particularly for the indigenous minority. In Alaska, it can be argued that the new system has resulted in improvements in schooling for Alaska Natives, and, in New Zealand, there is reason to hope for similar positive outcomes for Maori.

EMPOWERING MINORITIES: RECOMMENDATIONS

As several authors in this volume have already noted, researchers have spent the past 30 years developing theory about the causes of minority group school performance. Even after 30 years, many questions remain. Should educators wait another generation before taking action? If the answer to that question is "no," then how is an administrator or teacher to make sense out of the competing theories and viewpoints at this point in time?

Whatever applied approach educators take depends on the assumptions they make about the cause of the problems. If one accepts Ogbu's framework, one might easily conclude that more effort needs to go into educating parents about the long-term economic benefits of education and about ways in which parents can reinforce and support the work of the school. Parent educators might hope that such training would influence student retention rates and achievement as measured by test scores. On the other hand, if one accepts Erickson's approach, the conclusion might be to invest greater effort in training white teachers in cross-cultural communication. Priorities might be placed on the design of culturally appropriate classroom organization based on the work of Jordan et al. However, because academicians still know so little about the viewpoints of the groups in question, the best approach for the practicing educator is to rely on the judgment of local minority members themselves. Parents may choose to support programs of parent education, education for teachers in cross-cultural communication, or culturally appropriate classroom organization, but if these techniques are perceived as further impositions by the dominant majority rather than as options for possible selection by parents, implementation will be difficult if not possible.

The arguments for minority direction are clear. The specific techniques based on the theories that have been devised to date are not sufficient to bring about major changes in schooling for minorities. In many cases, the minority people themselves are demanding significant roles in directing their children's schooling. They have a right to that authority, and there are cases of minority directed schooling which are considered to be successful by the minority members themselves. These cases indicate that a critical element in successful schooling is the empowerment of parents to make choices about the direction of schooling for their children. When parents of *any* cultural group feel powerless, they may either withdraw support or actively oppose school policies. Parents support the schooling process only when they believe in positive outcomes of that process, and they must have the power to determine what constitutes or defines a positive outcome, to determine who school staff members should be, and to determine which programs should be chosen to lead to the goals they believe in.

Empowerment will not result in instant success. It took at least five years for Alaska's Native-directed schools to solve the initial problems they encountered, and, as in any other schooling situation in a constantly and rapidly changing world, when one set of problems is solved, new ones crop up. There are often conflicts that must be resolved within communities as to the appropriate goals of schooling. Empowerment of minorities will not solve all the problems, but empowerment is an essential precondition for success for many minority communities.

Minority direction is often viewed as a threat by members of established educational organizations, and interference from such organizations can have a devastating impact on minority initiatives. But, for those educators who are convinced of the need for minority direction, the following recommendations are offered.

The most obvious answer to the question of empowering minority people is for funding agencies to deliver funding to each school's elected board to manage, within guidelines, curriculum and staffing as they see fit.

For large schools with multicultural school populations, consideration should be given to allocating seats on the board to groups according to each group's proportion of the school population. One Maori school principal said:

> Democracy doesn't work for minorities. If you have democratic elections, the majority or dominant group will always win, and our views will never be represented.

His prediction was correct in the case of board of trustees elections in 1989 when nearly all seats went to Europeans. Mahuta has also described the difficulties encountered by Maori on the national level as the result of "tyranny of majority rule" (1989:14).

Another important device for insuring minority participation is to design teacher training programs specifically for minority members. There has been considerable argument against this approach—it is expensive, and minority people don't do as well on standardized tests—but certified minority teachers are essential to minority-directed schooling, and so it has to be done. The problems of cost and test scores must be dealt with in other ways than by eliminating teacher training programs for minority members.

If approached properly, parent participation and support can be encouraged and increased. In his earlier work, Ogbu described the patron/client and relationships between teachers and parents in Stockton (1974). We really have to get beyond such relationships if we expect minority members to join us in the school. School personnel need to see minority adults as partners, not clients, in the schooling endeavor, and interactions with parents also need to be structured in culturally appropriate ways.

For the educator who wants to involve minority parents in his or her school or classroom, the last resort is an advisory board. Parent advisory boards have been established in any number of schooling situations over the past 20 years: Indian education, bilingual education, special education, Headstart, university departments, and so on. Over that 20-year period, minority people have learned that advisory representation is tokenism of the worst sort. There is little authority or power in advisory status. There are distinguished minority educators who are refusing to serve in advisory capacities because their advice has not been heeded in the past.

On the other hand, advisory status may be better than nothing. If a concerned educator is unable to move the system to provide real authority for minority members in a particular situation, that educator can arrange an advisory group if and only if he or she will then act upon that group's advice.

PROFESSIONAL SUPPORT

Minority members generally recognize the need for trained professionals as participants. In many cases, they would prefer to have professionals from their own ethnic group but there are not enough professionals from their own group to meet the demand. Minority members are therefore willing to accept professionals from outside their own group provided that the professional is prepared to work on the minority group's teams.

All outside professionals need substantial training for cross-cultural understanding. There are a variety of training plans in operation around the United States and New Zealand. Some are terribly trivial. One workshop of course is not enough. Outsiders (even members of other minority groups) need to proceed through a substantial course of study to prepare them for work in schooling in specific settings (Harrison 1984).

Collaboration and consultation are the only useful ways for outside professionals to work in minority settings. Professionals have to approach local people as equals, respecting the insiders' knowledge of the culture, community, and children. Minority members are fed up with outside professionals who think they have all the answers, so consultation and collaboration are essential to constructive decision making.

Professionals must also be prepared to accept decisions when local people make them. Local people will sometimes make decisions contrary to professional opinion, and the outside professional who hopes to continue in the setting must be prepared to live with those decisions.

Finally, short-term efforts in development by outside professionals are useless. There are numerous examples in Alaska where a professional has spent a few days, weeks, or months getting a project started only to depart after a limited period of time. (The author regretfully confesses to having been a participant in such short-term commitments in the past.) The next year, another professional with another pet project spends a short time. The next year another and the year after another and so on. It is not at all surprising that Native Alaskans are skeptical and sometimes uncooperative when a new professional fad is presented to them. Unless an outside professional is willing to make a long-term commitment, he or she might as well stay home.

CONCLUSION

In summary, although the existing theories are useful, they are incomplete because they do not take sufficient account of the perceptions of minority members themselves. Members of these groups are demanding the power to direct their own schools and to solve the problems they perceive in their own ways. There are cases of minority-directed schools in Alaska, New Zealand, and the continental United States that are viewed as successful by minority members, and the particular cases seem to have little in common beyond the fact that they are minority-directed. In other words, the difference between success and failure may hinge on whether or not parents have the power to make choices about appropriate education for their children, not on specific instructional techniques. There are a number of ways of empowering minorities so that they can make appropriate choices, and appropriate roles for professionals in minority-directed schooling have been described.

The viewpoints presented here are based upon a limited number of cases. Systematic studies to determine the degree of success of minority-directed schools in general are needed. Presumably, there are cases of failure as well as cases of success, so an important dimension in future research should be to identify underlying conditions and specific structures in which programs have failed or succeeded. It has been pointed out that the New Zealand government and the national education system could either help or hinder the success of bilingual schools depending upon the degree of support provided for the development of Maori language materials, training of Maori speaking certified teachers, and in other areas (Harrison 1987). Certainly, the same issue—help or hindrance from existing educational agencies—would be a significant underlying condition for study in minority-directed schooling elsewhere.

Researchers are needed who are willing to emphasize the viewpoints of minority members. Taylor Branch, in his history of the American civil rights movement from 1954–1963, emphasized the tremendous effort invested by Martin Luther King and others in getting white authorities to pay attention to what was perceived to be the most important minority schooling issue of the day—desegregation of schooling (Branch 1988). Minority schooling issues will not be fully understood or resolved until members of the dominant society learn to *listen* to what minority people have to say.

In spite of the technological advances in anthropological research methods, long-term, live-in anthropologists are needed. Harry Wolcott has been correct in his insistence that we need the traditional methods of the anthropologist to provide holistic viewpoints if we are ever to find complete explanations and improvements in minority education (Wolcott 1982) And, for those researchers who are interested in what minority people have to say, the traditional live-in approach provides many advantages.

In the meantime, while researchers and theoreticians continue the search for explanations, schooling must go on, and there must be educators trained in anthropology who are willing to get on with the job working in minority communities doing the best that can be done with what we know (or think we know) at this point in time.

REFERENCES

Barnhardt, Carol
  1982   "Tuning-in": Athabaskan Teachers and Athabaskan Students. *In* Cross-Cultural Issues in Alaskan Education, vol. 2. Ray Barnhardt, ed. Pp. 144–164. Fairbanks: University of Alaska, Center for Cross-Cultural Studies.
Barnhardt, Ray
  1989   Two Cultures, One School: St. Mary's, Alaska. Fairbanks: University of Alaska.
  1990   Two Cultures, One School: St. Mary's Alaska. Canadian Journal of Native Education 17(2):54–65.
Branch, Taylor
  1988   Parting the Waters: America in the King Years 1954–63. New York: Simon & Schuster.
Harrison, Barbara
  1984   Training for Cross-Cultural Teaching. Anthropology and Education Quarterly 15(2):169–170.
  1985   Manokotak: A Case Study of Rural School Development in Alaska. Fairbanks: University of Alaska, Center for Cross-Cultural Studies.
  1986   Manokotak: A Study of School Adaptation. Anthropology and Education Quarterly 17(2):100–110.
  1987   Rakaumanga School: A Study of Issues in Bilingual Education. Hamilton, New Zealand: University of Waikato, Centre for Maori Studies and Research.
Hostetler, John A., and Gertrude Enders Huntington
  1971   Children in Amish Society: Socialization and Community Education. New York: Holt, Rinehart and Winston.

Madsen, Eric
  1983   The Akiak "Contract School": A Case Study of Revitalization in an Alaskan Village. Doctoral dissertation, Division of Educational Policy and Management, University of Oregon.
  1990   The Symbolism Associated with Dominant Society Schools in Native American Communities: An Alaskan Example. Canadian Journal of Native Education 17(2):43–53.

Mahuta, R. T.
  1989   Commemorative Symposium on Race Relations in New Zealand 150 Years After the Treaty of Waitangi. Paper presented to the Symposium, Rhodes House, Oxford, England.

Ogbu, John U.
  1974   The Next Generation: An Ethnography of Education in an Urban Neighborhood. New York: Academic Press.
  1978   Minority Education and Caste: The American System in Cross-Cultural Perspective. New York: Academic Press.

Van Ness, Howard
  1982   Social Control and Social Organization in an Alaskan Athabaskan Classroom. In Cross-Cultural Issues in Alaskan Education, vol. 2. Ray Barnhardt, ed. Pp. 165–191. Fairbanks: University of Alaska, Center for Cross-Cultural Studies.

Wolcott, Harry F.
  1982   Mirrors, Models, and Monitors. In Doing the Ethnography of Schooling. George Spindler, ed. Pp. 68–95. New York: Holt, Rinehart and Winston.

10

Constructing Cultural Difference and Educational Achievement in Schools*

Margaret A. Eisenhart and M. Elizabeth Graue

When culture and schools are talked about together in the United States, culture tends to be used as an explanation for why children from many nonmainstream homes—the culturally different—are less successful in school, on average, than mainstream children. Anthropologists of education have found important differences between the behaviors, communication patterns, and expectations of minority communities (the cultures of minority communities) and the culture of the school. Anthropologists have also found that when these cultural differences go undetected and unaddressed, minority children often have trouble understanding what is expected of them and how to interpret what happens to them at school. To these children, school is like a foreign culture, often including a different language or a different version of the language. Without help in translating between the two cultures, many minority children find themselves confused at the time they start school and behind their mainstream peers on achievement indicators from then on. Some educational anthropologists, investigating the differences between a particular minority culture and a school culture, have subsequently intervened to bridge the gap. They have found that even small in-school adjustments that are culturally sensitive to minority children's

* We are grateful to Katharine Cutts and Cheryl Ray for their assistance in reviewing some of the materials discussed in this chapter. We would also like to thank Evelyn Jacob and Cathie Jordan for their comments on earlier versions of this chapter.

experiences at home can improve minority students' academic achievement and attitudes toward school (Heath 1983; Jordan 1985; Moll and Diaz this volume; Vogt, Jordan and Tharp this volume).

In this chapter we want to draw attention to another explanation for student performance at school. We will show that growing up a member of a minority family and living in a minority community—by virtue of skin color, native language, religion, and so forth—is not the only means by which individuals share similar characteristics or learn the behaviors and attitudes they exhibit at school. Groups form and flourish at and around school, too. From their responses to the school, these groups may develop distinctive "cultural orientations," that is, more-or-less shared ways of interpreting the meaning of school experiences and their place in the school.[1]

We will focus on two properties of school-related groups. First, we point out that school-related group boundaries and cultural orientations may not match those attributed to ethnic, or minority, groups outside school. In our first example, about the way parents talk about their children's "readiness" for kindergarten, we demonstrate that some parents who "look" the same, that is, share the same skin color, the same native language, and the same religious and ancestral background (or in other words, have the same ethnicity), may develop different cultural orientations to school. In our second example, about black and white women on two university campuses, we demonstrate that students who look different sometimes share cultural orientations related to school. These two examples are intended to show that there is not a one-to-one correspondence between the way individuals look and the things they believe; individuals may look the same and not share some beliefs, or alternately, they may look different and share some beliefs.

Our second major point is that processes of school-related group formation and cultural differentiation occur around the things that happen in school. Using another set of examples, we show that groups and cultural differences may arise from the policies, labels or curriculum offerings of the school (Borko and Eisenhart 1986; Fordham and Ogbu 1986). Further, we suggest that school-related groups and orientations can be produced by students as they attempt to identify and distinguish themselves from their peers (Eckert 1989; Willis 1977). When students are identified or identify themselves at school, the groups that emerge can divide and reorganize ethnic groups in ways that families or communities do not. The particular dimensions of

---

[1] Our use of the term "cultural orientations" may be unfamiliar to some readers. By it, we mean shared (collective) ways of interpreting the world that are associated with social groups in a particular setting (Holland 1986). Later in the paper, we will use the term "cultural differentiation" to refer to the processes by which distinct orientations arise and are maintained. From this perspective, cultural differences are fundamentally ideational differences (with behavioral and attitudinal correlates) about the things that matter to a group (Eisenhart 1989).

group formation and cultural differentiation in school will vary depending on local conditions and interests, and though influenced in important ways by family and community, school-related groups and cultural orientations can take on a life of their own, with important implications for school achievement.

Our perspective will lead us to argue that those wishing to improve the academic achievement and school outcomes of minority students must investigate how students are placed or place themselves in the groups that arise in relation to school and what cultural orientations toward school these groups hold. Interventions should accommodate school-related groups and cultural orientations, as well as those associated with ethnicity.

SCHOOL-RELATED GROUP BOUNDARIES AND CULTURAL ORIENTATIONS

One Ethnic Group/Different Cultural Orientations

Among American social scientists, it is common to read that black Americans are "culturally different" from white Americans, Hispanic Americans from black or white Americans. Often, an assumption follows that *within* each group, members share many cultural characteristics, and that between-group differences are greater and more significant, especially when it comes to school performance, than within-group differences.

But studies of subgroups reveal a different picture. Subgroups of whites, for example, are recognizable in their relation to schools because they do not share knowledge and attitudes about schooling. Nor do they have equal power to affect their children's schooling. In their interactions with each other and with the school, they construct different interpretations of schooling. This process may begin very early in children's school careers.

An example comes from work on school readiness in three white Colorado communities located within 20 miles of each other (Graue 1990). Although "school readiness" is often thought to be reliably determined by following an established set of developmental indicators of a child's maturity, we began to suspect that the interpretation of readiness might vary by community as Graue began to conceptualize a study of academic redshirting.[2] In a descriptive study of age patterns in Colorado kindergartens (Shepard, Graue, and Catto 1989), it was found that the age ranges in these districts varied widely, with as many as 70% and as few as 0% of the children being overage for their grade placement. These variations were apparent not

---

[2] Academic redshirting occurs when children are held out of kindergarten although they are legally eligible to enroll according to their chronological age.

only across districts but across schools within a district. Taking kindergarten enrollment patterns as an indication of orientations to readiness, we found that the meaning of readiness was not the same everywhere, that features of the community and local school figured into decisions about whether a child was enrolled when eligible or held out for an additional year.

Analysis of Graue's data suggests that parents, teachers, and students in the three communities develop location-specific sets of ideas about when children are ready and what constitutes readiness. Their interpretations of early childhood education, its purposes and goals, vary. Differences in the meaning of readiness could be heard in the language used by participants in each setting. For example, parents were differentially articulate in the language of "school readiness." Parents of children about to enter one of the schools, Norwood, were anxious to talk with teachers and the researcher about the "facts" of their children's ages and school-related skills. One said about her daughter:

> She'll be 5 September 4th and I've talked to the teacher and she seemed to think that Katie was plenty ready because she can say her alphabet or most of it and count and her name and stuff.... I don't know if she'll be one of the youngest kids in the class—the other kids will have already been five. The preschool she goes to—they have a prekindergarten class and she didn't get to go in that because she wasn't four yet.... I thought that she seemed plenty ready to go into kindergarten. I went ahead and enrolled her and I thought going 3 years in preschool was a little much.

In contrast, white parents about to send their children to another school, Fulton, did not discuss "readiness" in terms of birth date, relative age or requisite skills. When asked about what she was thinking as her child approached kindergarten, one mother in this community focused on the possibilities that the school experience would provide:

> Because we live in a small town and I stay home with her, she doesn't have a lot of friends her own age. We're real excited about it as far as social reasons go. And then, of course we may be prejudiced like a lot of other parents, but we think that she's pretty smart for her age. We are looking forward to it because we think she'll do real good.... She's real willing to learn and we're just real enthusiastic about it.

Because it is in these uses of language that the meanings of readiness are developed and communicated in interaction among parents and with the school, ways of assisting and assessing readiness come to be different in each place. The parents at Norwood have one version of the language of readiness which focuses on age, sex, academic skills, and pressures to excel at school work. This meaning system corresponds with the one used at Norwood School and allows the parents to talk about and prepare their preschool children in terms of the academic indicators and attitudes valued by the school teachers and administrators. Parents and school personnel make decisions about whether to hold a child out based on their assessment of the child's relative position on their readiness scale. Fulton parents are much less able, by their language at least, to make this kind of assessment or decision. While their ideas about readiness also correspond to their school's ideas, they focus on the school as an opportunity for their children, like a gate that is open and waiting for the children to walk through. Holding out is not a strategy used by these parents, at least in part because they do not have a scale of academic skills to measure their children, and because they hope their children will enjoy, more than compete in, school work.

In sum, the cultural orientations—in this case the meaning of "readiness"—for interpreting, conducting, and negotiating school business—differ among these American whites. These differences exist even though they share many "background" characteristics and live very close together.[3]

Two Ethnic Groups/Same Cultural Orientation

Holland and Eisenhart (1988a,b, 1990) have written about the "culture of romance"—a meaning system of student peer groups at two universities. Derived from a cultural system of the wider society, the campus culture of romance flourished at both the black university, Bradford, and the white school, SU. On both campuses, the culture of romance was used by students to categorize women into groups according to their physical attractiveness and their ability to attract appealing men as romantic partners.

The interesting thing about this example is that the culture of romance was almost identically constructed by the black and white women. Their racial difference made little difference when it came to romance.[4] On both campuses, the women arrived at college with strongly expressed interests in school work and a career later. However, for all the women, interest in

---

[3] As might be anticipated, on average the two communities differ by social class: Fulton's families are predominantly working class while Norwood's are predominantly middle class. They do not, however, differ by ethnicity (by physical characteristics, native language, or religion; nor are they afforded a special status or identity in the U.S. sociopolitical system). Because of their shared ethnicity, we think that U.S. school officials, reformers, and researchers often (though not always) overlook or diminish any differences in cultural orientations, and their implications for schooling, in favor of those associated with ethnic groups. We raise this last point again later in the chapter.

[4] A few differences in the ideational systems of the black and white women were identified. See Holland and Eisenhart (1989) for a discussion of them.

romance came to take precedence over interest in school work. Although the black and white women had different ideas about the purposes and value of their college coursework (Holland and Eisenhart 1988b), the majority of women on both campuses ended up devoting the bulk of their time and energy during college to their romantic affairs. By graduation, most had little of themselves invested in school work and were not inclined to pursue additional schooling or the careers they had once envisioned.

To forestall stereotypical thinking about the origins and sources of school groups and the cultural orientations they exhibit at school, we think it is quite important for teachers and other observers of schools to realize that the distinction between minority and mainstream groups and their cultural orientations is not sufficient to account for some major ways in which school-related groups and cultural orientations affect the school performance of students. Using the familiar model of cultural difference, the groups and cultural orientations described in the examples given above would likely have been ignored because they exist in the absence of ethnic minority groups (the readiness example) or because they cross-cut ethnic group boundaries (the romance example). We believe that these emergent school groups and the meanings associated with them, in addition to students' background or demographic characteristics, must be understood as contributing in important ways to what students do at school and to their attitudes toward school and academic achievement (Eisenhart 1989).

To understand *how* such groups and cultural orientations affect student academic achievement, it is necessary to turn to the processes by which differences arise in and around schools. This is the topic of the next section.

THE PROCESS OF CULTURAL DIFFERENTIATION AROUND AND IN SCHOOLS

In social interactions in and around school, such as when people talk about when children should start kindergarten, differences like those between the Norwood and Fulton parents are much more than a casting of phrases. The orientation of the Norwood parents permits them to get their children ready for school in a way that the Fulton language does not and vice versa.

We cannot say, of course, what the eventual effect of these differences will be on the academic achievement of students from Norwood and Fulton. But we think their potential implications are important to draw out. The differences may anticipate what the children at each school have learned after a year of school, how much of it they know, and the feeling they have toward school. (Is it "felt" as a pressure cooker or a good time?) Should the differences persist over time, we would expect the gap between what the two sets of children know to increase. If these children were later to meet at the same middle or high school, to take the same standardized tests of academic achievement, or to compete for admission to college or for a job, we think that their differences could quickly become salient, with positive outcomes and the designation of "high academic achievement" more likely to go to Norwood students.

In this hypothetical example, we can speculate that a process of cultural differentiation may develop as people who interact about school readiness learn, use, or have access to different cultural or linguistic resources to think about and act with regard to the school. These differences would be drawn from and serve to reinforce different activities at school and different orientations toward schooling. They could eventually lead to quite different school outcomes, especially if students from different school-related groups are ever judged in relation to each other.

With the next set of examples, we examine processes of cultural differentiation in and around schools. The examples suggest that the process can take several forms.

Differentiating by Ability Group at School

Once children enter school, the school itself can extend or even initiate the process of cultural differentiation. For example, Borko and Eisenhart (1986) reported how reading experiences were differentiated in four second grades housed in a school with a fairly homogeneous population: mostly white, middle class from a small rural Appalachian county.[5]

In all four second grades at the school, students were officially divided according to reading ability into four reading groups. Research in these classrooms revealed that the high and low ability students came to differ in their experiences with and conceptions of reading. Each reading group, together with the teacher, seemed to be operating with a distinct and closed informational system. Each system had its own set of mutually supportive and reinforcing reading activities, student and teacher behaviors, student understandings of reading, and criteria for successful performance. For example, learning to read for low ability students was defined in terms of behavior and using correct procedures, while for high ability students it was related to global reading and comprehension strategies. Teachers focused on these group-specific meanings of reading in their instruction.

Implicit in these reading systems were differences in their definition and criteria of success. While the high ability group could apply its rules to other class activities with a positive payoff, the low ability group could not. Beyond

---

[5] This study has been described at length in Borko and Eisenhart (1986) and in Eisenhart (1989). The reader is referred to those articles for details omitted here.

their instructional uses, the groups for reading became the basis for the development of distinct views of reading success and its relationship to more general school success. These views, in turn, made movement between groups difficult because students had to construct a new meaning system to become part of the other group. Working harder would not be enough; they must come to think about reading in a different way, attending to a different set of information and skills. The closed system of the reading groups reduced low ability students' access to the opportunities given to the high ability group. Further, it encouraged one group to see itself as distinctly different from the other and to begin to apportion prestige and status, as well as knowledge, accordingly. Consequently, the students were internalizing differences among them, using the categories supplied by the school.

Differentiating by Activities at School

Another example of a similar process comes from Fordham and Ogbu's (1986) study of a black high school in Washington, D.C. The Capitol High student peer group appropriated school activities as a means of defining what it meant to be "black" versus "white." In this case, the school did not make this distinction for students; the students used the school setting and school arrangements to make the distinction meaningful in their everyday school activities. Certain activities, such as studying hard, excelling, and making good grades were singled out as evidence of "acting white." Speaking standard English, reading poetry, or trying out for the It's Academic Club were also categorized as "white." Other activities, such as being good at sports or cutting up in class, were interpreted as evidence of acting black or as oppositions to acting white, and thus were viewed as more desirable for blacks.

In a school that was 99% black, the influence of this black peer cultural orientation on students' orientation toward academic achievement was profound. Black students who acted "white" in school risked being ostracized by their peers, and few of the activities associated with school success were deemed appropriate for blacks. Thus, the majority of students gave up any interest they might have had in excelling at school work. The few black students who wished to do well in school despite their peers had to keep their academic achievements hidden behind school pranks or athletic ability, if they wanted to have any friends. In other words, school achievement came with a high price: give it up and fit in with one's peers or pursue it and risk losing one's peers. Not surprisingly few of the school's students excelled at school work.

In this example, the process of differentiation is developed by the students, not primarily to distinguish among themselves at school but to establish their collective identity as a group in relation to others in the larger society.

Unfortunately from the standpoint of school achievement and attainment, success in school is a devalued part of the identity these students construct for themselves.

Differentiation by Student Groups at School

Several studies illustrate how informal student groups differentiate themselves by the nature of their response to cultural features of their home communities and of the school. From the conjunction of cultural elements from home and school, at least some of these groups actively create their own cultural categories at school. Paul Willis (1977), for example, describes how some British, white, working-class boys at Hammertown School drew on certain ideas and practices from their white working-class community to forge a particular, oppositional response to their schooling. Beginning during the age period of American middle schools, a student group known as the "lads" emerged at the school. When they were at school, members of the group demonstrated behaviors such as having a "laff," smoking, drinking, and boasting of sexual exploits. They expressed attitudes such as a preference for manual (rather than mental) labor and an irreverence for formal authority. All these behaviors could be found in the homes and shop floors where adult members of this primarily working-class community lived and worked. By reproducing these behaviors in school where everyone knew they were inappropriate, the lads constructed and expressed their disdain for the school, its authority, and credentials. In this confrontation of selected community norms with the norms of the school, the lads produced, for themselves, a cultural system based on privileging some cultural orientations of the working class and opposing some school-sanctioned behaviors and norms.

At the same time, other working-class boys in the school, who would not or could not join the lads, drew on their orientations from the same white working-class community—orientations that were more consistent with middle class orientations. This group, dubbed "ear'oles" by the lads, had a peer group identity and associated cultural orientations at school too, but they conformed more closely to school norms than did the lads. Although drawing from the same working-class community, the lads and ear'oles took up different elements and used them to oppose each other at school.

The school outcomes for the boys were different too. The lads renounced the value of the school and thereby the credentials (good grades, a high school diploma) that might have permitted them to leave the working class. The ear'oles, in accepting the school's program including the need for good grades and a diploma as the best preparation for work, paved a way toward some social mobility by meeting the requirements for supervisory jobs, for higher education, and for middle-class consciousness. Although the seeds of disappointment, radicalism, and conformity were present (and later enacted) by some members of each group, the interpretations of later events and possibilities were quite different.

Willis emphasizes that the "class cultures" that came to distinguish the lads and ear'oles at Hammertown were in many ways peculiar to that site. Thus, there was no reason that working-class students in other locales or in the next generation would produce meaning systems exactly like those of the lads or ear'oles; the outcome was locally determined and always in doubt from one generation to the next. However, because other working class students would share *structural* characteristics with the lads and ear'oles, certain themes could be expected to persist across sites.

> Class cultures are created specifically, concretely in determinate conditions, and in particular oppositions. They arise through definite struggles over time with other groups, institutions, and tendencies. Particular manifestations of the culture arise in particular circumstances with their own form of marshalling and developing of familiar themes. The themes are *shared* between particular manifestations because all locations at the same level in a class society share similar basic structural properties,... [and] face similar problems. (Willis 1977:59)

Eckert's recent (1989) account of "jocks and burnouts" in an American high school makes some similar points. In it, she describes how a social division into jocks (who had a cooperative relationship with the school) and burnouts (who had an adversarial relationship with the school) emerged in daily interactions at Belten High. Like the lads and ear'oles, Eckert's jocks and burnouts drew selectively on their neighborhood and family experiences to turn ways of talking, behaving, dressing, identifying territories, and using illicit substances into indicators of distinct peer orientations at school. Also like Willis, Eckert emphasizes that community-based behaviors and norms were only the starting point for social-class differentiation within the school. Once outside norms and behaviors were brought to school by students, they became the focal points for further differentiation and competition between jocks and burnouts.

Similar to Willis, Eckert found that although the jocks drew upon middle-class cultural orientations while the burnouts drew upon working-class orientations, membership in each group was not consistently determined by class background (16% of self-identified jocks came from working class backgrounds; almost 50% of burnouts from middle-class backgrounds). Further, the students' career aspirations were more closely related to whether they identified themselves as a jock or a burnout than to their class backgrounds.

In Eckert's interpretation, the jock/burnout distinction is not primarily a matter of actual group membership; in fact, the majority of students said they belonged to neither group. Eckert views the distinction as a social organizational principle—a cultural dimension—for interpreting behavior and social identity at the school.

> Thus Jocks and Burnouts do not constitute clear groups or cliques; they are cultural categories, which define and unify collections of groups and cliques. The Jock and Burnout categories organize the ideologies of the groups within the social network of the school, aligning groups at different parts of the network according to key issues in the adolescent society. They are cultural foci rather than clearly defined groups, and their differences are organizing principles within the community rather than definitions of individuals or groups of individuals. (Eckert 1989:20)

In sum, cultural differences may arise from students' needs to locate themselves in their social worlds at school. Forging their own identities from the resources available to them and in response to their experiences of school, they reconstruct and sometimes create for themselves school-related groups and distinctive orientations toward school work.

SUMMARY AND CONCLUSIONS

From the examples we have given, it is clear that familiar indicators of cultural difference—skin color, native language, religious and ancestral background—are not the sole determinants of the behaviors, attitudes, and performance of students. Group boundaries and cultural orientations emerge in and around schools, organized around the factors that are or become salient there. Groups formed at school may divide ethnic or minority group members in different ways than do families or communities. And the cultural orientations of a school group may encourage members to think about school and act at school in ways that distinguish them from their ethnic counterparts in other school groups. Further, similar cultural orientations toward school can be produced in more than one ethnic group, such that members of various ethnic groups come to share orientations toward school. Such situations do exist, as our research has shown, and they are important to recognize because they affect how students feel about school and what they do there.

We realize, however, that such situations blur ethnic boundaries and thereby complicate treatments and remedies conscientiously designed to help targeted groups. Because the statistical trends are clear—some ethnic group members do consistently less well in school, on average, than their majority counterparts—explanations for the trend are sought, so that remedies may be proposed. Researchers find it easier to generate or test explanations if the group is assumed to be homogeneous. Similarly, schools and teachers find it easier to plan interventions, receive support for them, and implement them if the benefits of the program are thought to be generalizable to a large, "at-risk" group. However, these practices, as they are presently conducted in the United States, also contribute to stereotyping, in that they often lead to labeling, separating, and ranking of students by ethnic membership and to treating everyone within an ethnic group the same. Eisenhart experienced an extreme case of this when she worked at a black university. Because 99% of the students were black, the school could receive federal money for many remedial programs. Thus it set up an extensive program of remedial courses for freshmen. Within a few years, all freshman courses had become remedial, and all entering students, regardless of academic skills, were required to enroll in them. When remedies such as this one are applied across the board to members of ethnic groups, they may well miss their mark, or worse, they may depress, rather than encourage, students' interest in school.

We have also demonstrated that the processes of cultural differentiation occurring at school take several forms. Some children arrive at school with little that differentiates them, yet the school's policies of assessment, grouping, and ranking may create its own set of different groups and orientations. Other differences are produced primarily by the students, as they respond to the way the school treats them or they work out their own social identities among their peers.

There are several reasons why we think these processes of differentiation occur. First, different orientations are likely to arise in local communities because parents, teachers, and students negotiate the meaning of school primarily in their face-to-face dealings with each other; thus, the orientations formed in one setting will reflect its social organization. When members of one community encounter other orientations as a consequence of sending children to school (where they usually encounter other students from a larger and more heterogeneous area), a new social dynamic will be created and is likely to produce some new groupings of students and some changes in orientations.

Second, all schools use some form of student grouping and academic ranking system. Thus, every child finds him- or herself in some kind of school group, according to the school's assessment of the child's academic ability and potential. By this formula, some in-school groups are always disadvantaged relative to others: Some groups must be "low" groups; some must be "high." The organization and policies of schools do not, for example, permit teachers consistently to put all their students in a high group or to give everyone in the class an A. The requirement that schools group and rank students creates conditions in which school groups and distinct orientations toward school may form, regardless of ethnic group membership.

Further, students are affected in different ways by messages from home, their community, or the media about schooling. A few of the black students in Fordham and Ogbu's study were persuaded by the view that school success is an important step toward a successful adulthood; they worked hard to do well in school despite the peer pressure to do otherwise. Most of the students, however, learned from the experiences of adults around them and from their peers to question the school's claim that hard work and success at school translates into good jobs later. In other words, students' responses to school may differentiate the cultural orientations of ethnic group members, too.

Finally, students may need, for psychological or sociological reasons, to identify like-minded peers and distinguish them from others in order to develop their own social identities. This process may result in the cultural differentiation of an otherwise homogeneous group, as occurred among the working-class boys Willis studied and the mostly middle-class students in Eckert's study.

If these are the reasons, they are unlikely to go away any time soon, as they are deeply rooted aspects of American life and schools. We are optimistic, however, that the processes of differentiation can be recognized if we do not settle for the taken-for-granted markers of group membership. Further, we believe that if we can identify the groups that form within schools, we can work to create the conditions that foster more positive school outcomes. Shirley Brice Heath's (1983) work, for example, illustrates how teachers who understand some of the cultural orientations held in the communities from which their students come can create classroom activities that disrupt the normal pattern by which some children tend to be labeled "behavior problems," assigned to low ability groups, and come to dislike school. In her examples, a few teachers were able to raise both young students' and their parents' interest and enthusiasm for school. Similarly, the work of Cathie Jordan and her associates to understand and change the pattern of disinterested school performance among Hawaiian and Navajo children is encouraging. While their work is based on a more conventional definition of groups and cultural difference, the steps they took show that attempts to make education more culturally compatible work: When ethnic groups and their cultural orientations are accommodated by teachers, student achievement improves. Our appeal is to enlarge the scope of such interventions so that groups formed in schools and their cultural orientations also become the subject of research and intervention efforts. We want to apply the anthropologists' tools for understanding groups and cultures beyond familiar categories for distinguishing children at school so we can know more about students and hopefully produce more responsive environments for their education.

REFERENCES

Borko, Hilda and Margaret Eisenhart
    1986   Students' Conceptions of Reading and Their Reading Experiences in School. Elementary School Journal 86(5): 589–611.
Eckert, Penelope
    1989   Jocks and Burnouts: Social Categories and Identity in the High School. New York: Teachers College Press.
Eisenhart, Margaret
    1989   Reconsidering Cultural Difference in American Schools. Educational Foundations 3(2):51–68.
Fordham, Signithia and John Ogbu
    1986   Black Students' School Success: Coping with the "Burden of 'Acting White.'" The Urban Review 18(3):176–206.
Graue, M. Elizabeth
    1990   Socially Constructed Readiness for School in Three Communities. Ph.D. Dissertation, University of Colorado, Boulder.
Heath, Shirley Brice
    1983   Ways With Words: Language, Life, and Work in Communities and Classrooms. Cambridge: Cambridge University Press.
Holland, Dorothy
    1986   How Cultural Systems Become Desire: A Case Study of American Romance. Paper presented at the meeting of the American Anthropological Association, Philadelphia, PA.
Holland, Dorothy and Margaret Eisenhart
    1988a   Moments of Discontent: University Women and the Gender Status Quo. Anthropology and Education Quarterly 19(2):115–138.
    1988b   Women's Ways of Going to School: Cultural Reproduction of Women's Identities as Workers. In Class, Race, and Gender in American Education. L. Weis, ed. Pp. 266–301. Albany: SUNY Press.
    1989   On the Absence of Women's Gangs in Two Southern Universities. In Women in the South: An Anthropological Perspective. H. Mathews, ed. Pp. 27–46. Athens: University of Georgia Press.
    1990   Educated in Romance: Women, Achievement, and College Culture. Chicago: University of Chicago Press.
Jordan, Cathie
    1985   Translating Culture: From Ethnographic Information to Educational Program. Anthropology and Education Quarterly 16(2):105–123.
Shepard, Lorrie, M. Elizabeth Graue and Sharon Catto
    1989   Delayed Entry into Kindergarten and Escalation of Academic Demands.

Paper presented at the meeting of the American Educational Research Association, San Francisco, CA, April.

Willis, Paul
   1977   Learning to Labour: How Working Class Kids Get Working Class Jobs. New York: Columbia University Press.

11

Resistance and Compliance in Minority Classrooms

John D'Amato*

Student compliance with at least the main part of teacher directions and requirements is a major part of the foundation upon which academic engagement and achievement are built. While it is not the only ingredient in the mix that produces student learning, it is certainly a necessary one; and when student resistance to teacher demands markedly outweighs compliance, teaching and learning founder.

This chapter is an interpretation of the process of resistance to school among Hawaiian children and certain other minority populations; it attempts to relate this process to cultural and sociostructural variables. The chapter starts by briefly describing Hawaiian children's beginning-of-the-year challenges to teacher authority and the potential outcomes of these challenges. It then reviews current theory on minority resistance to school. Next, it outlines an alternative theory, focusing especially on the issue of variability in the outcome of the relatively intense forms of resistance offered by Hawaiian children and other members of the category that Ogbu has labeled "castelike minorities." Why resistance in some cases is only a passing phenomenon, while in others it becomes permanently embedded in the life of the classroom is the key question raised by this chapter.[1]

---

*John D'Amato is a cultural anthropologist, who formerly worked at the Kamehameha Early Education Program of the Kamehameha School and now is an attorney.
[1] The primary ethnographic data presented in this chapter come from eight years of studying interaction between teachers and young Hawaiian school children from low-income families. Over the course of this time, 6 preschool, 7 kindergarten, 2 first-grade, 5 second-grade, and 5 third-grade classrooms were studied. Most were studied for two to four

HAWAIIAN CHILDREN AND THE PROCESS OF "ACTING"

The beginning of the year in Hawaiian classrooms,[2] as in most, if not all American classrooms, consists of a period of time during which the children and their teachers define their relationship with one another, settling the issue, among others, of who will control the classroom. From the children's perspective, this is a time in which the teacher is on trial—does she[3] or does she not possess the qualities of a worthy incumbent of her role? Is she or is she not worthy of respect? From the perspective of teachers, this is a time for "shaping" the children's behavior and for meeting the "testing," that is to say, the challenges from the children, that they all come to expect (cf. Beynon and Atkinson 1984; Dumont and Wax 1976:210-212; Roberts 1970; Wax 1976:218).

In Hawaiian classrooms, this beginning-of-the-year process has three phases: a honeymoon phase, a contentious phase, and a resolution that emerges from the contention.

The honeymoon phase may last for as long as a week or as few as ten or fifteen minutes. During the honeymoon phase, the children are more or less on their best behavior and show attentiveness and friendliness to the teacher. But they are also quite alert to the teacher's actions and the significance which the group begins to attach to these actions. This phase appears to be an evaluative one during which the children arrive at a preliminary consensus as to what kind of a person they perceive the teacher to be.

The second, contentious phase is called "acting" by the children. The name is suggestive, for Hawaiian children first encounter this term at home in their relationships with their parents, other adult kin, and older siblings

---

hours per day two to three times per week; one cohort of children and their teachers received almost daily study for a period of two years. In addition to classroom studies, sociometric studies were done of peer relationships in eight classes, and about 500 hours were spent observing playground interactions and interviewing children about relationships with peers and teachers. The data gathered during these eight years consist of transcripts of videotapes and audiotapes, fieldnotes, sociograms, and notes and tapes of interviews with teachers, children, and parents.

[2] By "Hawaiian," I mean an identity claim made by individuals whose ancestors include people who resided on the Hawaiian Islands prior to the arrival of Captain Cook. I thus mean the term to have only a weak racial connotation and to represent primarily a socio-cultural identity projected by individuals who participate in social networks identified as Hawaiian ones. By "Hawaiian classrooms," I mean classrooms in which two-thirds or more of the students are Hawaiian as defined above. See D'Amato (1986) for an analysis of Hawaiian social networks as the locus of a distinctive Polynesian culture.

[3] The feminine gender is used, not in reaction to sexism, but to represent reality: All of the teachers studied were female and, indeed, virtually all of the elementary and preschool teachers in the schools studied were female.

and cousins. Their superiors use the term in both an approving and disapproving fashion. As a term of approbation, it refers to playful challenges of authority, such as joking or clowning around, which tend to show mettle, wit, and a certain *joie de vivre*. As a term of disapprobation, it refers to acts demonstrating disrespect (D'Amato 1986).

In the classroom, "acting" begins with indirect and playfully mischievous challenges which fall into three general categories. The first type of playful challenge involves play with the parameters of legitimate performances so as to produce actions which are legal in form but subversive in intent; this type of "acting" includes doing playful versions of legitimate responses, initiatives, and teacher evaluations. For example, children may make loud and tumultuous demonstrations in reacting to a visual aid to which a teacher might have welcomed a moderately enthusiastic response. In answering a yes or no question, children may form themselves into opposing teams, do contending cheers of "yes!" and "no!" and then laugh at the effect they have produced. In doing playful versions of legitimate initiatives, children may create traffic jams in the bathroom, slowly grind pencils down to the eraser, take three-point shots at the rubbish can, and do scolds of peers so histrionic that they are usually much more disruptive of classroom order than whatever it was that the peers were doing. In exploiting rights to do teacher evaluations, children may take enormous delight in anything interpretable as a teacher misstep or occasionally produce derisive commentary on class proceedings, saying, "Ah, junk!" for example, when the next lesson topic is introduced.

The second major category of playful challenge consists of outrageous actions, the more outrageous and conspicuous, the better. Examples include jumping off tables, hiding under tables, disappearing into closets in the middle of instruction and then dramatically reappearing, sailing airplanes or doing cartwheels across the room. These actions differ from the exploitation of legitimate terms in that they pre-empt the group's attention and thus have the effect of briefly seizing control of the situation from the teacher.

The third type of playful challenge is a lively stream of playful peer contention—joking, teasing, disputing, and the like—which competes with the lesson for peers' attention and both influences and is influenced by lesson events. A conspicuous success in answering a question, for example, may be followed by boasting to peers, stimulating countermoves on their part. Alternatively, peer contention may move from the flow of peer interaction into the lesson itself. Very commonly, for example, other children will echo a response to the teacher, voice a contrasting response, or dispute the correctness of a response. Playful peer contention is typically the most volatile aspect of the "acting" process.

Together, peer contention, outrageous actions, and playful forms of legitimate actions undermine the flow of lessons. The often comic and sometimes derisive effects of these actions mock the serious, instrumental character of instruction and the teacher's claim to an identity capable of inspiring obedience in children. In consequence, "acting" tends to make the teacher's definition of what is going on come "unstuck" from the situation (D'Amato 1986).

The intensity of "acting," however, varies from class to class and leads ultimately to widely divergent outcomes. The proximate source of this variability appears to be the preliminary evaluation which the children have made of the teacher in the honeymoon phase. With some teachers, "acting" is mild to begin with and never progresses much further than group play with answer turns and background peer playfulness. In such classrooms, "acting" is almost reduced to a ritual. The children do what they need to do to show the teacher and each other that they have spunk, but then settle into the routine. To be sure, this resolution of "acting" into compliance is not perfect—"acting" ripples through the classroom now and again throughout the year. But the ripples do not collect into waves because the children themselves monitor and control the process, sanctioning peers who threaten to go too far. In these classrooms, there is never a question as to who is legitimately in control. It is not too much to say that the support of the children in such classrooms typically becomes a source of great pleasure to teachers. Hawaiian children can be uncommonly sweet and gentle, and demonstrative in their affections, and these qualities are regularly cited by experienced teachers as among the greatest rewards of their careers.

With other teachers, however, the process of "acting" is radically different from the beginning and leads to a radically different outcome. Playful "acting" quickly gives way to direct and open challenges, both of the teacher and of other children; eventually these challenges escalate to open conflict, including fights between children, yelling matches featuring strong insults between children and teachers, and even physical struggles between children and teachers, as, for example, when teachers attempt to restrain children from fighting, from leaving the classroom, or from some similarly impermissible undertaking. Resolution of "acting" in such classrooms amounts to the routinization of enmity. Children learn that the ultimate result of allowing conflict to build to climax in the classroom may be punishment at home; teachers learn that the ultimate result of too rigid an insistence upon a presumptive right to exercise authority may be extremely unpleasant encounters with parents of students and equally unpleasant, if less direct, suggestions from colleagues and superiors that they themselves are to blame for whatever problems they may have. Owing to the unpleasantness of these ultimate results, teachers and children come to restrain the full expression of their frustrations with one another and the situation. They avoid disturbances which will attract attention from outside the classroom;

inside it, they find themselves living in a tense and hostile atmosphere, waging a kind of cold war with one another devoid of civility, let alone generosity. Once this mood has set in, teachers and children appear powerless to change it. Their loss of trust in and respect for one another lasts the entire year. In such circumstances, children come to hate school, and teachers, their jobs.

CULTURAL DIFFERENCE AND CASTELIKE MINORITY THEORIES OF RESISTANCE

Two questions that fairly leap out of the phenomenon of "acting" and similar phenomena among other populations of school children are, first, why does such intense resistance occur, and second, how is it possible that it can lead to such disparate outcomes.

The theories which presently dominate attempts to answer these questions for minority children are two—the cultural difference theory and the castelike minority theory developed by Ogbu. Each of these theories provides a useful perspective and has contributed important distinctions and concepts, including the ideas of cultural conflict and of castelike minority status. Neither perspective, however, gives adequate answers.

Cultural difference theorists provide a type of processual explanation of resistance in minority classrooms. They argue that minority children behave in terms of a set of norms learned at home, and that conflicts and other problems develop in minority classrooms owing to cultural differences between home and school (e.g., Boggs 1985; Erickson and Mohatt 1982; Philips 1972). From this perspective, phenomena like "acting" represent a kind of interactional self-defense used by minority children to combat the cultural affronts inflicted upon them in classrooms. The children behave in the way they do because teachers have behaved in the way they have (Boggs 1985; Dumont 1972; Erickson and Mohatt 1982; Philips 1972).

The castelike minority position provides a type of sociostructural explanation of resistance in minority classrooms. This position argues that in racially organized systems of social stratification, oppressed racial groups or "castelike minorities" develop attitudes of warranted cynicism regarding the social mobility functions of institutions like schools; practice a group-wide, "oppositional culture" in dealing with the representatives of such institutions (Ogbu 1985); learn survival skills appropriate to the nature of their structurally limited opportunities; and socialize their children in these matters (Ogbu 1982a, 1982b). In consequence, children of castelike minorities have no reason to believe in the value of school and are committed to resist teachers both as a duty of minority group membership and as a function of the survival skills they have learned (Ogbu 1982b). From this perspective, conflict between teachers and children of castelike minorities is not a problem which develops within classrooms; it is instead a sociostructural problem which merely finds expression there. The children behave as they do because the society has behaved as it has.

There is evidence to support both of these positions on resistance in minority classrooms, but each stumbles over certain troublesome and crucial facts. First, neither position accounts for the fact that resistance to school is not a phenomenon restricted to minority children, but occurs among all school children for whom we have close ethnographic accounts. Resistance occurs in some surprising places—for example, among Japanese school children (Rohlen 1983) and even, under certain conditions, among decidedly upper-middle-class Jewish American school children (Schoem 1982).

Second, neither position can account for the facts marshalled by the other. As Ogbu (this volume) points out, the cultural difference position cannot explain why certain immigrant children excel in school despite the cultural differences which ought to separate them from their teachers. If cultural discontinuities between home and school are as critical as cultural difference theorists claim, then surely these children should also fail (Ogbu 1982a). On the other hand, the castelike minority position is unable to explain why the children of castelike minorities do not always reject their teachers. Au and Mason (1981) have documented this fact in a compelling way by means of videotaping two teachers teaching reading on alternate days to the same group of Hawaiian second graders. Both teachers were experienced, but one was new to Hawaiian children. The lessons she taught became shambles; in the lesson taught by the other teacher, however, the same children were as well-behaved as children ought to be. If sociostructural considerations are as critical as castelike minority theorists claim, then these children should have practiced "oppositional culture" with both teachers, not just one. Au and Mason (1981) argue convincingly that the difference between the two sets of lessons has to do with a difference in the interactional rules followed by the two teachers.

Underlying the limited explanatory reach of the two theories appears to be a shared theoretical weakness. Each of the theories looks at processes in school from the perspective of states of affairs outside school—from the point of view of the norms held by culturally distinctive minority populations as a matter of historical accident, or from that of the oppositional norms developed by oppressed minorities in adapting to exploitative economic and political structures. In order to establish links between these external states of affairs and school processes, each theory relies upon typifications of minority school children and of teachers, positing that the children, acting as such children do, and their teachers, acting as such adults do, interact themselves into predictable difficulties. The problem is that these actors do not always behave as the typifications say they are supposed to behave.

Minority children do not always behave at school in terms of norms learned at home; castelike minority children do not always wage war against their teachers; school staff do not always act in ways that reproduce class structures and the majority culture. To be sure, one is always reduced to typifications in theorizing about social phenomena. But the theories must be supple enough to encompass known variability in the phenomena and to provide some means for understanding how, in processual terms, the "same" situations can produce widely divergent results. Social processes in classrooms are not mechanical ones, produced by automata; no social process is. They are emergent, developmental, and highly dynamic processes capable of working their way to variable outcomes. No one would dispute the enormous influence of cultural and class variables upon the processes of minority opposition and resistance to education. But what is needed for an adequate understanding of these processes is a theoretical framework capable of accounting for both their emergent and dynamic character and their massive regularities.

In outlining and exploring some elements of such a theory over the balance of this chapter, I propose to begin by framing the issues somewhat more broadly and inclusively than is usually the case in studies of minority resistance to school. It seems apparent that in order to bridge adequately the range of facts that have been established concerning the phenomenon of resistance to school, a theory of castelike minority resistance to school must be able to account for three facts. It must be able to account, first, for the generality of the phenomenon of resistance to school, since it is clear that resistance occurs among virtually all populations of school children; second, for variability in the intensity of resistance to school, since, the generality of the phenomenon notwithstanding, it is clear that castelike minority children offer resistance of greater intensity than do most other children; and third, for variability in the outcomes of the relatively more intense forms of resistance offered by castelike minority children, since it is also clear that these forms of resistance do not foreclose the possibility of compliance. In building a position to address these issues, this chapter will draw from the work of educational sociologists, from that of Ogbu, and from that of the cultural difference theorists, in that order. The chapter will take the position that challenges to teacher authority are inherent in the institution of school; that sociostructurally determined beliefs about the value of school have the effect of intensifying tests of teacher authority through their influences upon the peer group cultures of school children; and that cultural discontinuities between teachers and minority school children usually have the effect of causing tests of teacher authority to escalate to resistance and conflict. Rather than to cultural contrasts between home and school, however, this chapter will relate the escalation of classroom conflict to intermediate cultural discontinuities between the world of school as defined by adults and the world of school as defined by children themselves. The chapter will argue, in essence, that the source of variability in the outcome of castelike minority resistance to school is the fit, or lack of it, between adult and child versions of school social order: between teacher-defined social structures and processes and the children's own peer-defined peer group structures and processes (D'Amato 1986).

THE ROOTS OF RESISTANCE: SCHOOL AS THE SOURCE OF ITS OWN PROBLEMS

Challenges or tests of teacher authority are an exceedingly general phenomenon (e.g., Beynon and Atkinson 1984; D'Amato 1986; Dumont and Wax 1976; Furlong 1984; Kileff 1976; McDermott 1974; Philips 1972; Roberts 1970; Schoem 1982; Tripp 1986; Wax 1976; Williams 1981). So general is the phenomenon that Waller (1961) seems certain to have been correct in arguing that the source of resistance to school must be the features of schooling rather than the particular cultural or sociostructural characteristics of the children who attend school.

Three features of schooling appear to be primarily responsible for engendering resistance from children: School is compulsory and otherwise constraining; instructional interaction is contentious; and children are taught as groups with the consequence that they encounter and react to the compulsory and contentious aspects of school as groups.

As Waller (1961:292–316) observed with acuity, schools attempt to exercise power over children. Children are compelled to attend school, and during the schoolday, teachers are supposed to take control over children's lives, giving them places to be, things to do, and ways to interact with adults and also with each other. The element of compulsion and unequal distribution of power inherent in these facts always appears to create an opposition between teachers and children and to lay basis enough for some degree of struggle (Waller 1961; cf. Beynon and Atkinson 1984; D'Amato 1986; Roberts 1970).

The processes of classrooms provide children with additional motivation for resistance. Teachers are supposed to get children to participate in instruction. But as Jackson (1968) points out and as the analyses of Bossert (1979) and Mehan (1979) confirm, this means eliciting public displays of knowledge and competence which are then publicly evaluated as to worth. Since an implicit if not explicit dimension of teachers' evaluations of children's performances is the relative worth of a performance compared to those of other children, "instructing children" in fact means requiring them to compete—to vie with one another in structures of peer contention defined, managed, and judged by teachers (D'Amato 1986). Teachers, in effect, try to get children to contend with one another for awards of teacher and group recognition. A teacher's right to do this may itself be challenged by children, for instruction so defined very regularly gives rise, not only to pleasure, but also to affront.

The fact that children are taught in groups, thirdly, means that their experiences of school politics are shared, group experiences. This, in turn, appears to lay the foundation for the establishment of resistance to teachers as a group norm and group duty and thus as a reaction which comes to be motivated largely by peer relationships. In the Hawaiian case, acceptance by and status within the peer group ride to a large extent on proving willingness to discharge the obligation of living up to the norm of resisting the teacher. To "act," or at least to show sympathy for those who do so, is to assert a claim to membership and to a certain status in the children's peer group. To shun the rite of "acting," on the other hand, is to betray the side and lose rights to the loyalty and support of peers (D'Amato 1986). In Hawaiian classrooms, in short, the test of a teacher has at least as much to do with children's peer relationships as it does with their relationship to school and teacher, for the dynamics of these relationships encourage resistance. The evidence is that, elsewhere as well, children's peer relationships drive the process of resistance to school (e.g., Beynon and Atkinson 1984; Dumont and Wax 1976:210-212; Roberts 1970; Wax 1976:218).

This characterization of the sources of resistance to school suggests certain hypotheses concerning the phenomenon of compliance. If attending school is costly to children owing to loss of personal autonomy and to the affronts suffered when public sanctions are administered for behavior which has been deemed "inappropriate" by a teacher or when the evaluation of a performance is poor, it follows that if children nonetheless comply with school, then the perceived benefits of school must in some way outweigh the costs. Owing to the group dimension of resistance, it also follows that the perceived benefits of school must be credible to the class as a whole, that the peer group as a whole must perceive some sort of credible, counterbalancing benefit to school. This last point deserves emphasis: If resistance is an expression of the group, then compliance must also be a group expression and will fail if it is not. Again, the Hawaiian case is instructive. In Hawaiian classrooms, resistance does not subside a little at a time, now one child, now another deciding to behave; instead, resistance deflates more or less all at once, if it deflates at all.[4] The reason that resistance is concluded by the group

---

[4] In Hawaiian elementary classrooms, the last children to toe the line are boys who wish to vie for the status of being the "toughest" boys of the class. They are the last, not because it takes longer for them to be won over, but because by showing that they are the children least willing to comply, they stake a public claim to being the toughest in the class (D'Amato 1986).

as a group seems to be that individual children cannot readily accept the authority of a teacher until it is clear that peers do so as well, for to accept a teacher's authority in the absence of a consensual basis for this acceptance within the peer group is to lose face among peers. Conversely, in order to accept the authority of a teacher, children as a group must possess some sort of credible group rationale for justifying to themselves their own acts of participating in the classroom and insulating themselves from the charge that they have merely capitulated to the will of the teacher (D'Amato 1986). If this account applies not only to Hawaiian school children but to school children generally, then it follows that the key to whether beginning-of-the-year resistance yields to compliance is the capacity of children to locate a rationale that will enable them to accept the costs of school and to control their own peer relationships. Without such a rationale, the dynamics of children's reactions to the politics and contests of school seem to push them almost inevitably into conflict with teachers and with one another. With such a rationale, however, they are able to hold their resistance within the norms of interaction imposed upon classrooms by teachers (D'Amato 1986).

Some generalizations concerning the intensity of resistance to school are also suggested by this characterization of the sources of resistance. It should follow that children will resist school the more intensely the less probable it seems to them at the outset of the year that they will arrive at a group conclusion that the benefits of compliance outweigh the costs of school. And, as is argued below, rationales for seeing value in school are not equally available to children.

STRUCTURAL AND SITUATIONAL RATIONALES FOR ACCEPTING SCHOOL

School can be said to have value in two senses—intrinsic value, having to do with rewards of the experience itself, and extrinsic value, having to do with the instrumental value of school achievement in the attainment of other ends. Each sort of value can support a rationale for accepting school. These rationales will be termed situational and structural rationales, respectively.

As the work of Ogbu and his colleagues demonstrates, school can have structural significance for children in the sense of having known or presumed implications for states of affairs beyond school. Thus, some groups of children may see successful participation in school as a precondition for entry to college and high-status careers; or they may see success in school as a precondition for maintaining acceptance and approval in relationships within household, kinship, and other private social networks. Where the external rewards for compliance and sanctions for resistance are sufficiently compelling, the structural implications of school performances may be said to provide children with a structural rationale for limiting group opposition and resistance to school politics and for justifying to themselves participation in instructional contests and other relatively constraining and divisive school processes. As Ogbu's work indicates, the availability of this rationale to children varies primarily with matters of family history, race, ethnic, or national history, class structure, and caste structure. Where school success has been associated with social mobility, as in the case of the middle and upper classes, the need to succeed in school is emphasized in home-life networks, and children take for granted the value to their futures and to present social relationships of positive teacher evaluations and other markers of school success. Similarly, where school success is viewed as a viable means of improving social status, as is the case in many immigrant populations, the value of school success is again taken for granted by both adults and children (Ogbu 1978). School, however, tends to have little credible structural significance for castelike minority children (Ogbu 1978) and for majority children of lower socioeconomic strata (Wilcox 1982). It also has limited significance for children placed at the low end of academic hierarchies (Lacey 1976) and for children attending schools adjudged by them not to provide adequate or pertinent education (Schoem 1982).

As suggested by work in the cultural difference tradition, school events also have situational significance for children in the sense of having implications for identities, relationships, and other states of affairs within the flow of school life itself, and this situational significance also influences children's behavior in school. School dynamics may be such as to render school an intrinsically enjoyable process. Thus, children may view participation in lessons and other school processes as a means of maintaining valued relationships with teachers and peers and of gaining access to experiences of mastery and accomplishment (Bossert 1979; D'Amato 1986). On the other hand, the dynamics of school processes may have primarily negative meanings for children. Where the situational rewards for compliance and sanctions for resistance are sufficiently compelling, the implications of school performances may be said to provide children with a situational rationale for limiting group opposition and resistance to school and for justifying participation in school processes.

Children can have access to both structural and situational rationales for accepting school, to one but not the other, or to neither. The especial intensity and volatility of castelike minority children's resistance has to do with the fact that they typically have access to neither sort of rationale. Owing to the fact that their racial and ethnic experiences will not support structural rationales for accepting school, their resistance to school is always relatively intense from the outset; owing to the fact that their experiences at school will also typically not support situational rationales for accepting school—a quite different matter—their resistance tends to escalate to conflict.

The following sections elaborate upon and attempt to disentangle the phenomena of intensity of resistance and outcomes of resistance by examining in some detail the effects upon children's peer culture of the presence or absence of structural rationales for accepting school.

WHEN THE STRUCTURAL SIGNIFICANCE OF SCHOOL IS STRONG

Where the structural implications of school are compelling for children, the balance of power in classrooms lies squarely in the hands of teachers. This is so because children's own beliefs about the structural significance of school mean that the things teachers control are things that the children need. Older children know with clarity that grades, evaluations, placement in "high track" classes, and other records and indications of performance in school will have lasting implications for their lives. Accordingly, children in this situation apply themselves to the work and contests of education, accept its politics with little more than token opposition and resistance, and appear willing to tolerate even extremely punitive classroom events; they must if they wish to acquire the things teachers have to dispense. Conversely, they cannot make classroom constraints, sanctions, and instructional contests rallying points for manifest and collective resistance to teachers, and, in general, cannot permit issues in peer relationships and other "personal" matters to intrude into classroom operation. They have too much to lose, individually and collectively, in organizing a strong peer group, resisting teachers, and attracting unfavorable evaluation. The children instead tend to construct their peer cultures around the politics of school, organizing themselves in terms of teacher standards and teacher indications of relative peer standing (Bossert 1979). To provide these children with a credible group rationale for accepting school, teachers may need to do little more than remind children of the world outside the classroom and of the significance of school events within this world (Wilcox 1982).

Rohlen's (1983) account of students at Nada, an elite high school in Japan, substantiates this characterization in the case of older students. Most students at Nada have a good chance of being accepted at top universities. Succeeding in this is extremely important to the students because they know that attending a top university has lifelong effects. Consequently, the students display only token opposition and resistance to teachers and show little reluctance to vie against each other in competitive classroom exercises. Of a history lesson at the school, Rohlen (1983:19–20) noted that,

At the front is a group of boys whose hands shoot up in response to virtually every question, their faces alert and serious—caricatures of classroom virtue....The answers to the teacher's questions are notable. Sometimes someone gets one wrong, and there is jovial snickering from friends nearby, but most of the time the students' replies are crisp, detailed, and on the mark.

Wylie's (1976) description of a French school in the rural village of Peyrane illustrates the parallel effects of a different type of structural acceptance of school. Wylie argues that children at this school behave well and perform as well as they can academically mostly to avoid bringing shame upon their families.[5] Of the children, Wylie (1976:95) writes:

> They are courteous, docile, gentle, cooperative, respectful....Above all they have a sense of dignity and social poise. Regardless of what complaining parents say, the children of Peyrane appear to accept the social yoke that is placed on them. The teachers rarely have to punish a serious infraction. Their principal disciplinary efforts are directed toward insisting on courtesy and neatness, and towards repressing restlessness and talking out of turn.

To assume that children at Peyrane and Nada have no problems with school, however, is to romanticize classroom politics. Children's own beliefs about the structural implications of school place children at the Nadas and Peyranes of this world so deeply in the control of teachers that they are willing to try to tolerate most any situation.

Warren's account (1976) of a school in the German village of Rebhausen gives some flavor of this. "Teachers, along with the mayor and clergy,...occupied the apex in village society," and most parents gave unquestioned support to the school as a socializing institution (Warren 1976:110,114). In this context, teachers clearly dominated classrooms. Children had little choice but to endure disciplinary and instructional processes which could be quite punitive:

> The content of the student's learning experiences is almost always rigidly controlled by the teacher....The recitation process is, in this respect, particularly significant. Lines of communication run almost exclusively between individual students and the teacher, with the latter controlling and directing the content of the communication....In one

---

[5] See also Hostetler and Huntington's account (1976) of an Amish school. Children here, too, seem interested mostly in fitting into the community and avoiding disapprobation; they are very compliant in the classroom (Hostetler and Huntington 1976:196): "The classroom runs smoothly, for [the teacher] does not pretend that the children make the decisions. An Amish teacher quietly tells a child what to do and he does it."

sense students are, in the classroom, isolated from each other intellectually and therefore more vulnerable to and dependent on the dictates
of the teacher.

The almost limitless power of the teacher seems to affect the kind of
respect he displays towards students. One has the feeling that the
respect [of the teacher] must be earned either through academic
performance or through appropriate behavior. There is little psychological protection in the classroom for those who have difficulty measuring
up to acceptable standards. Their exposure is constant, with few
avenues of relief available. (Warren 1976:113)

The situation does not seem so cold at Peyrane. Again, however, there is an
unquestioned belief in the value of school (Wylie 1976:89), and the
consequence of this belief is again that teachers dominate classrooms.
Children's peer relationships are weak relative to their relationships to the
teacher, and children seem compelled to try to tolerate the processes of
school, even when punitive (Wylie 1976:92, 93):

The first day I attended Madame Girard's class I was shocked at the
way in which she insisted on discussing her pupils with me in front of
them. After each child in the Preparatory Course recited she stopped
the recitation to give me an analysis....

"There's an intelligent little one....She works hard, too. It's a
pleasure to teach a child like that..."

"There's Renee. Not stupid, but lazy. She sits there distracted with
her mouth open all day. And untidy! You can't expect much of that
kind of girl..."

"Poor Marie. She tries, but—I think all is not right." She tapped her
forehead significantly with her forefinger. Marie squirmed in her seat
and looked...unhappy..., but the recitation and the commentary
moved on until all the children had had their turn.[6]

---

[6] See also Wylie's account (1976:96) of dictation in one classroom:

The most usual punishment and apparently the most effective one lies in shaming
a child by isolating him and pitting the rest of his society against him....

A scene that took place in Madame Vernet's room one day after she had given a
dictation was typical....

"Ah, Monsieur, you arrive just at the right moment," she said, "just look at this
dictation of Laure Voisin. Have you ever seen anything so careless, so untidy?...Stupid! It's only stupidity—and I used to think she was fairly intelligent....And lazy....She prefers to sit there and dream! And to think that this girl
insists on presenting herself for the *certificat primaire!* I wouldn't shame the school or
her parents by letting her try...."

The other children laughed mockingly...Laure winced and tears came.

"That's right. Now you cry. As though that would help you."

These accounts óf Nada, Peyrane, and Rebhausen tell much the same story regarding the influence of structural issues upon the peer cultures of children and their willingness to accept school. For children in these locales, performance at school holds strong implications for regard within the family and community. In these circumstances, children are compliant with teachers, displaying only token opposition and resistance. Children accept participation in competitive classroom processes and seem concerned mainly to elicit favorable and to avoid unfavorable teacher evaluation. Congruently, the children's peer relationships are weak relative to their relationships with teachers. In at least the French and German communities, children are also willing to tolerate extremely punitive classroom processes. As both Wylie and Warren make clear, however, children do this not because the processes are not painful to them but because the links between home and school are such as to give them no choice.

WHEN THE STRUCTURAL SIGNIFICANCE OF SCHOOL IS LIMITED

An altogether different situation prevails where school holds limited structural significance for children. Here, children's beliefs about links between school and home and school and the future no longer place power in the hands of teachers. Owing to the children's sheer numbers and to their relative freedom from structural constraint, the balance of power in the classroom lies in their hands. Wolcott (1974:411,416), for example, gives an account of how his Kwakiutl students socialized him to what he regarded as a "deeply entrenched pattern of pupil hostility toward the teacher:"

> My pupils were good teachers and their techniques were effective. The methods they used to socialize me included giving slow, reluctant responses..., ignoring my comments..., mimicking my words or actions, constantly requesting to leave the classroom to go to the toilet, and making me the target of spoken or written expletives.

Of the children's behavior with peers, Wolcott (1974:414,415) notes:

> Teasing and bullying were very disruptive elements in class....I could not make them help each other, be patient toward each other, or socialize each other toward such teacher-approved purposes as keeping the classroom quiet so pupils could read, working quickly enough to allow time for other activities, or letting younger pupils join in the recess play of the older ones.

Teachers of Hawaiian children give very similar accounts. A widely experienced teacher described in the following way her first year's introduction to Hawaiian children's group dynamics (D'Amato 1986:18,19):

I taught for three days in the morning. The first two days were fine....The third day...four [boys] began to show signs of not cooperating at all. You know, I'd ask them to do something and they'd just sit down and refuse to do it....

By the second week I was a basket case. Literally....I acted like I didn't know what I was doing, and so they figured they were in control, and they were to a certain extent....

I'd go home in tears every day....I had to work to like the group as a whole because at that point I hated every one of them....I was so uptight about that group. I mean I've never ever had a group like it....There was...constant interfighting....Who did this and who did that—that was more important than the education and the reading and that. The social interplays took far more precedence....From the playground in, there could be five fights within two minutes and you just didn't have enough hands, you know, to take care of them all.

Even a day's experience in minority classrooms can be intense enough to make a teacher question the human qualities of the children. Ellis (1976:118), for example, quotes a note from a substitute teacher who worked one day with "a group of black boys, enrolled in a 'remedial' class":

This is better than a trip to the zoo; they don't let you inside the cage. This group is beyond belief....We didn't get any books opened. I just sat here and tried to keep them inside of their cage and from killing each other.[7]

But it is not only in minority classrooms that one sees conflict and hears teachers reacting in this way to children. Rohlen gives an account of classroom events at a low-ranking Japanese high school. Students at this high school need diplomas in order to get employment, but good grades are not a concern; they know already that they will not be going to universities (Rohlen 1983:40):

A young male teacher is trying to explain English grammar to a class of largely inattentive students. One girl is brushing a friend's hair; several students are staring out the window; others are passing around movie magazines; and a handful of boys in the back talk incessantly. The teacher tries to make jokes, but they are too witty for the students, and he laughs alone. In fact, it seems he is lecturing to himself.

---

[7] Ellis (1976:118) attributes the content of the note to racism; without denying this possibility, one may wonder whether there was not something else going on as well.

Schoem gives an account of a religious school at which Jewish students received instruction in Judaism and Jewish values. The students found this instruction relatively pointless. Schoem's account (1982:314) is particularly telling since these same children were reported to be highly successful, socially and academically, in their secular elementary schools:

> There were not infrequent cases of students openly mocking the teacher's comments, interrupting discussions with what were intended as rude remarks, hiding in closets, walking on tables, throwing paper airplanes across the classroom, and intimidating and scapegoating certain individuals until they would cry.

The similarity of these phenomena across cultural, class, and minority lines suggests that the classroom itself can harbor all that is required to turn any group of children into combatants of teachers and of one another. When children neither fear nor value the structural implications of school, they appear free to confront the premises and politics of school openly and directly. Owing to this, a systematic transformation of classroom politics seems to occur.

First, the teacher's routine exercise of power has the effect of unifying and politicizing the children and their peer group. When the teacher commands, forbids, or otherwise constrains, children no longer tolerate the situation as relatively isolated individuals. They are free to attend to the fact of constraint and to their collective experience of constraint, and they react accordingly, demanding that teachers justify formal power inequities and prove personal entitlement to positions of authority. The children become aware of their power as a group, are intolerant of strong assertions of teacher authority, and resist the status of dependency presupposed by such assertions. In ethnographic accounts of school children who do not fear or value the structural implications of school, one hears repeatedly that the children feel they are put down or treated like babies at school (Clark 1976:256; Gallimore, Boggs and Jordan 1974; Tripp 1986:141; Williams 1981:217) and that the road to sustaining interaction with the children involves some form of power sharing.

Second, children are much more absorbed by peer relationships, organize these relationships to a much greater extent, and are willing to pursue issues in peer relationships whether or not this means disrupting lessons. Less concerned with the teacher, the structural implications of her evaluations, and influencing these evaluations, children are much more concerned with the immediate potentials of the here and now and therefore almost necessarily with each other. Though school may be relatively pointless for these children in terms of its structural implications, it is not meaningless; the children give it meaning through development of and play with peer relationships. Correlatively, there is every reason for the children to pursue developments in these relationships, whatever the teacher definition of the situation, for the worth of school to children is now determined primarily by relative success at demonstrating a capacity to influence and maintain a certain standing in the peer group (cf. Dumont and Wax 1976; McDermott 1974; Philips 1972; Roberts 1970; Wax 1976; Williams 1981).

Third, because the teacher is no longer the center of influence in the classroom, the children are not constrained to organize their peer relationships on the basis of her norms and indications of relative status and do so instead on that of their values and evaluations (D'Amato 1986; McDermott 1974; cf. Bossert 1979; Labov 1982). This is not simply a formal difference. Peer relationships defined and managed by peers are everywhere somewhat similar to one another and somewhat different from peer relationships defined and managed by adults or other superiors. The characteristic dynamic of the former is rivalry, of the latter, competition (D'Amato 1986). Rivalry and competition are similar to one another in being types of peer contention in which players try to win, but are quite different in their goals, processes, and values. In competition, one wins by establishing clear superiority over peers, typically through a judgment rendered by some sort of official standing above and beyond the fray. This game of peer contention celebrates disparity and has the effect of producing social differentiation, a hierarchy of achievement. Rivalry, on the other hand, is based upon the ethic of egalitarianism. One wins this contention by showing that one is as good as anyone else, that no one is better than oneself; the assertion of parity is legitimated by the judgment of peers. Joking, and the audience response to joking, is the paradigm for the process. Rivalry levels; it celebrates parity, and its successful management depends upon keeping the play with emergent differences among peers from disturbing overall premises of balance and equality within the peer group (D'Amato 1986; cf. Labov 1972). Strong commitments to maintaining appearances of balance in peer relationships have been noted for Hawaiian (Boggs 1985; D'Amato 1986; Gallimore, Boggs and Jordan 1974), Cherokee (Dumont and Wax 1976), Oglala Sioux (Wax 1976), Odawa (Erickson and Mohatt 1982), Warm Springs Indian (Philips 1972), and black American school children (Goodwin 1982), all of whom typically lack structural rationales for accepting school.[8]

---

[8] Typically, rivalrous peer dynamics at school mirror rivalrous peer dynamics in home life social networks. Hawaiian children, for example, first learn rivalry through their socialization to a generational system of interaction in which peers tend to interact with peers and to avoid interaction with superiors or juniors. As argued elsewhere (D'Amato 1986), this type of social structure and its associated dynamic constitute an adaptation to conditions of limited opportunity for individual social mobility. It should be noted, however, that rivalrous dynamics have also been reported for Japanese (Rohlen 1983) and for American White

The dynamic of rivalry plays a decisive role in a fourth aspect of the transformation of school politics, that of children's intolerance of standard classroom practices. Worldwide, most standard instructional practices amount to methods of producing conspicuous winners and conspicuous losers in the classroom; they constitute forms of competition. Typically, children face the teacher as a group; they usually speak one by one in response to teacher initiatives; and the teacher evaluates the worth of a response before the audience of the speaker's peers, declaring, in effect, who has won and who has lost and how children stand relative to one another (Bossert 1979; Mehan 1979; Roberts 1970). Children are able to cope with the competitiveness of this situation to the extent that it reflects their own peer dynamic and lies within the tolerance of their norms for managing that dynamic. For children whose peer dynamic is rivalry, however, the competitive dynamic of traditional classrooms is wholly unacceptable because it runs exactly counter to the basic premises of their peer relationships. For these children, the competitions staged by teachers are not interpretable as ordeals of introduction to the interactional engine that drives society; the practices instead appear inhumane, some would say, "barbarous" (Dumont and Wax 1976), for their only notable effect is the divisive one of introducing differentiation into the peer group and of damaging or upsetting individual children's claims to parity with their peers. Consequently, whereas children for whom school holds strong structural significance seem willing to try to tolerate even extremely punitive processes, children who do not see structural value in school commonly take moral stands against even the most routine of teaching practices, using playful tactics to subvert these practices or directly and hotly contesting a teacher's right to interfere in peer affairs. Conversely, when these children do vie in competitive instructional contests, they are highly likely to experience conspicuous victories or defeats, which, in view of their peer values of egalitarianism, lead almost certainly to peer conflicts (D'Amato 1986).

Owing to the transformation of politics in classrooms in which children neither fear nor value the structural implications of school, beginning-of-the-year tests of teacher authority feature intense, group-driven resistance which can easily escalate to bitter, year-long feuding. The description by Wax (1976:218) of Oglala Sioux children's resistance conveys the intensity of the phenomenon and the seeming helplessness of teachers before it:

> The school is where the peer group reaches the zenith of its power....the power of the peer group may rise to the extent that the

---

(Clark 1976) and Jewish school children (Schoem 1982) who do not fear or value the structural implications of school. This would appear to show that in the right circumstances school is capable of independently teaching children the dynamics of rivalry.

children literally take over the school....As observers, we could not but marvel at the variety and efficiency of the devices developed by Indian children to frustrate the standard process of formal learning: unanimous inattention, refusal to go to the board or writing on the board in letters less than an inch in height, mumbled and inarticulate responses, whispered or pantomimic teasing of victims called on to recite, and in some seventh and eighth-grade classes, a withdrawal so uncompromising that no voice might be heard in the classroom for hours but that of the teacher, plaintively asking questions or giving instructions to which nobody responded.[9]

As Wolcott (1974:419) notes of his own year of living dangerously,

No one, teacher or pupils, ever let his guard down very far. If we were not at any one time engaged in a classroom skirmish, it was only because we were recovering from a prior one or preparing for the next. On the last day of school I reflected that I had not won a battle; instead I felt that all year long I had had a tiger by the tail, and we had merely crossed some kind of symbolic finish together.

The evidence, however, is that the resistance of castelike minority children does not inevitably escalate to conflict (e.g., Au and Mason 1981; Boggs 1985; D'Amato 1986; McDermott 1974; Roberts 1970). As Ogbu argues, it is true that castelike minority children do resist with greater intensity than is the norm and that the intensity of their resistance is related ultimately to sociostructural facts. But it is not true that these same facts mean that resistance will always escalate to conflict. The question of why resistance escalates turns upon a third matter, that of the potential of school experience to hold intrinsic value for children.

PEER GROUP STRUCTURE AND CLASSROOM STRUCTURE

That the relatively intense resistance mounted by castelike minority students does not always escalate to conflict must mean two things. It must mean, first, that classroom experiences themselves can be sufficiently valuable to

___

[9] See also the account of Dumont and Wax (1976:210-212) of Cherokee resistance:

The Cherokee students respond to the pressures of alien educators by organizing themselves as The Cherokee School Society....In any educational transaction, the Cherokee School Society is actively judging the competence of the teacher and allowing him a corresponding function as a leader....For the Cherokee School Society has created within the formal confines of the institutional classroom another social edifice, their own "classroom," so that at times there appears to be not simply a clash of cultural traditions but a cold war between rival definitions of the classroom.

children to outweigh the costs associated with school and to support a credible, group rationale for accepting school. It must also mean, second, that the mere lack of structural reasons for accepting school is not by itself enough to cause resistance to escalate to conflict. Where resistance does escalate, the cause of the escalation must have to do with a concatenation of factors—the failure of the society to provide the children with structural reasons for accepting school, and equally the failure of school to provide the children with experiences worth sustaining.

The question is, what distinguishes classroom situations which trigger conflict from ones that do not? What determines the availability to children of situational rationales for accepting school?

If one approaches this question from a social science, as opposed to a psychological science, perspective, it seems reasonable to suppose that the intrinsic value of school experiences to children, and thus the availability to them of credible situational rationales for accepting school, must turn on the relationship between the structure and social dynamic imposed upon the classroom by the teacher and the structure and social dynamics of the children's peer relationships. Where there is a fit between the two, then it should follow that classroom processes will support rather than conflict with peer values and forms of contention, buoy rather than interfere with the claims of individual children to membership and status in the peer group, and, in diffuse ways, provide children with experiences the risks of which are stimulating, rewarding, and fun. Where there is not a fit, on the other hand, the reverse should follow, with the result that the classroom will have the potential to become as much a scene of punishment, humiliation, and cruelty for the children, as it does for their teachers.

If it is the case, as has been argued in this chapter, that rivalry is the characteristic peer dynamic of castelike minority children and others who possess limited access to structural rationales for accepting school, it follows that if the classroom is to provide these children with a rationale for accepting school, then its processes and structures must be consistent with the rivalrous dynamics of the children's peer group. This, in turn, must mean a transformation of the standard competitive processes of American classrooms.[10]

Whatever this theory's applicability to other populations of castelike minority children, its main contentions are supported in the case of Hawaiian children. Teachers who attempt to impose competitive structures and processes upon Hawaiian children stimulate rebellion and lasting ill will. On the other hand, teachers who adapt classroom culture to the

---

[10] What is required in order for compliant children to find the classroom a source of valuable experiences is an equally important question. It is beyond the scope of this chapter, but it needs to be addressed if the romanticization of majority children's experiences at school is to be avoided.

children's peer culture, transforming competitive structures and processes into ones consistent with the children's own rivalrous structures and processes, ultimately succeed in eliciting compliance from them. The general lesson that should be drawn from this contrast is that it appears to be pointless for teachers to persevere with modes of authority and forms of instructional practice which presuppose a gift of power that has not been made. Castelike minority children will not adapt their relationships to the teacher's idea of what their peer culture should be; it is she who needs to adapt to them. Where she does, she provides the children with classroom experiences worth sustaining, and worth defending from the process of resistance.

Specific alterations of classroom practice that are illustrative of an adaptation by the teacher to rivalrous peer dynamics include certain changes in instructional sequences, in classroom organization, and in evaluation of student performances, both positive and negative. As has been detailed by Au and Mason (1981), effective teachers make use of participation structures having "open" features. In these structures, turns are permitted to overlap, children who have been nominated to speak are not required to speak, children who have not been nominated are not forbidden to speak, and speakers are entitled to complete, elaborate, and build upon others' performances. The result is not chaos but a process of measured contention in which individual performances do not provide bases for claims of special merit or demerit, are not readily evaluable against each other, and may be inserted as the need of maintaining parity with peers requires—a result wholly consistent with rivalry and its preference for parity and the play with small status differences autonomously from the control of superiors. One-at-a-time, question–answer–evaluation rules of performance in lessons, by contrast, are rules of competition; they constitute interaction so that individual performances are distinct and can be evaluated against each other and abstract standards of performance. This form of interaction is fiercely resisted by Hawaiian children, especially owing to its strong tendency to stir up trouble in their peer relationships and to turn the children against each other (D'Amato 1986).

A second change introduced by successful teachers, also consistent with Hawaiian children's rivalrous dynamics, is replacing whole-group instruction with small-group instruction, in which one group of children receives direct instruction while other groups of children work on tasks independently. Whole-group instruction masses attention upon individual performers and is therefore inherently riskier than small-group instruction. In any classroom, a teacher who stands at the front of a classroom before a phalanx of desks, controlling conversation and other aspects of interaction in face-to-face fashion, asserts conspicuous dominance over children and makes herself an easy target, her control readily subverted. A child required to perform in such a context will bear the weight of the attention of all of his or her peers, and may easily become a target of teasing or worse. In whole-group instruction in Hawaiian and other castelike minority classrooms, these potentials for problems are all regularly realized, particularly fully at the beginning of the year (D'Amato 1986). Another problematic aspect of whole-group instruction is that it assumes that the children of a class can all participate together in the same interactional process. This assumption is not justified where, as in the Hawaiian case, children will not subordinate their rivalries to the instructional process and where the structure of those rivalries typically involves relationships of formal opposition, like gangs, which radically diminish the possibility that the children will be able to sustain harmonious, whole-group processes (D'Amato 1986; cf. Bossert 1979).[11]

Small-group instruction defuses all of these aspects of the situation. It makes it possible for a child to perform in something less than the glare of full audience attention, and it reduces the teacher's visibility as a figure of authority. It enables her to experiment with the composition of work groups so as to avoid problem groupings and by that means to demonstrate to the children appreciation of and sensitivity to their peer relationships. A small group organization also makes it possible for her to legitimize something that the children will do anyhow, namely, interact with their peers. In Hawaiian classrooms organized on a small-group basis, the peer interactions which occur in the groups not receiving direct instruction tend to be harmless, easily modulated by the children themselves, and often related to school work. It is only when the teacher forbids the interactions, as she almost must in the whole-group context, that they become interferences (D'Amato 1986; cf. Bossert 1979).

A third alteration is that negative and positive evaluations are handled in a way that accords with rivalrous dynamics. Praise is not meted out according to a merit calculus but is distributed so that everyone gets some share of praise for performances (Au and Mason 1981) and so that the shares are more or less even. Criticism of lesson performances is rare. This prevents teacher evaluations from disturbing appearances of parity among children and inducing imbalances that cannot be ignored. Correlatively, directives (Erickson and Mohatt 1982) are framed so that they do not shame children in front of their peers. Means of accomplishing this include "privatizing" directives (Erickson and Mohatt 1982) so that peers do not participate

---

[11] As discussed elsewhere (D'Amato 1986), the features of the structure of Hawaiian children's classroom peer groups can include opposed gangs, assumptions about gender enmity, and positions like that of the class "bull" for which both boys and girls may contend. Events in lessons can easily trigger disputes across formal lines of organization and put children with conflicting identity claims in public opposition to each other.

directly in such events (cf. Edelsky, Draper and Smith 1983), using small groups and other types of classroom organization which reduce the size of the potential audience to directives and children's replies (cf. Bossert 1979), focussing directives upon groups or subgroups of children rather than individuals (Erickson and Mohatt 1982), and using forms of directives that do not compel immediate compliance with specific actions but leave the definition and timing of compliance up to children themselves (D'Amato 1986).

These alterations in standard practice, however, are merely illustrative. More important than the particular changes in classroom practice made by teachers, is the result apparently achieved thereby: the establishment of a classroom culture consistent with the children's peer group culture and thus of a situational basis on which the children can justify extending compliance.

CONCLUSION

This chapter has taken the view that the source of processes like "acting" lies neither in oppressive social structures nor in cultural differences but in the politics inherent in schooling. Sociocultural considerations exacerbate these politics for some minority children by cutting them off from societal rewards for classroom compliance and achievement; in a sense, however, the lack of structural rationales for accepting school is liberating. It frees children to express reactions to the experience of compulsion and to the punitive aspects of instruction. In the case of such children, cultural compatibility between teachers' and children's ways of doing things is essential, but less for cognitive than for political reasons. It is not so much that the children are cultural dopes, unable to escape the unconscious patterns of their natal cultures (cf. Erickson and Mohatt 1982), as that they are ingenious and principled politicians, who have every right to make the uncompromising demand that the teacher appeal to them on the basis of their own peer values and peer culture.

If the analysis developed in this chapter is correct, then children's classroom peer groups should fall somewhere along two continua—a continuum of structural acceptance of school and one of situational acceptance of school. Educational social scientists should probably be most concerned with telling the stories and advocating the causes and interests of children on the "wrong" end of the situational continuum: both those who must suffer through classrooms quietly and those who make such grand and courageous protests.

REFERENCES

Au, K. H. and J. Mason
   1981   Social Organizational Factors in Learning How to Read: The Balance of Rights Hypothesis. Reading Research Quarterly 17:115–152.
Bateson, G.
   1965   Naven. Stanford, CA: Stanford University Press.
Beynon, J. and P. Atkinson
   1984   Pupils as Data Gatherers: Mucking and Sussing. In Readings on Interaction in the Classroom. S. Delamont, ed. Pp. 255–272. London: Methuen.
Boggs, S. T.
   1985   Speaking, Relating, and Learning: A Study of Hawaiian Children at Home and at School. Norwood, NJ: Ablex.
Bossert, S.
   1979   Tasks and Social Relationships in Classrooms. Cambridge: Cambridge University Press.
Clark, W. W., Jr.
   1976   Violence in Urban Public Education in the United States. In The Anthropological Study of Education. C. J. Calhoun and F. A. J. Ianni, eds. Pp. 251–265. Paris: Mouton.
D'Amato, J.
   1986   We Cool Tha's Why: A Study of Personhood and Place in a Class of Hawaiian Second Graders. Unpublished doctoral dissertation, University of Hawaii, Honolulu.
Dumont, R. V., Jr.
   1972   Learning English and How to be Silent: Studies in Sioux and Cherokee Classrooms. In Functions of Language in the Classroom. C. B. Cazden, V. P. John, and D. Hymes, eds. Pp. 344–369. New York: Teachers College Press.
Dumont, R. V., Jr. and M. L. Wax
   1976   Cherokee School Society and the Intercultural Classroom. In Schooling in the Cultural Context. J. I. Roberts and S. K. Akinsanya, eds. Pp. 205–216. New York: David McKay.
Edelsky, C., K. Draper, and K. Smith
   1983   Hookin' 'Em In at the Start of School in a "Whole Language" Classroom. Anthropology and Education Quarterly 14(4): 257–281.
Ellis, H. G.
   1976   Theories of Academic and Social Failure of Oppressed Black Students: Source, Motives, and Influences. In The Anthropological Study of Education. C. J. Calhoun and F. A. J. Ianni, eds. Pp. 105–126. Paris: Mouton.
Erickson, F. and G. Mohatt
   1982   Cultural Organization of Participation Structures in Two Classrooms of Indian Students. In Doing the Ethnography of Schooling: Educational Anthropology in Action. G. Spindler, ed. Pp. 132–175. New York: Holt, Rinehart & Winston.

Furlong, V. J.
   1984   Black Resistance in the Liberal Comprehensive. *In* Readings in Interaction in the Classroom. S. Delamont, ed. Pp. 212–236. London: Methuen.
Gallimore, R., J. W. Boggs, and C. Jordan
   1974   Culture, Behavior and Education: A Study of Hawaiian-Americans. Beverly Hills, CA: Sage.
Goodwin, M. H.
   1982   Processes of Dispute Management among Urban Black Children. American Ethnological Society 9(1): 76–96.
Hostetler, J. A. and G. E. Huntington
   1976   The Amish Elementary School Teacher and Students. *In* Schooling in the Cultural Context. J. I. Roberts and S. K. Akinsanya, eds. Pp. 194–205. New York: David McKay.
Jackson, P.
   1968   Life in Classrooms. New York: Holt, Rinehart & Winston.
Kileff, C.
   1976   The Rebirth of a Grandfather's Spirit: Shumba's Two Worlds. *In* Schooling in the Cultural Context. J. I. Roberts and S. K. Akinsanya, eds. Pp. 129–140. New York: David McKay.
Labov, W.
   1972   Rules for Ritual Insults. *In* Rappin' and Stylin' Out: Communication in Urban Black America. T. Kochman, ed. Pp. 265–314. Chicago: University of Illinois Press.
   1982   Competing Value Systems in the Inner-city Schools. *In* Children In and Out of School. P. Gilmore and A. Glatthorn, eds. Pp. 148–171. Washington, DC: Center for Applied Linguistics.
Lacey, C.
   1976   Intragroup Competitive Pressures and the Selection of Social Strategies: Neglected Paradigms in the Study of Adolescent Socialization. *In* The Anthropological Study of Education. C. J. Calhoun and F. A. J. Ianni, eds. Pp. 189–216. Paris: Mouton.
McDermott, R. P.
   1974   Achieving School Failure: An Anthropological Approach to Illiteracy and Social Stratification. *In* Education and Cultural Process: Toward an Anthropology of Education. G. D. Spindler, ed. Pp. 82–118. New York: Holt, Rinehart & Winston.
Mehan, H.
   1979   Learning Lessons. Cambridge, MA: Harvard University Press.
Ogbu, J. U.
   1978   Minority Education and Caste: The American System in Cross-cultural Perspective. New York: Academic Press.
   1982a Cultural Discontinuities and Schooling. Anthropology and Education Quarterly 13(4): 290–307.
   1982b Equalization of Educational Opportunity and Racial/Ethnic Inequality. *In* Comparative Education. P. G. Altbach, R. F. Arnove, and G. P. Kelly, eds. Pp. 269–289. New York: Macmillan.

1985   Variability in Minority School Performances: A Problem in Search of an Explanation. Paper presented at the 84th American Anthropological Association Meeting, Washington, DC.

Philips, S. U.
1972   Participant Structures and Communicative Competence: Warm Springs Children in Community and Classroom. *In* Functions of Language in the Classroom. C. B. Cazden, V. P. John, and D. Hymes, eds. Pp. 370–394. New York: Teachers College Press.

Roberts, J. I.
1970   Scene of the Battle: Group Behavior in Urban Classrooms. Garden City, NY: Doubleday.

Rohlen, T. P.
1983   Japan's High Schools. Berkeley: University of California Press.

Schoem, David
1982   Explaining Jewish Student Failure. Anthropology and Education Quarterly 13(4): 308–322.

Tripp, D. H.
1986   Greenfield: A Case Study of Schooling, Alienation and Employment. *In* Alienation from School. P. Fensham, ed. Pp. 27–159. London: Routledge & Kegan Paul.

Waller, W.
1961   The Sociology of Teaching. New York: Russell and Russell. (Original work published in 1932)

Warren, R. L.
1976   The School: Authority, its Sources and Uses. *In* Schooling in the Cultural Context. J. I. Roberts and S. K. Akinsanya, eds. Pp. 104–114. New York: David McKay.

Wax, R. H.
1976   Oglala Sioux Dropouts and their Problems with Educators. *In* Schooling in the Cultural Context. J. I. Roberts and S. K. Akinsanya, eds. Pp. 216–226. New York: David McKay.

Wilcox, K.
1982   Differential Socialization in the Classroom: Implications for Equal Opportunity. *In* Doing the Ethnography of Schooling: Educational Anthropology in Action. G. Spindler, ed. Pp. 268–309. New York: Holt, Rinehart, & Winston.

Williams, M. D.
1981   Observations in Pittsburgh Ghetto Schools. Anthropology and Education Quarterly 12(3): 211–220.

Wolcott, H. F.
1974   The Teacher as an Enemy. *In* Education and Cultural Process: Toward an Anthropology of Education. G. D. Spindler, ed. Pp. 411–425. New York: Holt, Rinehart & Winston.

Wylie, L.
1976   The School at Vaucluse: Educating the French Child. *In* Schooling in the Cultural Context. J. I. Roberts and S. K. Akinsanya, eds. Pp. 84–104. New York: David McKay Company.

12

Failure's Failure

David Smith, Perry Gilmore, Shelley Goldman, and Ray McDermott

When faced with an irremediable disaster like an earthquake or a hurricane, it is sometimes comforting to explain the phenomenon as if giving voice might also give control or at the least help absolve us of responsibility. Minority school failure is a disaster of sorts. Our country is increasingly and dangerously divided between those who have and those who have not, and schools, through their power to impose failure on selected groups of individuals, are a principle mechanism for assigning people to their respective niches. This being the case, explaining school failure not only delivers little control, it risks making things worse.

Natural disasters come on their own schedules, and we must learn to cope with their inevitability. School failure, on the other hand, should be more tractable. In the final analysis, it behooves us to deal with school failure as a social creation, an institutional fabrication, a mock-up, and a game that takes our attention and diverts it from the inescapable side effects of our actions. School failure is inevitable in an educational system in which everyone is encouraged to do better than their neighbors. This is the case in contemporary America, but it does not have to be so. In the American system, there are presently two ways for students to go through school: One is to succeed and the other is to fail. Success and failure define each other more than they define the children they label. They define each other statistically (only half can be above grade level, and half below) and administratively (tracking). Most importantly, success and failure are used to define each other interactionally in the classroom. Our children must use the mutual definition of success and failure to guide their way through daily classroom rounds. Knowing full well that the ascription of either success or failure awaits their every move, students spend their time in school arranging when to be seen knowing something and, more perniciously, arranging not to get caught not knowing something.

Explanations of school failure, while generally offered in the spirit of making things better, have concentrated on ways to diagnose and predict problems that individual children might have in school. They have failed to take the notion of failure itself as problematic. While our efforts at explanation have led to a robust testing industry and an important niche in the academy for researchers who focus on the problem of school failure, they have also added to the general trivializing and demoralizing of the teaching profession, done little to empower people who might do battle with the ascription of individual success and failure, and contributed only negligibly to our understanding of the phenomenon. In fact, efforts to explain school failure institutionalize its existence as a field of inquiry and reify it as a cultural category not amenable to solution. It may be possible to reorganize the institutional world enough to empty cultural categories (this has happened to most kingships over the past 200 years), but continuing attention to explaining the phenomena within a category still in use—in this case individual or group failures—only lends credence to and tacitly strengthens the category itself.

The message in the title of this chapter is that school failure has become one of the mainstays of American culture, and that most of our efforts to deal with it—both our explanations and our attempts to confront it in the classroom—are subverted into promoting the proliferation of failure. It is hard to get beyond the failure of school failure as a useful category in the institutional lives of our children. As a category for describing reality, failure has failed us. More than providing a description of reality, it creates reality. Increasingly, everything we do in the name of minority education seems to be in the service of strengthening the category of failure.

We could do without more explanations of school failure (Cazden 1982; McDermott 1987), just as we could do without more explanations of concomitant institutionally arranged and often empty categories such as dropouts (Fine 1986; Gilmore and Smith 1989; Trueba, Spindler, and Spindler 1989), illiterates (Gilmore 1986; Harman 1987; Shuman 1986; Smith 1985, 1986), the learning disabled (McDermott in press; Mehan in press; Mehan, Hertweck, and Meihls 1986), and the inarticulate (Gilmore 1983, 1985; McDermott 1988). "School failure" and its mutually constitutive companion in making things worse, namely, "school success" cause us great trouble and get us little in return. It is time to stop locating, describing, documenting, measuring, remediating, and explaining both.

That failure is a fabrication is a point well made by Moll and Diaz (this volume) in their account of how quickly failure can be reorganized into learning on a local level. Once the threats of failure and the pressures of success are pushed aside, once we recognize that the task of schooling is not to explain which students do or do not learn, learning becomes easy for most. This will require the dismantling of the elaborate apparatus we have erected for documenting the failures of our children and redirecting the energies taken by that enterprise into organizing more learning. Moll and Diaz show us that failure is task-specific and institutionally fragile in the sense that it could always be otherwise, that the same behaviors, the apparent failing behaviors, could be made into instances of people working together accomplishing tasks promoting productive lives in the wider community (see also Newman, Griffin, and Cole 1988).

We do not underestimate the enormity of the task this proposed shift entails. The ubiquity of moments available for the ascription of success and failure in American classrooms creates great problems for teachers. It is difficult enough to organize children to learn under classroom conditions. American school teachers must do much more than teach, in the traditional sense. They must organize classrooms so that children do not have to spend the bulk of their learning time arranging to not get caught by failure. There is little room in usual classrooms for not knowing things, and, in classrooms without room for not knowing, there is a great constraint on learning. Our children do not go to school to learn to read and write, but to play the success and failure game with reading and writing.

As a motivating force in our children's lives, the success and failure game may have had some utility at a different time in our history. In an expanding, full employment economy, for example, the consequences of the game may be minimized, as in the Japanese grade school. But when an arbitrary device for encouraging motivation becomes reified into a classificatory schema defining social statuses, not just in school, but far beyond into the adult work lives of the children, the nature of the game has been transformed. Success and failure are now used to ascribe social status early in life, and these statuses are documented in school records that follow the children from school to other institutions, effectively locking them into particular tracks. Under such circumstances it is difficult to teach—if teaching is seen as organizing classrooms to assure learning.

In the sections that follow, we offer some stories about the ways that failure's failure has been confronted. We present these stories fully aware of the difficulties teachers face in risking even the smallest such confrontation. Teachers who would like to have less failure in their classrooms are clearly resisting strong pressures to intensify efforts to seek out, document, and sort more and more children into the failing pile. The teachers in our stories were more, rather than less, successful in their confrontations, but even their achievements were modest. We offer the stories to show that confronting failure in our schools is possible.

A first step in the confrontation must be the recognition by teachers that the criteria for distinguishing success and failure are arbitrary and that children are routinely labeled as school failures without regard for their potential in other settings. This first step, however, is a huge one requiring more than simply changing labels. It entails a radical shift in perspective, a reordering of conceptual reality revealing possibilities not allowed for under traditional arrangements predicated upon the ineluctability of success and failure.

Even a radical shift in perspective, however, does not mean that the day is won. From any point of view the ingrained, and interlocking challenges posed by race, class, and gender bias pervading the classroom are both complex and delicate. Erickson and Shultz (1982) provide an example of this delicate complexity in carefully documenting the many problems even a good counselor must confront in a simple interview with one student in a single session.

We offer our stories, therefore, not because they constitute easy or failsafe recipes for dealing with failure as a pervasive classroom presence. We write not as experts peddling truth, but as practitioners and observers who have seen many teachers, in a variety of class and cultural settings, both in the United States and elsewhere, skillfully and sensitively open their classrooms to the possibility of learning by all of their students (Smith 1981). We offer their stories in the hopes that, to paraphrase the haunting language of Sean O'Casey's *Autobiographies,* "they may bring some strength to the weakness and some softness to the pain."

We have divided our stories into two kinds. Those in section I address some of the mechanisms—competition, tracking, and tests—that make failure so ever present and seemingly intractable to our schools. Competition, tracking, and tests come easily to the American classroom. We worry about their misuse and their institutional consequences. We could put them to far better use if we envisioned education as dedicated to the good of the community as a whole and not just for the social success and mobility of individual children.

The second section illustrates confrontations with failure's failure in multicultural settings. We do not think that cultural differences per se explain school failure anymore than do cultural deficiencies (D'Amato 1987; Gilmore and Smith 1982; McDermott and Gospodinoff 1979). Whether conceived as the result of communicative mishaps or as the result of the sort of alienation that might result from generations on the bottom of the social hierarchy, minority school failure can be focused on only in social systems that have already arranged for school failure and minority status to be points of focus. If anything needs to be explained, or better, confronted, it is the system that makes school failure a career option open to so many. Cultural differences can only lead to school failure if schools are in the business of producing massive school failure. Minority status, be it manifest in communicative codes or attitudes about job ceilings, may exacerbate the situation by providing the excuse to inflict failure, but it cannot be the cause.

This being the case, the conventional strategy of confronting the problem through endless explanations is clearly futile. We must instead confront the very idea of school failure, seeing it for what it is, manifestations of classism and of racism. It is incontovertable that the all American school failure problem hits minority communities in particularly hard ways, and the stories offered in the second section, illustrating ways in which failure has been confronted in classrooms serving minority students, are important for this reason.

STORIES ABOUT CONFRONTING SOME OF THE MECHANISMS UNDERLYING FAILURE'S FAILURE

Balancing Cooperative and Collaborative with Competitive Classroom Activities

In order to situate the problems of school failure, one of the realities that must be considered is the difficulty of teaching children in a society that celebrates competition in the classroom. The use of competition to build institutional records moves identity enhancement and degradation to the forefront of classroom life. Furthermore, given that we have a society deeply divided by race and class inequalities, forced competition can exacerbate the inequalities. In theory, competition may be a fine way for equals to hone their skill. It is not a fine way for children momentarily less equal than their peers on some task to catch up and to display their potentials.

When half the children in our society are in various ways failing at school, and later failing at other life paths, it is necessary to worry about the institutional consequences of competition. It is time to balance competition with collaborative activities in the classroom. It is time to emphasize learning as participation in, and contribution to, a community. (See Lave and Wenger 1990 for an account of learning as apprenticeship and participation.)

Competition is definitional of the American classroom (Goldman and McDermott 1987; Spindler and Spindler 1990). Even the basic exchange of turns at talk generally take the shape, in the classroom, of question, answer, and evaluation (Cazden 1988; Mehan 1979). A child in our schools is never far from the press of evaluation and comparison. No sooner does the individual teacher get such pressures removed from the classroom, but they come storming back again in the form of principal inquiries, parental demands, standardized tests, entrance requirements for next schools, and a wide range of special purpose tests.

Competitions can even engage an entire state's population of school children. The popular nation-wide competition called "The Battle of the Books" is a case in point. A list of recommended award-winning and classic books are sent out to schools. Students read the books and are challenged to answer what often amount to trivia questions about events, characters and circumstances in the books. Classroom teams compete within schools, and schools compete with one another in state and nation-wide competitions which are talked about widely. Although it might be difficult to identify the usefulness of the learning that is organized by such a contest, Americans are not likely to be called on to do so. A competition of almost any kind is assumed to be doing some kind of good: focusing the students, for sure, and mobilizing them to new achievements. Just what the achievements are and how they might relate to the ongoing needs of the community, is left unexplored. If the state does not organize the competition, the rest of us do the job. Pressures to compete are everywhere.

In a highly "successful" junior high school in New Jersey, hundreds of competitive moments could be noted in the course of a single week (Goldman 1982).

"Who knows?"

"I do. I do."

"What is it?"

"Thomas Jefferson had red hair."

"Very good."

American schooling exists between the "Who knows?" and the "Very good." "Who knows?" is the cant of the American classroom, and with it comes the more troublesome question, particularly if someone is keeping records: "Who doesn't know?" The warp and the woof of American education: "Who knows?"/"Who doesn't know?" The cant and the can't.

We have worked in and studied a number of schools where teachers have attempted to reduce competitive activities and displays. This proves extremely difficult. If the teachers did not organize competition, the children or parents predictably did. It takes a whole community of persons to support each other enough to construct an environment in which there are other ways of proceeding. Competition is not only considered to be motivating, it can bring a certain kind of order to the classroom. One reason the reliance on competition is comfortable and easy for us is that the connections between our classroom-level games and large-scale student failures are not readily apparent to individual school practitioners who work in relative isolation (Lortie 1975).

Confronting Competition. In a Black Muslim classroom in New York City, a group of boys were working at their desks on a math problem (27−9 = ?). The teacher was sitting in front of the room. One boy was struggling with the problem at the board; in particular, he was having trouble carrying the one from the tens column over to the ones column. A boy from the back of the room raised his hand and said: "Sister Cynthia, I don't do it that way. I do it invisible, like in my head." Apparently, he did not have to carry the one from the tens column for calculating "9" from "27." In the competitive American classroom, both children are potentially a problem. One is behind, the other ahead; one is slow and must catch up, the other too fast and must be kept busy. One is to be encouraged, the other to be applauded. The teacher approached the situation in a most unusual way: "Knowledge is only useful so you can share it with your brothers. So cross out that two and carry the number so I can see it." This is a significant response. It involves the community; it involves learning for a reason other than being smart. What would it take for most Americans to have community needs as their reflex response to classroom problems? The Black Muslim school was in some ways organized in contrast to and in defiance of American culture, and alternatives to competition were momentarily available there.

Teachers can begin to organize more of the activities in their classrooms around the idea of cooperation. Children can work together to achieve an end instead of being pitted against each other. Students can be put to a task to figure out ways to maximize their talents and resources to get the job done. Research on cooperative learning in the classroom has demonstrated that, when students work with each other to complete tasks, they learn more, and that both slower and faster students benefit academically from the interactions, especially if status differentials are accounted for in the planning of the activities. In addition, a great deal of research has focussed on how cooperative work groups can function maximally in the classroom (Slavin 1983; Cohen, Lotan, and Leechor 1989).

Looking at this body of research and curriculum work, talking with others who work on it, and spending staff development time on it might be helpful. We have seen teachers orient to the idea that they can help students more if they reduce competition and increase cooperation in their classrooms.

The Problems of Moving to Cooperative Classrooms. We examined the developing nature of cooperative learning in a classroom when we field-tested a science curriculum in a sixth grade in New York City (Newman, et al. 1989; Goldman and Newman in press). As part of the program, students worked in collaborative science groups throughout the year. The collaborative work included science laboratory experiments, data analysis, and report writing activities. The students adapted to collaborative work in quite nice ways. Students in each group structured their roles and responsibilities vis-à-vis each new task without concern for how tasks were broken up in other classroom groups. They began to identify their work as accomplishments of the whole group rather than of particular individuals. Our data are full of instances of individual children responding to teacher questions using pronouns referencing the group. The teacher asks, "Juan, tell me what you got as a reading on the thermometer," and Juan answers, "Our group's was 75."

Students appeared to adapt to collaborative activity more easily than their teachers. The teachers preferred more traditional methods. The teachers were accountable for individual student grading and they often required individual reports from each lab group member as information about each student's participation. The students, nonetheless, filled out their individual lab reports together. We have seen teachers get the best results when they didn't evaluate the outcomes of cooperative activities in a competitive way. Despite the growing set of data supporting the educational value of collaborative assessments, a system that continues to uncritically demand individual grades as a bottom-line outcome still serves to constrain teacher efforts.

Collaborative Traditions in the Soviet Union. In our conversations with Soviet students training to become teachers, we hear reports of a long tradition of collaborative learning in Soviet schools. They report that in classes, students are expected to give each other answers whenever they can, even while completing classroom tests. When asked if their teachers get angry, they laughed and asked, "Why would the teacher be angry if we could learn it?" Classroom tests do not carry the weight they do in our system. Tests that are used to direct academic careers, such as university entrance exams or finals, are clearly marked as individual tasks.

In the United States, we do not make these distinctions, and consequently, teachers are given little room to develop cooperative teaching arrangements. (This situation also reflects an apparent difference between Russian and American notions of teacher. We see and treat ours as mere technicians, charged only with implementing decisions made by others. In the Russian system teachers seem to be viewed more as professionals, responsible for the educational decisions called for in the classroom.) Despite the constraints imposed by our technistic approach to schooling, it is possible for teachers to get good results if they separate their cooperative activities from the overall competitive agenda of schools enough that students are not torn between a real cooperative classroom experience and one overlaid on a thinly disguised competitive assessment agenda.

It is possible for a society to use competition in ways detrimental to its own development. Imperial China had one of the most demanding and arbitrary examination systems ever documented (Miyazaki 1981), although the Vietnamese may have adapted it in an even more stringent form (Hodgkin 1976). Most cultures make an easier peace with competition than we do. Contemporary Japan serves as an example. It is an intensely competitive society, particularly in the high school years, during which any student who wants to do well in the world has to go to after-school (*juku*) schools and study harder than most Americans consider possible (Rohlen 1980). The earlier years, however, are much less competitive and so too, surprisingly, the daily round in public high schools; competition is reserved for tests against faceless others. Face-to-face contacts are directed to building and tending to attachments and responsibilities with the people closest at hand (Rohlen 1983, 1989).

The Japanese system is no fun, and we are not recommending it. Teenagers, in particular, have a fairly horrible life. But it is not at all certain that an ethnographer working in Japan would find "pain" to be a useful key category, as McLaren (1986) did, in the description of the lives of Toronto seventh graders. Detroit, East Palo Alto, and Bethel may require even more attention to suffering. We need a better balance.

Minimizing Tracking into Ability Groups

One highly visible consequence of competition is the practice of tracking students of apparently different capabilities and potentials into different streams. In early schooling, ability tracking is usually limited to in-class groups and various special education programs. In the later years, various layers of success and failure are organized more dramatically into separate classrooms, programs, and schools. Although it is definite that these groupings reflect the class and racial hierarchy of the wider social structure, there is no evidence that this tracking reflects the actual potentials of the children so divided.

Everyone involved in schooling eventually has an unpleasant experience with the tracking system, usually involving the patently arbitrary assignment of individuals one is personally acquainted with to a particular slot. Local-level battles can be mounted and won, and various children can be transferred from one slot to another, particularly in middle-class neighborhoods where parents have the political power to have their children moved from one program to another.

Changing Tracks. The mother of an eighth-grade child who had spent three years in special education requested that she be mainstreamed. The learning specialists thought it better to keep the girl in special education classes, but the mother persisted. Finally, after a difficult meeting, it was agreed that the girl would return to the regular classes and her progress would be monitored carefully. The principal admitted privately that, if a parent vigorously challenged a tracking assignment, he would honor the request regardless of teacher or special education recommendations. Parents, he said, knew their children's learning potentials better than anyone in the school could. In the case at hand, after six months, the girl was holding her own in the mainstream (Goldman, 1982).

Pressuring the School. One mother of four had three of her children doing well in a special magnet school program. Her youngest, however, had problems gaining entrance. The fourth-grade teacher explained that the child's third-grade test scores had not been good, and, though he was doing better in her class, he did not belong in the faster paced magnet school. The mother argued to no avail that her son had had difficulties with the third grade teacher. She agreed that her youngest was not performing as well in school as her others had and wanted him switched precisely to get him on the right track. She went to the principal and pleaded. He said that the acceptance list had already been prepared and that nothing could be done to include her son. When the school failed to help her, the mother turned to her church and was, in turn, connected to a local politician. When the published list of magnet school choices came out, the boy was included. He did quite well in the magnet school and soon scored high on standardized tests (Gilmore 1982).

Although the tracking system can be malleable on a case-by-case basis, tackling it on a schoolwide basis is a different matter. It is here that the real struggle begins. If parents organize against tracking, the teachers can resist. If the teachers organize against tracking, the school board can resist. If parents, teachers, and the school administration organize against tracking, the local school board or the state is likely to complain that the school has dropped its standards.

The many levels and ways that change can be resisted suggests the investment our communities have in the school failure game. Our schools continue to thrive on the fiction that everyone is supposed to do better than everyone else. That, of course, not being possible, the fiction is maintained by our ability to document the relative success of some and the failure of others, the arbitrary standards notwithstanding.

The Difficulties of Reducing Tracking. Language arts teachers in a success-ful suburban middle school decided that the school's heavy tracking practices brought students more stress than necessary. They decided that tracking segregated and stigmatized students and kept the "slower" students from dealing with the most stimulating content and the most creative teaching. These suspicions were supported by re-search showing that if students worked in heterogeneous groups, both the fastest and the slowest students made significant progress. After many meetings, they conceived a "no sort" reading and language arts program for incoming sixth graders. The new program featured team teaching of heterogeneously grouped classes, and a literature-based curriculum with student self-selection into reading group levels. The program was structured to allow every student a high grade for complete work regardless of ability or level. The teachers implemented the program in September. By winter, the program was challenged by the school board, and the staff was required to justify the program at a school board meeting. Two parents of "gifted" children objected (to school board members) that children of lesser ability were slowing down the class. The school board eventually endorsed the program, but the teachers felt that the justification process was demoralizing. To keep the school board at bay, they found themselves trying to influence the students on their choice of groups at the start of new units. Group size, discipline, and student ability worked their way back into the list of considerations teachers brought to the group process.

In American schools, failure is always being made possible. Without it, there are no recognizable success stories. Theoretically, of course, everyone could succeed, but in a society that celebrates competition, this kind of success would be hollow indeed. Tracking helps to remove the lowest achievers at each new level and to intensify constantly for those who stay, both the pace and the consequences of the success and failure game. Both games are fueled by testing practices, particularly standardized tests, the recognized and authoritative tools of assessment (Goldman, 1982).

Reorganizing Assessment Practices

Any teacher attempting to confront failure's failure must do battle with the ways we have of assessing our children's school progress. Critiques of standardized testing have been numerous and intellectually devastating, but the testing institution persists, relatively unscathed. Teachers, children, parents, and administrators all demand to know what kind of progress children are making in school, and this appetite for evaluation is not easily brushed aside.

As a nation, we continue to believe that if we want to know if students have learned something, we should give them a test. Our testing services and an enormous population of middle-class professionals give a credence to the practices and results of tests and grades. The marketplace that eventually employs the children continues to assume, against considerable evidence, that performance on standardized tests and school grades are the best measures of potential. Our commitment to testing is not matched by an equal commitment to figuring out how tests can be made a part of learning activities, used to help students participate more, and to legitimize the kinds of thinking and problem-solving skills needed to live in an increasingly technocratic world. We can work for new kinds of assessments in the long run, but in the meantime we must work to mitigate the consequences of the tendency to test.

> *Teaching to the Test.* Tenth-grade biology students at a highly rated northern California school receive chapter tests and final exams. The exams include multiple choice, matching, and true-false items. The tests are constructed by the teacher and scored by a machine, which also gives item-by-item analyses with which teachers make future tests harder or easier. Most items test science vocabulary, although a few ask students to put concepts to work. This was the best that testing technologies could offer. College biology majors and teachers to whom we showed the tests were amazed at how much content was being covered (over 200 items on one test that covered 17 chapters) and concerned that much of it did not convey a sense of what they thought "Biology" was. The tests were running the curriculum, and not the other way around.

There are testing programs that do not dominate classroom content and interaction and, perhaps more importantly, that are not used to divide a classroom into differentially successful groups.

> *Giving Students Control Over Testing.* In a labor union literacy program in NYC, most of the workers had failed in school and were afraid of tests. We did not want to scare people out of the program, but we had only ten weeks to prepare the workers for an extremely difficult state examination (at the eleventh-grade reading level). A colleague (David Harman) suggested a two-part alternative that worked nicely. Part one: We made up the first tests with the most elementary questions. Any item everyone got right one week was put on the next week's test, until the men were all doing well on tests with many items. Part two: For the

first three weeks, we adopted the test questions from the manual; for the second three weeks, we took the questions from the teachers (who were union members who had already passed the test); and for the last four weeks, we used questions made up by the students. The students were amazed at how hard their questions were (one item asked for eleven pieces of information). In learning how to make up tests, they learned how to take them (Goldman and McDermott 1987).

Too often the limitations of traditional assessment techniques hide just what students are actually capable of doing. One solution is to look at students in their lives outside the classroom, where it is not difficult to find them being smart far beyond what can be imagined inside the classroom.

Recognizing Student Capabilities. In an after-school literacy program in NYC, we worked with teachers, children from their school, and the children's families. For much of the time, the teachers helped children and adults with homework and word-processing skills. For part of the time, however, the teachers were asked simply to observe the children with their parents and siblings doing various things from working with computers to preparing snacks. Sometimes the teachers were surprised to see that some children, who seemed quite immature and incompetent in the classroom, were actually quite mature and competent in the family program. What was the difference? The problem was not that the children could not learn in school, but only that the classroom organizes a narrow range of ways to display competence. Teachers who can notice other kinds of learning in their students may be able to organize more of it back into the classroom.

The learning children do on their own is remarkable enough for us to wonder how we could possibly find ways to fail them in school. From the language used by two five-year-old boys in an isolated hillside of East Africa (Gilmore 1979, 1983) to the speech play of black, adolescent girls and boys in American cities (Gilmore 1985; Goodwin 1990; Shuman 1986), ethnographic findings on learning in out-of-school settings reveal not only the competence of the children, but a deep understanding of their social worlds. Let's examine the unique story of the two boys and their communicative ingenuity:

Discovering the Integrity of Children's Talk. For 15 months, two young boys, Sadiki, a six-year-old Kenyan of the Samburu tribe and Colin, Perry Gilmore's five-year-old American son, were friends and neighbors on a ranch in Kenya where Gilmore was conducting research with the Gilgil Baboon Research Project. Soon after the children started spending their days together and becoming inseparable friends, it became obvious to others that the boys were speaking fluently and frequently with each other, but in neither English nor Swahili. When their verbal interactions were examined as legitimate linguistic and sociolinguistic phenomena, what would have sounded like nonsense to most adults turned out to be a full-fledged pidgin language that allowed the two boys to communicate with each other without adults understanding what they were saying. This language, their language, expanded as they learned more of each other's first languages, and it remained their language of choice for the entire fifteen months they were together (Gilmore 1979, 1983).

Although not every observation of children outside the classroom will deliver anything as startling as a pidgin for two, it is equally true that most every glance at the world of children would not deliver the kinds of cognitive failures that are so often made manifest in our schools. Competencies can never be separated from the environments that have called them forth, and it seems that the world outside the classroom calls forth more competencies than most classrooms.

Attention to what students seem to know rather than what by some arbitrary standard they seem not to know is at the heart of good teaching. Turning that attention into new assessment techniques may be the challenge before all good teachers in the coming decades. Parents need to know that their children are making progress. Unfortunately, they will settle for the simple knowledge of how their children are doing relative to other children by whatever standards have been invented by a distant testing service. Teachers cannot afford to do the same. They must continue to please the parents and offer some account of their skill, while at the same time coming up with measures that are better tuned to the learning the children are being asked to do in school and, more importantly, the learning they will be asked to do after they leave school. That is a terribly hard job for teachers, but it is essential if failure is not going to continue succeeding at failing half the next generation.

STORIES ABOUT CONFRONTING SCHOOL FAILURE AMONG MINORITY STUDENTS

It is easy to imagine how cultural diversity within a school or classroom can cause difficulty for teachers. The teacher in the multicultural classroom must communicate with children across differences in values, perceptions, languages, and communication styles. Because all borders leak (especially cultural and linguistic borders), with time and some sensitivity, the effects of these differences can be lessened. In the course of weeks, sometimes months, individuals from different groups often learn to adjust to each other to work successfully together. After they get to know each other, after they get by the communicative mishaps that plague initial cross-cultural interactions, then the real difficulties become apparent. The social pressures that hold groups at odds within the political and economic arena are not easily erased by classroom teachers. Establishing a spirit of cooperation or becoming culturally sensitive will not be enough. The troubles that brought about the necessity of an African American child spending half the year in Mississippi with mother's sister and half the year in Chicago with mother's mother will not go away because the white teacher no longer makes arrogant assumptions about the disorder of the African American family under difficult economic circumstances (Stack 1974). The troubles that brought a Mexican child to San Jose for education are not altered tremendously by the Anglo teacher understanding a little better how turns to talk are allotted in the child's home. Sensitivity may be essential, but it is not a sufficient condition for dealing with culturally different children in ways that make schooling more palatable. Our sensitivity must move beyond knowledge about cultural differences to direct grappling with the problems that keep children from minority cultures alienated. Sometimes small-scale confrontations with the social order in the name of learning can go a long way.

Crossing Institutional Borders. One colleague of ours (Seth Chaiklin) began writing over electronic mail with two sixth-graders at a Harlem school. He was careful to address their concerns and ideas. As they introduced new topics for discussion, he often responded by asking for more explanation or by relating how comments reminded him of his own experiences. This started a mentoring relationship that lasted the school year and beyond. The three correspondents were quite revealing of their thoughts and feelings about various personal and school-related issues, and many of their writings made reference to the girls' native cultures (Malaysian and Jamaican). This pattern held even when they were discussing science and mathematics, and the girls used the communicative resources of their home cultures to discuss the topics under study. It seemed to be understood that the adult and the children could and would be different and at the same time listen respectfully to each other.

At other times, it seems much harder to cross cultural borders, and efforts to do so sound like "lip-service" to cultural differences. This is particularly true in classrooms, where it seems to take a great deal more work to be culturally sensitive. The lip-service side of multicultural education can be heard in the writing voice of a young Native Alaskan woman studying to become a teacher in rural Alaska:

> *The Effects of Superficial Levels of Sensitivity.* I have experienced ... (what Chester Pearce termed) racist "microaggression" within my school, maybe not intentionally caused, but nonetheless very real. For example, the attitude of many teachers portrayed a sense of low expectation; a sense of demeaning spirit to my own culture. Our school was almost sterile to my home life, my community, our beliefs, values. High expectations were always there for the non-Native students, many of these being the teachers' offspring.
>
> Many students came away "brainwashed" believing that we could never be as intelligent as the others. I may sound racist; this is not my intention as I am merely sorting out feelings that have lain submerged for a long time.
>
> There is currently a very important need in our school system. Teachers must be able to instill within the students a sense of self-esteem and pride for being who they are. This is needed so that our youth can develop into strong individuals, so crucial for the survival through ordeals we face in our society today. Our education system must include a cultural base process which emphsizes Native world view, social roles, Native professional development and research (Gilmore 1987).

How might a person gain a sensitivity to all that would be needed to bridge the gap? And what activities might follow from such sensitivity? A second Native Alaskan student offers some harsh advice while expressing concern about a new administrator in a rural village school district. The problem with the administrator was "she came straight from New York." When asked why that was a problem, she said:

> If someone had given her a pair of moccasins and she had walked from New York to Alaska, she might have known something when she got here (Gilmore 1987).

Experience is the proper teacher on matters of intercultural sensitivity, and it takes an intense and unrelenting commitment to realize the size of the social structural problems faced when we simply wish to make contact with each other.

In addition to practicing a deep respect for cultural differences in ways of knowing and acting, we have seen teachers infuse their classrooms with what is important in the lives of their students' communities, and make this the heart of their educational programs. In every community we have studied we have met and observed teachers who can locate resources, events, ideas, and actions in their students' communities and build heavily on their presence through curriculum. Students can develop skills in the course of studying their own communities, and actively contribute to life in them by applying their school learning to their improvement. And finally, we have seen teachers who work with people in the community outside of the school make better use of children both while they are in school and afterwards. These goals may be more attainable than they seem.

Connecting School and Community Life. An alternative junior high school in New York City was founded on the principles stated above. The school operated around themes central to the field of human service, and every student participated in an internship two mornings a week at a service setting within the community. The internship experiences students had in day care, senior citizen centers, community action agencies, health care settings and local businesses provided the common themes around which a great deal of the in-school, academic curriculum was constructed. All of the students, for example, had to assess their own strengths and interests in order to apply them in the service setting, they had to work in groups, and they had to supervise others for part of their internship days. Many content area activities and practices were generated to correspond with, and incorporate, these themes. The connections made were very exciting. Teachers knew what was happening in different corners of the community by making visits to the sites, supervising students, and incorporating the requirements of different settings into classroom lessons. Students were needed in their community, and many of them came to be relied upon at their internships or contributed new ideas or practices. Some internships led to summer jobs and in one case to employment for a student's mother (Goldman and McDermott, 1987).

The success of the above program cannot alter the fact that the school was surrounded by a violent drug culture and massive poverty in one of the nation's more infamous inner-city communities. Most of the children left the junior high for quite selective high schools, but not all of them completed the road to success. The opportunities for failure in that community far outweighed the chances for success, and even the best high school options afforded few guarantees. Their problem, however, was not that they were culturally different, nor that they saw no future in school work. When offered the opportunity to participate in the mainstream they did, and they prospered. When that opportunity was removed, they prospered less. Teachers are not just content specialists. They must be social change experts. Teachers are not just responsible for teaching. They must also help to create the conditions under which teaching and learning are possible. They must construct curricula that connect the resources of the local community to the opportunities of the wider world. Sometimes this is done more easily in out-of-school settings.

Breaking the Constraints of Schools. Some students from a minority community in northern California began to participate in an after-school club at a nearby research and development laboratory concerned with understanding learning. The club was designed to get new multimedia presentation tools into the hands of children for the purpose enhancing their learning. The tools enabled children to build multimedia presentations on different social and environmental science topics using video, sound, texts, graphics and animations. The club setting had some advantages: Students could work on presentations of choice without concern for curriculum requirements; the nonschool site would give students maximum interaction with sophisticated equipment, developers and researchers; and typical classroom constraints, such as size of the group, selection by grade level, and school schedules, could be avoided. The students generated multimedia compositions on endangered species, local real estate development proposals, the local wetlands environment, and adolescent culture. Presentations were delivered to many audiences including club members, other students, teachers, and the town council. Teachers from the school, only peripherally involved, found the project so interesting and exciting that they wrote proposals and received funding that enabled them to transfer the multimedia tools to their classrooms. Some of the students and teachers received summer employment at the research center experimenting with the multimedia tools together (Allen 1990).

During the summers, the University of Alaska, College of Rural Alaska conducts a program that has become a profound and moving experience for participants that has served as a successful technique for breaching cultural barriers to learning.

Shifting to Turf. Rather than attempting to simply sensitize teachers and students to cultural differences, three university classes of potential teachers, school administrators, and rural social workers are brought to a rural village accessed only by riverboat. The week of activities is under the direction of village elders and consists of traditional village activities—making a fishwheel, clearing brush, building shelters, sewing, basket-weaving, gathering herbs, bark and roots, dancing, story-telling, cooking, and so on, culminating in a traditional potlatch. Students and faculty live in tents for the duration, some of them bringing their own children to mingle with the many native children.

Both students and faculty have to deal with unfamiliar learning and teaching styles and the acceptance of new roles, which are often unclear and difficult to adapt to. Indeed, despite the patience and obvious care taken by the villagers to be good hostesses and hosts, some students find the whole experience stressful.

Since this week is the middle week of three-week intensive courses students are enrolled in, the third week is devoted to unpacking and making sense of the experience. Inevitably these discussions reveal a profound new respect for what our schooling must look like to native students and for the ways of doing learning and teaching indigenous to village lifeways. No longer is it easy to define the villagers as merely "them" in contrast with "us"—the ones who occupy the center. Not only is the issue of cultural difference addressed by this experience, but a step is made toward redefining the borders, toward recognizing the arbitrariness of notions of the center and the fringes (Smith, in preparation).

This last point is central to the major thesis of this chapter. So long as we either tacitly or overtly assume that the goal of successful education is the adoption of one way of doing things, accepting one view of reality, of adapting to one particular turf, we make failure the only possible human response to schooling for large numbers of students. The stories we have presented represent attempts by educators not just to be sensitive to cultural differences, but to find ways of being with students that legitimize and support them as they are.

In summary, these stories would suggest that if we are serious about confronting school failure in cross-cultural contexts, we must be careful to stop turning our cultural differences into cultural borders. And when we do, we need to step back and figure out what forces outside of the classroom make our person-to-person relations so difficult. We need to be aware that different cultural groups have differential access to the institutional and intellectual resources of the larger community behind and outside of the school system.

Miscommunication between teachers and students of different cultures is no accident. Communication problems across cultures are the accomplishment of and are constrained by the relations of cultural groups in the larger society and the development of circumstances that make school a place to succeed in or fail for students of any particular cultural groups.

CONCLUSIONS

For the most part, public school practices in the United States are predicted upon assumptions of incompetence. When it comes to the demonstration of competence, the burden of proof is placed upon the student. Furthermore the standards by which the judgments are made prove to be culturally alien to many students. Given the entrenched status of the success and failure game, the systematic ways in which it disadvantages minority students, and its interconnectedness to the larger society, finding alternative ways to arrange schooling presents formidable challenges to teachers. Nonetheless, our stories indicate that it is possible to find some alternative arrangements.

Our stories reveal at least four helpful practices teachers can use in their classrooms to mitigate the power of the failure/success game so painfully characteristic of our schools. Teachers can: (a) balance cooperative and collaborative learning experiences with competitive ones; (B) minimize tracking and maximize opportunities for all students; (c) employ assessment strategies that focus on student participation rather than on isolated skills; (d) and find respectful and open ways of incorporating other cultural perspectives and different ways of knowing in their classrooms.

REFERENCES

Allen, Christina
  1990   Mediaworks: The Role of a New Technology in Growing New Communities-of-Practice. Paper delivered to a NATO Conference on Computer-Based Learning Environments and Problem Solving.
Cazden, Courtney B.
  1982   Can Ethnographic Research Go Beyond the Status Quo? Anthropology and Education Quarterly 14: 33–41.
  1988   Classroom Discourse: The Language of Teaching and Learning. Portsmouth, NH: Heinemann.
Cohen, Elizabeth, Rachel Lotan, and Chaub Leechor
  1989   Can Classrooms Learn? Sociology of Education 62: 75–94.
D'Amato, John
  1987   The Belly of the Beast: On Cultural Differences, Castelike Status, and the Politics of the Schools. Anthropology and Education Quarterly 18: 357–360.
Erickson, Frederick and Jeffrey Shultz
  1982   Counselor as Gatekeeper. New York: Academic Press.
Fine, Michelle
  1986   Why Urban Adolescents Drop In and Out of Public High School. Teachers College Record 87: 393–409.
Gilmore, Perry
  1979   A Children's Pidgin. Sociolinguistic Working Paper, no. 64. Austin: Southwest Educational Development Laboratory.
  1982   "Gimme Room": A Cultural Approach to the Study of Attitude and Admission to Literacy. Unpublished doctoral dissertation. University of Pennsylvania.

1983   Ethnographic Approaches to the Study of Child Language. The Volta Review 85: 29–43.

1985   "Gimme Room": School Resistance, Attitude, and Access to Literacy. Journal of Education 167: 111 –129.

1986   Subrosa Literacy. *In* The Acquisition of Literacy. Bambi Schieffelin and Perry Gilmore, eds. Pp. 155–168. Norwood, NJ: Ablex.

1987   Academic Literacy in Cultural Context: Issues for Higher Education in Alaska. Paper presented at the American Anthropology Association meetings Chicago, Illinois.

Gilmore, Perry and David M. Smith

1982   A Retrospective Discussion of the State of the Art in Ethnography in Education. *In* Children In and Out of School: Ethnography and Education. Perry Gilmore and Allan A. Glatthorn, eds. Pp. 3–18. Washington, DC: Center for Applied Linguistics.

1989   Mario, Jesse, and Joe: Contextualizing Dropping Out. *In* What Do Anthropologists Have to Say About Dropouts? Henry Trueba, George Spindler, and Louise Spindler, eds. Pp. 79–92. Philadelphia: The Falmer Press.

Goldman, Shelley

1982   Sorting Out Sorting. Unpublished doctoral dissertation, Teacher College, Columbia University.

Goldman, Shelley and Ray McDermott

1987   The Culture of Competition in America. *In* Education and Cultural Process. George Spindler, ed. Second edition. Pp. 282–299. Prospect Heights, IL: Waveland Press.

Goldman, Shelley and Denis Newman

in press   Electronic Interactions: How School Conversations are Organized Over the Wires. Interactive Learning Environments.

Goodwin, Marjorie

1990   He-Said-She-Said. Bloomington: Indiana University Press.

Harman, David

1987   Illiteracy: A National Dilemma. New York: Cambridge Book Company.

Hodgkin, Thomas

1976   Scholars and the Revolutionary Tradition: Vietnam and West Africa. Oxford Review of Education 2:

Lave, Jean and Etienne Wenger

1990   Situated Learning: Legitimate Peripheral Participation. Report No. IRL90-0013. Palo Alto, CA: Institute for Research on Learning.

Lortie, Dan C.

1975   Schoolteacher: A Sociological Study. Chicago: The University of Chicago Press.

McDermott, Ray

1987   The Explanation of Minority School Failure, Again. Anthropology and Education Quarterly 18: 361–364.

1988   Inarticulateness. *In* Linguistics in Context. Deborah Tannen, ed. Pp. 36–68. Norwood: Ablex.

in press   The Acquisition of a Child by a Learning Disability. *In* People in Action. Seth Chaiklin and Jean Lave, eds. New York: Cambridge University Press.

McDermott, Ray and Kenneth Gospodinoff
  1979   Social Contexts for Ethnic Borders and School Failure. *In* Nonverbal Behavior. Aaron Wolfgang, ed. New York: Academic Press.

McLaren, Peter
  1986   Schooling as Ritual Performance. Boston: Routledge and Kegan Paul.

Mehan, Hugh
  1979   Learning Lessons. Cambridge, MA: Harvard University Press.
  in press   The Construction of an LD Student. *In* People in Action. Seth Chaiklin and Jean Lave, eds. New York: Cambridge University Press.

Mehan, Hugh, A. Hertweck, and J.L. Meihls
  1986   Handicapping and Handicapped. Stanford, CA: Stanford University Press.

Miyazaki, Ichisada
  1981   China's Examination Hell. New Haven, CT: Yale University Press.

Newman, Denis, Shelley Goldman, Deborah Brienne, Isaac Jackson, and Sol Magzman
  1989   Computer Mediation of Collaborative Science Investigations. Journal of Educational Computing Research 5: 151–166.

Newman, Denis, Peg Griffin, and Michael Cole
  1988   The Construction Zone: Working for Cognitive Change in School. New York: Cambridge University Press.

Rohlen, Thomas
  1980   The Juku Phenomenon. Journal of Japanese Studies 6: 207–242.
  1983   Japan's High Schools. Berkeley: University of California Press.
  1989   Order in Japanese Society: Attachment, Authority, and Routine. Journal of Japanese Studies 15: 5–40.

Shuman, Amy
  1986   Storytelling Rights. Philadelphia: University of Pennsylvania Press.

Slavin, R.E.
  1983   Cooperative Learning. New York: Longman.

Smith, David M.
  1981   Ethnographic Monitoring: A Way of Understanding by Those Who Are Making Schooling Work. The Generator 12: 69–92.
  1985   Illiteracy as a Social Fault. *In* Literacy and Schooling. David Bloome, ed. Pp. 55–64. Norwood, NJ: Ablex
  1986   The Anthropology of Literacy. *In* The Acquisition of Literacy. Bambi Schieffelin and Perry Gilmore, eds. Pp. 261–275. Norwood, NJ: Ablex Publishers.
  in preparation   The Cultural Politics of Education in Alaska.

Spindler, George and Louise Spindler (with Henry Trueba and Melvin Williams)
  1990   The American Cultural Dialogue and its Transmission. Philadelphia: The Falmer Press.

Stack, Carol
   1974   All Our Kin. New York: Harper.
Trueba, Henry, George Spindler, and Louise Spindler, eds.
   1989   What Do Anthropologists Have to Say about Dropouts? Philadelphia: The
           Falmer Press.
Varenne, Herve
   1983   American School Language. New York: Irvington Publishers.

Part V

Policy and Practice Considerations

13

Ethnography and Policy: A Catalytic Combination for Change

David M. Fetterman

Ethnographers and policymakers all too often believe that they work at cross purposes and come from separate worlds. In fact, ethnography and policy share a long history and a rich tradition. The relationship between these two disciplines traces back to both academic and applied anthropological work, although applied anthropological endeavors have a stronger track record. The work of Spicer, Holmberg, Tax, Spradley, and many others has demonstrated ethnography's relevance for policy. More recently, ethnographic educational evaluators have established a tight link between educational policy and ethnography. In this chapter, a national ethnographic evaluation of dropouts and ethnographic studies of gifted and talented education provide specific first-hand examples of how ethnography has informed policy decision making on many levels. The lessons learned from these policy-relevant studies serve to inform our current debate about the various explanations of minority students' school performance, placing it in a larger context.

THE APPLIED TRADITION

The question of whether ethnography and policy decision making can be combined is moot; the two have been combined for years. A brief list of historical examples of how ethnography and policy have walked hand in hand provides insights into the rich tradition that practicing anthropologists have established. The examples range from studies of a semifeudal Indian hacienda in Peru to an investigation of tramps on skid row in Seattle, Washington. The list underscores ethnography's historical relevance for policy.

Historical Examples

Edward Spicer was involved in both policy formulation and execution. He served as a program facilitator in the implementation of the War Relocation Authority during World War II. He was a cross-cultural interpreter, attempting to find out what Japanese Americans thought about the relocation camps. His task required sensitivity, political dexterity, and an appreciation of different cultural orientations in order to avoid misinterpretations that might have resulted in charges of disloyalty during wartime. Spicer also served as an ethnographer/policymaker as an Office of Economic Opportunity project director. He used ethnographic knowledge of the Yaqui community to help mediate agency programs to meet the needs of the Yaqui Indians[1] (see Spicer 1976).

As a joint enterprise between Cornell University and the Peruvian government, the Vicos project, Allan Holmberg's work, stands out as a notable achievement in planned organizational change. The project successfully transformed a semifeudal Indian hacienda in Peru into a democratic community within five years (see Holmberg 1958; ct. Doughty 1987). His work had considerable impact in the policy arena, shaping the transformation of many other similar hacienda communities in Peru. In addition, this ethnographic effort produced contexts in which Mestizos and Indians were able to interact under conditions of social equality, thus influencing traditional notions about segregation and prejudice.

As an ethnographic researcher, Sol Tax (1958) directly influenced the community policy of the Fox Indians. He clarified issues and listed options for change in the community. The decision to select and implement an alternative remained in the hands of the Fox. However, Tax, functioning as an ethnographer, served as a significant catalyst in policy development and implementation.

Ethnographic fieldwork has also significantly influenced policies concerning such issues as the social function of ghettos, minority unemployment, the causes of poverty, ethnic affairs, and the structure and function of family services[2] (see Gans 1962; Liebow 1967; Bott 1957; Hicks and Handler

---

[1] Spicer's efforts were not always successful, but they represent a significant step in the development of the interrelationship of ethnography and policy.

[2] Angrosino and Whiteford (1987) discuss how anthropologists assist in the process of policy formation by conducting ethnographic work. Their studies of community-based treatment for mentally retarded and emotionally disturbed clients—together with a fact-finding advocacy group designed to trace how the loss of federal monies affected health care to children—served to question the existing conception of policy formation. They demonstrated how policy developed at the initiation of the community-based program, rather than of the federal bureaucracy. They also demonstrate how practicing anthropologists can have an impact on policy at the local level—often the foundation of state and national policies.

1987; Valentine 1966; Lewis 1966). Ethnographic concepts and techniques have yielded much in the area of dealing with public drunkenness and mediating sentencing (Spradley 1970, 1973). Spradley's success in eliciting the viewpoint of tramps on skid row in Seattle helped develop a blueprint for change to stop the phenomenon of the jailhouse "revolving door."

Pelto and Schensul (1987) provided recommendations to the Federal Bureau of Education for the Handicapped about parental involvement in special education decision making, focusing on the placement of children in special education classes. They also illustrated how ethnographic work generated recommendations that influenced legislation. Wulff and Fiske (1987) produced a collection of award-winning case studies in which anthropological knowlege was successfully applied to real-world problem solving, including policy formulation, implementation, and evaluation.

Ethnographic Educational Evaluation

Ethnographic evaluation has made a sigificant contribution to policy decision making.[3] Ethnographic educational evaluation highlights ethnography's contemporary role in policy decision making, drawing on examples ranging from a study of disadvantaged youth in an Israeli town to analyses of bilingual bicultural preschool curriculum models in California, New York, Texas, and Wisconsin. Two national case studies provide depth to the discussion and explore specific policy implications.

Smith and Robbin's (1984) U.S. Department of Education-funded study of four federal elementary and secondary education programs provided a contextualized picture of parental involvement. Their efforts also illustrated clearly the compromises and tradeoffs requisite in policy research, while informing policy decision making.[4] In a study of disadvantaged youth in an Israeli town, Goldberg (1984) highlighted the importance of matching a research site to appropriate policy research questions (and the hazards of a mismatch). In a study of a school for the deaf sponsored by the Department of Health, Education, and Welfare (now the Department of Health and Human

---

[3] These contributions can be found in a multitude of areas and on various levels. For example, Maxwell, Bashook and Sandlow (1986) combined ethnographic and experimental methods to study physicians' participation in medical care evaluation committees at Michael Reese Hospital and Medical Center in Chicago. The work contributed to an understanding of the educational processes that occur in these committees, benefiting physicians, administrators, and patients. Pitman and Dobbert (1986) illustrated the value of using ethnography to evaluate a teacher training program in a day care center at a private urban college.

[4] Similarly, forcussing on the limitations of the federal government to make comprehensive change, the U.S. Office of Education-funded Rural Experimental Schools Study provided an insight into policy decision-making processes that was as valuable as the final assessment of the program (Messerschmidt 1984).

Services), Hemwall (1984) demonstrated the value of ethnography in exploring the policy question of mainstreaming the hearing-impaired. In a nonprofit research and demonstration organization-sponsored study, Simon (1986) used anthropological theory and ethnographic research methods and analysis to examine how youth employment and training programs and public incentives affected hiring decisions. An ethnographic understanding of the hiring process enabled the ethnographers to develop "marketing tools" to demonstrate how hiring youth would benefit employers. Studstill (1986) used ethnographic techniques to evaluate ten secondary schools in Zaire. The study was specifically designed to inform policymakers and to recommend ways to decrease extremely high student attrition. Chesterfield (1986) studied bilingual bicultural preschool curriculum models in California, New York, Texas, and Wisconsin for the Head Start Bureau of the Administration for Children, Youth and Families. This study's qualitative analysis furnished information about issues of concern to teachers, program, staff, and policy planners. For example, the qualitative data documented how some children used a majority of English in the classroom by the end of the year—even though the test data continued to judge them as dominant Spanish speaking in the classroom. Ferrell and Compton (1986) used ethnographic techniques to evaluate a school district's gifted and talented education program. Their work had an impact on students, parents, teaching staff, and the district's administration and Board of Education. They recommended the development of job descriptions for teachers, specification of how the gifted and talented program curriculum differed from the basic curriculum, and development of improved approaches to the identification of gifted minority students. Similarly, Marotto's (1986) ethnographic study of in-school truancy had an impact on students, teachers, school administrators, and the Board of Education. His work had an impact on the school's disproportionate number of minority suspensions.

Quantitative researchers, including Cronbach (1982) and Hoaglin et al. (1982), have reinforced ethnography's position in policy decision making by acknowledging a role for qualitative research in policy and evaluation studies. Numerous quantitative and qualitative researchers—including Cook and Reichardt (1979), Fetterman (1982a, 1988a, 1988b, 1989a, 1989b), Goetz and LeCompte (1984), LeCompte and Goetz (1982), Patton (1980), Smith and Louis (1982), and Weiss and Rein (1972)—have also made a case for the value of ethnographic and case study methods in the pursuit of knowledge about policy issues of implementation and change in school systems. See Firestone and Herriott (1984) for a discussion about multisite qualitative research and federal policy decision making.

A more detailed discussion about two ethnographic evaluations further illustrates the link between ethnography and policy decison making. The first case focussed on a national ethnographic evaluation of dropouts. The second study focuses on gifted and talented students in the United States and cross-culturally.

A *National Ethnographic Evaluation of Dropouts.* The author conducted the ethnographic evaluation of the U.S. Department of Education- funded (through the National Institute of Education) national program for dropouts and potential dropouts: the Career Intern Program (CIP). The formative and summative reports stemming from the ethnographic evaluation had a sigificant impact on the survival and potential prosperity of the CIP schools.

The CIP schools offered students a high school diploma and a career-oriented education. The schools were designed to handle both academic and personal problems. The CIP schools had as many counselors as it had teachers, recognizing that management of personal problems was essential to the program's academic mission. CIP schools successfully placed former dropouts in college and career-oriented positions, instead of dishwashing jobs. It represented one of the few exemplary programs for disenfranchised and economically disadvantaged minority youth in the late 1970s and early 1980s.

The CIP study represented an important shift in emphasis from the urban educational anthropology research of the previous decade because it focused on school success for minority youth rather than on school failure. It differed from the traditional ethnography of schooling in incorporating findings from a multidisciplinary evaluation effort. The research concerned not a single school, but an entire demonstration project in several sites across the United States. The analyses examined classrooms, program components, community environments, local and national affiliates, government agencies, and evaluators. The study differed also in its multidimensional emphasis, discussing federal involvement, evaluation design, and the role of reinforcing world views (Fetterman 1981a). It expanded an understanding of the process by which values and ideas are passed on from one generation to the next. In providing educational evaluators with a model of detailed description on several levels, the ethnographic component of the study demonstrated the means of contextualizing data. By locating data more precisely in a multilevel context, educational evaluators and ethnographers can arrive at a more comprehensive interpretation of its meaning. The CIP study also demonstrated how ethnography can be adapted to the language, timelines, and political concerns of policymakers, including advocacy (see Fetterman 1987, 1989a).

Policy Implications. The CIP study had a policy impact on many levels. During the study, the federal sponsors considered closing one of the schools. They were concerned that the program was not serving the target population because of low attendance: approximately 60% to 70%. This concern was legitimate, from their perspective, because they did not want to waste taxpayer money. The attendance in the CIP school was somewhat lower than that in neighboring urban high schools. However, the author reminded the sponsoring agency that the baseline with which to compare 60% to 70% attendance was zero attendance. These students were systematically different from the students attending the neighboring urban high school. The CIP students had routinely skipped school when enrolled in the neighboring urban high schools. The contextualized data helped policymakers make a more informed decision about the program. In this case, ethnographic data ensured that the program would continue serving former dropouts.

The most significant policy implications of the study, however, involved the concepts of replicating schools and of using the experimental design in studying dropouts. The federal government's goal was to replicate an existing exemplary program throughout the United States. It expected an almost clone-like duplication of the original program. The ethnographic report stated that this expectation was conceptually off target. Replication is a biological, not an anthropological or sociological concept. Programs take on new shapes and forms in the process of adapting to the demands of their environments. Studying how these programs respond to their differing environments would have been more fruitful than noting whether they were in or out of compliance with a given model. The ethnographic report specifically recommended that "the process of adaptation should be the focus of inquiry" (Fetterman 1981b).

A second, and more controversial, policy impact involved the use of the experimental design in federal evaluations. One part of this study included a treatment-control design. Students were required to pass specified tests for admission into the program. Half the candidates were randomly assigned to the treatment group—admitted to the alternative high school—while the other half were denied admission. The ethnographic portion of the study concluded that this behavior was maladaptive and inappropriate. Ethically, the use of the treatment-control design was problematic because it prevented dropouts from taking the first step back into the educational system. Parents referred to this rejection as a "slap in the face." Methodologically, the design had serious flaws: It was not double-blind. The teachers, counselors, and administrators providing the program knew that they were delivering the treatment. The students admitted to the program knew that they were receiving the "treatment" and thus received a positive treatment. No true control group existed. Students who passed the entrance tests but were selected as part of the control group knew they were not participating in the program or treatment. Thus the "control" group was actually a negative treatment group. In addition, because the control group had little incentive to return for posttesting, the students who did return represented a biased sample, producing misleading comparisons with the treatment group. All these forms of reactivity and contamination severely undermined the credibility of any outcome. (See Fetterman 1982a, for a detailed discussion of this problem.)

The study (Fetterman 1981b) delivered a strong set of recommendations to policymakers:

1. Abandon the use of randomized treatment-control designs to evaluate social programs, particularly when ethical standards have been violated. All available program positions should be filled; individuals should not be excluded from participation for the sake of constructing a control group.
2. Reevaluate the selection of an experimental design when methodological requirements cannot be met. The most significant methodological concerns in this case involve constructing a negative treatment group instead of a control group, and comparing groups without considering the effects of differential attrition at posttest time. (See Fetterman 1982a; Tallmadge 1979.)

These recommendations were made during a period in which evaluators and policymakers were attempting to legislate the use of specific evaluation designs, "especially randomized experiments." During the same period, academia was demonstrating much resistance to criticism of this sacred cow in educational research. (See Fetterman 1982b for a detailed discussion about academic resistance to substantive criticism.)

As a result of this ethnographic study, program sponsors made and implemented a variety of additional policy and programmatic recommendations. The findings and recommendations provide another demonstration of ethnography's relevance for educational policy. The relevance of ethnography for policy, however, extends beyond the written word. One of the ethnographer's most important roles may be as a consultant for policy questions. In the case under discussion, both government policymakers and program officials asked the ethnographer for information and advice regarding both short- and long-term intervention strategies.

Researchers have a moral responsibility to serve as advocates—after the research has been conducted—if the findings merit it. In this case, the evaluators disseminated the generally positive findings to appropriate individuals in governmental and quasi-governmental institutions. Future funding for the program depended on the dissemination of the evaluation findings and the recommendations of various agencies. The evaluation team also prepared a Joint Dissemination Review Panel Submission substantially based on the ethnographic findings to improve the program's credibility and its chances of securing future funding. This task was accomplished in the face of significant resistance: It was politically hazardous to favor social programs during this period. These actions were in accord with Mills' (1959) position that:

> There is no necessity for working social scientists to allow the potential meaning of their work to be shaped by the "accidents of its setting," or its use to be determined by the purposes of other men. It is quite within their powers to discuss its meaning and decide upon its uses as matters of their own policy. (p. 177).

Gifted and Talented Education and Policy Implications. During a study of dropouts and potential dropouts, the author identified a handful of gifted and talented students from limited-English-speaking and lower socioeconomic class groups. This study evolved into a decade of work on the gifted and talented in the United States and abroad. These efforts culminated in the publication of a book for both the lay person and the professional in the field: *Excellence and Equality: A Qualitatively Different Perspective on Gifted and Talented Education* (Fetterman 1988a). The book depicted the plight of gifted and talented children in a system geared toward the mean—an attempt to inform an educated and concerned citizenry about these children's special needs and individual differences. It discussed mythologies supporting neglect and explored simplistic conceptions of democracy that equated equality of rights with equality of ability and results. Comparisons of gifted selection procedures with athletic selection procedures helped to dispel the myth that Americans are equally egalitarian in all arenas. This work was primarily ethnographic in nature and successfully informed policy makers on the state and national level.

A review of all 433 gifted and talented programs in California, reported in *Excellence and Equality,* resulted in continued funding and overall program improvements, including legislation maintaining a broad conception of giftedness. As a result of a cross-cultural review of gifted education worldwide—and of the author's recommendation that the U.S. government establish a national gifted and talented center—he received an apppointment to a U.S. Department of Education panel to select a consortium to create a national gifted and talented education research center. Highlighting the disenfranchised, the author specifically recommended that the center focus on identifying gifted and talented children who may not be identified through traditional assessment methods. This group includes the limited English speaking, the economically disadvantaged, handicapped, and women. As an instance of a recommendation becoming a reality, in this case, ethnography had an impact on various policy levels and provided both the groundwork for change in terms of concrete policy recommendations and the actual construction and implementation of policy recommendations in terms of participation in the selection process of a national center for the gifted.

Policy decision making is both an art and a craft (Wildavsky 1979). It is fundamentally a political process in which research—ethnographic or otherwise—plays one part. The exchange of information, however, does not presuppose a substantial voice in policy decisions; it only ensures participation in the game. The insights and findings of the most capably conducted research are useless if researchers abdicate their responsibility and choose not to play in this game.

PLAYING THE GAME

Playing the game does not mean behaving unethically. On the contrary, it requires honesty, candor, and commitment. Educators, anthropologists, and well-informed public citizens have an obligation to take a position and to become involved in addressing the social and educational problems that lie at their doorstep.

Participation in the process of decision making is what playing the game is all about. Sensitivity to the decision maker's worldview can enhance one's effectiveness. The CIP and gifted studies were successful because they overcame traditional obstacles by translating academic language into bureaucratese, internalizing the dynamics of policy decision making, producing results in a timely fashion, assuming the role of advocate when appropriate, and providing the type of process information useful to policy decision makers. The role of language, timeliness, and advocacy merit specific attention.

Language

Language is a powerful force that can shape thoughts and influence minds. The most intricate, carefully crafted speech will fall on deaf ears if it is not spoken in a language the listener understands and appreciates. To be effective the individual must learn to speak many languages and accept other views of reality (see Fetterman 1989a). The language may be bureaucratese, the focus administrative, and the reality or worldview widely disparate from that of the people one works with on a daily basis, but policymakers have a need for and a right to knowledge.

Policymakers funding the CIP and gifted research needed executive summaries about the studies' findings and recommendations written in their own language. The author recognized that, as Cronbach stated, "when an avalanche of words and tables descends, everyone in its path dodges"

(Cronbach et al. 1980:184). The thorough and scholarly investigation (the basis for the executive summary) was also reported in a lengthy technical report for program personnel and policymaker staff members. In addition, articles and books about dropouts and gifted children came out of the study and served to educate and inform a concerned citizenry, with the aim of influencing other policymakers from the grass roots.

Timeliness

One of the most important features of the federal and state policymaker perspective is timeliness. Knowledge is power, and information is required at prespecified periods to assist in the decision-making process. The CIP and gifted studies attempted to recognize and adapt to these needs.

The studies were completed within the specified periods of time to allow for maximum policy impact. In addition, interim reports were produced and delivered without jeopardizing complex research relationships or the quality of work. In fact memoranda and other interim communications improved the accuracy of the effort, because they provided a reality check on the accuracy and appropriateness of the interim findings and recommendations. The author was also responsive to policymaker inquiries in the middle of the research effort. Shifting political pressures forced well-intentioned policymakers to seek information before agreed-on timelines. The decisions would have been made with or without the desired input. However, policy decision makers preferred some imperfect and imprecise information to no information at all.

Advocacy

A few examples of the advocacy role adopted (after the research was conducted) have been discussed. The CIP study included the dissemination of generally positive findings to appropriate policymakers and the preparation of a Joint Dissemination Review Panel Submission. The gifted studies culminated in a book recommending that the U.S. government establish a gifted and talented center. In addition, the author took an active role in selecting a consortium to create such a center.

There are many appropriate roles to adopt. Educators and anthropologists can seek the assistance of unions, public relations offices, and lobbyists to represent them in the policy arena. Politically savvy researchers can work with senators and representatives. For example, Hess (1989) presented testimony to the Elementary, Secondary, and Vocational Subcommittee of the U.S. Home Committee on Education and Labor. He testified in support of an act to establish a National Demonstration Project of Educational Performance Agreements for School Restructuring that would provide local schools with more flexibility in the use of federal funds, in exchange for commitments to improve student performance.

Anthropological knowledge can shed light on classroom practices as well as on the dark and often mysterious political corridors. The same tool required to navigate inside the school district can be used to navigate around the Capitol. Sensitivity to the insider's perspective, whether student or politician, can go a long way in increasing one's effectiveness.

A COMMON THREAD

A common thread running through this collection is the attempt to explain the school performance of minority students. Ogbu (1978, 1987) clearly demonstrates the power of the anthropological lens, using his secondary discontinuity approach. This approach argues that minority groups that were forced to come to the United States (in a subordinate or caste-like role) do poorly in school, while minority groups that made the choice to come to the United States (as immigrants) frequently do well in school. Ogbu argues that subordinate groups' poor performance in school is both "a reaction and an adaptation to the limited opportunity available to them to benefit from their education" (Ogbu 1974:12). He focuses on labor market influences and job ceilings for minority groups to explain poor school performance.

Erickson's (1984) focus on the role of cultural differences complements Ogbu's societal level analysis. The cultural difference approach states that differences between mainstream and minority cultures result in cultural conflicts that inhibit proper academic achievement of minority youth. The style of interaction, language use, and cognition become the focus of inquiry as well as explanation. They are also useful levers of change for practitioners.

These approaches are both useful, addressing different elements of the same problem at different levels of analysis. Arguments suggesting that one approach is better than another, valid or invalid, are off target. A more constructive approach is to focus on how anthropology can help us alleviate or solve our most pressing social problems. In this case, the contrast between these two approaches is more apparent than real, reflecting our current level of understanding. A synthesis of these approaches in the future should strengthen the policy relevance of anthropological works in this area (see Fetterman 1990). Ogbu's and Erickson's complementary top-down and bottom-up approaches illustrate the scope of what anthropology has to offer, shedding some light on the school performance of minority youth.

A detailed analysis of the policy implications of Ogbu's and Erickson's work is beyond the scope of this chapter; however, each approach has policy implications. Both approaches highlight the cultural influence of teachers and the need to sensitize teachers to these cultural forces at work—on both macro and micro levels. In addition, these approaches help inform educational policies about individual differences and levels of intelligence in remedial, average, and gifted classrooms. These approaches fight educational neglect by replacing deficiency theories for minority youth and dispelling the mistaken notion that gifted children will make it on their own. In general, Ogbu's approach speaks to powerful forces of institutional racism and job ceilings. Erickson's work captures the delicate interpersonal gatekeeping structures that close the door to minority youth. Both confront the same fundamental issue of equality of opportunity.

Zeuli and Floden (1987) provide a useful service, highlighting the tenuous relationship between research and practice. Anthropological research, like educational research in general, must be contextualized and collaborative to have a real and lasting impact in practice. Time is required to determine what sociocultural and socioeconomic factors are at work in the local setting before intervention is prescribed and implemented. "Teachers will not know in advance which patterns of interaction will be prevalent in their students' communities, and which of those lead to learning difficulties, because they differ from the dominant school culture" (Zeuli and Floden 1987:10). Moreover, communities may be ethnically and socioeconomically similar, but they are not identical. As the author noted in arguing against replication, this variation requires adaptation of policy and practice, not blind conformity to an ideal approach. Teachers and researchers need to work together to understand the levers of change and to "buy into" the problem and solution. This interaction further refines both an understanding of classroom behavior and strategies to alter behavior.

The author's work with the CIP study relied on a close collaborative relationship with teachers, students, parents, and administrators. Descriptions of events as well as strategies to improve curricula, rules and regulations, and school climates were shared with participants. Their feedback and participation in the process improved the accuracy and effectiveness of the ethnographic effort. Moreover, participants helped adapt policies and programmatic recommendations to each school program across the country—as they evolved from the study.

Similarly, Fetterman's gifted research found that "the majority of gifted educators realize that no single program or curriculum model can serve all gifted children. There are, however, some gifted educators who have not recognized that the search for a single, all-encompassing gifted program is comparable to the search for the Holy Grail. The idea of a single program belies the fundamental tenet of gifted education—to serve the individual needs of the student" (Fetterman 1988a:29–30). Just as no single program serves the needs of any identified population, so no single theory can or should be applied to all children.

CONCLUSION

Anthropological tools represent only one approach to removing the barriers to equal educational opportunity. However, they are a powerful force when combined with policy decision making. The leap from policy to practice is often difficult, but not impossible. Ethnography already has an established tradition in the policy field. Lessons learned from that relationship can be applied to a host of educational concerns. Sensitivity to context, language, timeliness, and political concerns is imperative if a policy impact is desired. A few of these concerns have been highlighted in this discussion. As members of a global community, we can enable our children to achieve their full potential only if we continue to toil in the educational vineyards.

REFERENCES

Angrosino, M. and L. Whiteford
   1987   Service, Delivery, Advocacy, and the Policy Cycle. *In* Appled Anthropology in America. E. Eddy and W. Patridge, eds. Second Edition. Pp. 482–504. New York: Cambridge University Press, 1987.
Bott, E.
   1957   Family and Social Network. New York: Free Press.
Chesterfield, R.
   1986   Qualitative Methodology in the Evaluation of Early Childhood Bilingual Curriculum Models. *In* Educational Evaluation: Ethnography in Theory, Practice, and Politics. D.M. Fetterman and M. Pitman, eds. Pp. 145–168. Beverly Hills, CA: Sage.
Cook, T. and Reichardt, C. (Eds.)
   1979   Qualitative and Quantitative Methods in Evaluation Research. Beverly Hills, CA: Sage.
Cronbach, L., S. Ambron, S. Dornbusch, R. Hess, R. Hornik, D. Phillips, D. Walker, and S. Weiner.
   1980   Toward Reform of Program Evaluation. San Francisco, CA: Jossey-Bass.
Cronbach, L.
   1982   Designing Evaluations of Educational and Social Programs. San Francisco, CA: Jossey-Bass.
Doughty, P.
   1987   Vicos: Success, Rejection, and Rediscovery of a Classic Problem. *In* Applied Anthropology in America. E. Eddy and W. Partridge, eds. Second Edition. Pp. 433–459. New York: Cambridge University Press.
Erickson, F.
   1984   School Literacy, Reasoning, Civility: An Anthropological Perspective. Review of Educational Research 54(4):525–544.
Ferrell, B. and D. Compton
   1986   Use of Ethnographic Techniques for Evaluation in a Large School District:

The Vanguard Case. *In Educational Evaluation: Ethnography in Theory, Practice, and Politics.* D.M. Fetterman and M. Pitman, eds. Beverly Hills, CA: Sage.

Fetterman, D.M.

1981a Blaming the Victim: The Problem of Evaluation Design and Federal Involvement, and Reinforcing World Views in Education. Human Organization 40(1):67–77.

1981b Study of the Career Intern Program. Final Report—Task C: Program Dynamics: Structure, Function, and Interrelationships. Mountain View, CA: RMC Research Corporation.

1982a Ethnography in Educational Research: The Dynamics of Diffusion. Educational Researcher 11(3):17–29.

1982b Ibsen's Baths: Reactivity and Insensitivity (A Misapplication of the Treatment-Control Design in a National Evaluation). Educational Evaluation and Policy Analysis 4(3):261–279.

1987 Ethnographic Educational Evaluation. *In* Interpretive Ethnography of Education: At Home and Abroad. G.D. Spindler, ed. Pp. 79–106. Hillsdale, NJ: Erlbaum.

1988a Excellence and Equality: A Qualitatively Different Perspective on Gifted and Talented Education. Albany: State University of New York Press.

1988b Qualitative Approaches to Evaluation in Education: The Silent Scientific Revolution. New York: Praeger Publications.

1989a Ethnographer as Rhetorician: Multiple Audiences Reflect Multiple Realities. Practicing Anthropology 11(2):2, 17–18.

1989b Ethnography: Step by Step. Newbury Park, CA: Sage.

1990 Review of *Accommodation without Assimilation: Sikh Immigrants in an American High School,* Ithica, NY: Cornell University Press, by M. Gibson. American Anthropologist 92(1):218.

Firestone, W. and R. Herriott

1984 Multisite Qualitative Policy Research: Some Design and Implementation Issues. *In* Ethnography in Educational Evaluation. D.M. Fetterman, ed. Pp. 63–88. Beverly Hills, CA: Sage.

Gans, H.

1962 The Urban Villagers. New York: Free Press.

Goetz, J. and M. LeCompte

1984 Ethnography and Qualitative Design in Educational Research. New York: Academic Press.

Goldberg, H.

1984 Evaluation, Ethnography, and the Concept of Culture: Disadvantaged Youth in an Israeli Town. *In* Ethnography in Educational Evaluation. D.M. Fetterman, ed. Pp. 153–173. Beverly Hills, CA: Sage.

Hemwall, M.

1984 Ethnography as Evaluation: Hearing-Impaired Students in the Mainstream. *In* Ethnography in Educational Evaluation. D.M. Fetterman, ed. Pp. 133–152. Beverly Hills, CA: Sage.

Hess, G.A.
1989   Testimony in Favor of: Educational Performance Agreements for School Restructuring. Testimony Presented to the United States House of Representatives Committee on Education and Labor Subcommittee on Elementary, Secondary, and Vocational Education. Chicago, Illinois: Chicago Panel on Public School Policy and Finance.

Hicks, G.L. and M. Handler
1987   Ethnicity, Public Policy, and Anthropologists. *In* Applied Anthropology in America. E. Eddy and W. Partridge, eds. Second Edition. Pp. 398–432. New York: Cambridge University Press.

Hoaglin, D., R. Light, B. McPeek, F. Mosteller, and M. Stoto
1982   Data for Decisions: Information Strategies for Policymakers. Cambridge, MA: Abt Books.

Holmberg, A.
1958   The Research and Development Approach to the Study of Change. Human Organization 17(1):12–16.

LeCompte, M. and Goetz, J.
1982   Problems of Reliability and Validity in Ethnographic Research. Review of Educational Research 52:31–61.

Lewis, O.
1966   The Culture of Poverty. Scientific American 215:19–25.

Liebow, E.
1967   Tally's Corner. Boston, MA: Little, Brown.

Marotto, R.
1986   "Posin' to Be Chosen": An Ethnographic Study of In-School Truancy. *In* Educational Evaluation: Ethnography in Theory, Practice, and Politics. D.M. Fetterman and M. Pitman, eds. Pp. 193–211. Beverly Hills, CA: Sage.

Maxwell, J., P. Bashook, and L. Sandlow
1986   Combining Ethnographic and Experimental Methods in Educational Evaluation: A Case Study. *In* Educational Evaluation: Ethnography in Theory, Practice, and Politics. D.M. Fetterman and M. Pitman, eds. Pp. 121–143. Beverly Hills, CA: Sage.

Messerschmidt, D.
1984   Federal Bucks for Local Change: On the Ethnography of Experimental Schools. *In* Ethnography in Educational Evaluation. D.M. Fetterman, ed. Pp. 89–113. Beverly Hills, CA: Sage.

Mills, C.
1959   The Sociological Imagination. New York: Oxford University Press.

Ogbu, J.
1974   The New Generation: An Ethnography of Education in an Urban Neighborhood. New York: Academic Press.
1978   Minority Education and Caste: The American System in Cross-cultural Perspective. New York: Academic Press.
1987   Variability in Minority Responses to Schooling: Nonimmigrants vs. Immigrants. *In* Interpretive Ethnography of Education: At Home and Abroad. G.D. Spindler, ed. Pp. 255–78. Hillsdale, NJ: Lawrence Erlbaum.

Patton, M.
  1980   Qualitative Evaluation Methods. Beverly Hills, CA: Sage.
Pelto, P. and J. Schensul
  1987   Toward a Framework for Policy Research in Anthropology. *In* Applied
         Anthropology in America. E. Eddy and W. Partridge, eds. Second Edition.
         Pp. 505–527. New York: Cambridge University Press.
Pitman, M. and Dobbert, M.
  1986   The Use of Explicit Anthropological Theory in Educational Evaluation: A
         Case Study. *In* Educational Evaluation: Ethnography in Theory, Practice,
         and Politics. D.M. Fetterman and M. Pitman, eds. Pp. 78–100. Beverly Hills,
         CA: Sage.
Simon, E.
  1986   Theory in Education Evaluation: Or, What's Wrong with Generic-Brand
         Anthropology. *In* Educational Evaluation: Ethnography in Theory, Practice,
         and Politics. D.M. Fetterman and M. Pitman, eds. Pp. 51–77. Beverly Hills,
         CA: Sage.
Smith, A. and Louis K. (Eds.)
  1982   Multimethod Policy Research: Issues and Applications. American Be-
         havioral Scientist 26(1):1–144.
Smith, A. and Robbins, A.
  1984   Multimethod Policy Research: A Case Study of Structure and Flexibility. *In*
         Ethnography in Educational Evaluation. D.M. Fetterman, ed. Pp. 115–132.
         Beverly Hills, CA: Sage.
Spicer, E.
  1976   Anthropology and the Policy Process. *In* Do Applied Anthropologists Apply
         Anthropology. M. Angrosino, ed. Pp. 118–133. Southern Anthropological
         Society. Athens, GA: University of Georgia Press.
Spradley, J.
  1970   You Owe Yourself a Drunk: An Ethnography of Urban Nomads. Boston:
         Little Brown.
  1973   The Ethnography of Crime in American Society. *In* Cultural Illness and
         Health. L. Nader, and T. Maretzki, eds. Pp. 23–34. Washington, DC:
         American Anthropological Society.
Studstill, J.
  1986   Attrition in Zairian Secondary Schools: Ethnographic Evaluation and
         Sociocultural Systems. *In* Educational Evaluation: Ethnography in Theory,
         Practice, and Politics. D.M. Fetterman and M. Pitman, eds. Pp. 101–118.
         Beverly Hills, CA: Sage.
Tax, S.
  1958   The Fox Project. Human Organization 17(1):17–19.
Valentine, C.
  1966   Culture and Poverty: Critique and Counter Proposals. Chicago: University
         of Chicago Press.
Weiss, R. and M. Rein
  1972   The Evaluation of Broad-aim Programs: Difficulties in Experimental
         Design and an Alternative. *In* Evaluation Action Programs: Readings in

Social Action and Education. C.H. Weiss, ed. Pp. 236–249. Boston: Allyn and Bacon.

Wildavsky, A.
1979   Speaking Truth to Power: The Art and Craft of Policy Analysis. Boston: Little, Brown.

Wulff, R. and S. Fiske
1987   Anthropological Praxis: Translating Knowledge into Action. Boulder, CO: Westview Press.

Zeuli, J. and R. Floden
1987   Cultural Incongruities and Inequities of Schooling: Implications for Practice from Ethnographic Research? Journal of Teacher Education 38(6):9–15.

14

Contexts of Education, Contexts of Application: Anthropological Perspectives and Educational Practice

Cathie Jordan and Evelyn Jacob

This book has presented some perspectives that educational anthropology has to offer on minority education. It has paid special attention to the problematic issues of academic achievement and student compliance. It has emphasized perspectives that differ in some ways from those of psychology and educational science, the disciplines more usually associated with formal education in the United States.

The anthropological perspectives which have been discussed here have implications for policy and practice. Ogbu's work suggests that removing the job ceiling (or the higher education ceiling) for nonimmigrant minorities could help their performance in school. Harrison's work suggests that giving minority parents more control of their children's schools could be significant. The chapter by Gilmore et al. suggests reducing competition and increasing cooperation within our school systems might contribute to academic achievement. Erickson's and D'Amato's theoretical stances and the research of Vogt et al. suggest that culturally compatible classroom practices can be important for student who do not have a "structural rationale" (D'Amato's terminology) for schooling. These are but a few examples of such applied implications of theory and research.

However, there is no automatic link between theory and research and either policy or practice. For research or theory to become policy or practice people must make political and personal decisions in specific contexts. Knowledge must be translated into action.

The previous chapter (Fetterman, this volume) focused on how anthropology and anthropologists might influence educational *policy.* This final chapter examines the application of the research and theory, principles and methods (collectively termed *perspectives*) of educational anthropology to educational *practice,* particularly practice in minority education.[1]

The chapter will begin by examining some of the assumptions underlying the application of anthropology to educational practice. It will then explore different contexts in which educational practice and anthropological perspectives may interact, and discuss examples of interaction in each context. Finally, it will examine some factors which appear to be common to effective application in all contexts.

ASSUMPTIONS UNDERLYING APPLICATION

Every effort to affect educational practice is undergirded by assumptions arising from the knowledge and experience being brought to bear. (See Chapter 2 of this volume.) In the case of anthropology and minority education, the most important of these assumptions address four questions: (1) What are the major problem areas in the practice of minority education? (2) Where is the proper locus of change; that is, who or what is expected to be changed in order to mitigate the problems? (3) What kinds of solutions are looked for, at what level of generality? (4) What are the goals of change?

The definition of problem areas arise from the observation that schools, as they are ordinarily set up in the United States, fail *some* children as a necessary part of their operation (Gilmore et al., this volume). In most schools and in all normed tests of achievement, it is assumed that there will be a range of achievement among students and that for some children to succeed, others must fail. In addition, schools fail *minority* children in disproportionate numbers. Thus, minority children experience academic underachievement disproportionately. In some cases at least, this appears to

---

[1] Not all educational anthropologists are comfortable being directly involved in applying anthropology to practice. In part, this is because one of the first principles of ethnography, anthropologists' primary research methodology, is to interfere as little as possible with the culture, society or context being investigated. Despite these traditional dictums against intervention, some educational anthropologists have been willing to enter into the applied arena in the United States, particularly when the focus is on intervening in the formal educational system, not on changing students or their families. Several factors influence their participation: The educational system is usually seen as a part of the anthropologists' own culture; there is often a felt need for change in the educational system on the part of the members of both school culture and minority culture; and there are obvious inequities in many formal educational settings, particularly when these involve the education of minority populations.

be attributable to the fact that students refuse to comply with the requirements of teachers and schools, and that they make this choice because there
are neither external (Ogbu, this volume; D'Amato, this volume) nor internal
(D'Amato, this volume) reasons sufficient to elicit compliance and to
counteract the pressure toward absorption in peer agendas. In other cases, it
appears that even when compliance is achieved, academic underachievement may still persist (Tharp and Gallimore 1976). So, in the opinion of the
authors, the most important problems in minority education are academic
underachievement, correlated in many cases with student noncompliance
with teacher demands. These are accompanied, in turn, by teacher–student
tensions and by feelings of unhappiness and of being devalued, often held by
students, parents, community members, teachers, and administrators alike.
In such situations, no one wins.

A traditional response to individuals or groups who end up on the failing
end of the failure/success continuum in school has been to try to change the
students, and often, when a disproportionate number come from an identifia-
ble ethnic or cultural group, to attempt to change the students' families or
communities as well. Parent education programs for minority parents, for
example, frequently are based on the assumption that if children experience
failure in school, the socialization practices of their parents need to be altered
to conform more closely to those of school-successful populations, usually
middle class Anglos. Anthropological perspectives widen the focus of
attention, at least in the case of disproportionate academic underachievement by a group of children, to include the *contexts* of educational failure—
that is, the classroom, the school, the institution of schooling, and the
relationship of formal education to other social factors. Such perspectives
suggest that changing contexts that produce (or even demand) failure is at
least as likely to contribute to changed outcomes as attempts to change whole
populations of people and their cultures to conform more closely to the
culture of the school.

Many traditional approaches to developing practice in minority education
have tended to assume that, allowing for individual differences, all populations of children could be treated as if they were the same. This kind of
approach looks for universal solutions to educational problems. It is program-
oriented and expects educational programs that are effective for one
population to be effective for other populations. It assumes that there is such
a thing as "just good teaching" and that "good teachers," by using tried and
true practices, can be good teachers whatever the setting or the student
population.

Anthropological perspectives suggest that solutions to educational problems will be population- and situation-specific, and that what is good
educational practice for one population and in one setting may not be good
educational practice for another population or in a different setting. Such an

approach expects variability among populations and thus in the programs that are effective for them. It looks for local, population-specific solutions, rather than universally effective programs. It assumes that what are generalizable about solutions are the processes that lead to them, not necessarily particular programs or practices. It assumes that "good educational practice" does not exist outside of a particular educational context, and that "just good teaching" is not *just* good teaching at all, but a complex process of combining information from a number of different sources to produce practice well adapted to the population and setting at hand.

On one level, the major goal of applied work in education is similar for all disciplines—to enable all students to learn effectively. What is perhaps unique about the perspectives of educational anthropology is an expectation that this is most likely to happen, especially in the case of minority populations, not only by helping children, families, and communities to adapt to the demands of schools and schooling, but also by educational practice being shaped and changed by children, families, and communities. Anthropological methods and concepts can be used to enable both parts of the effort. They can be used in developing: (1) processes and strategies with which to understand better the culture of classrooms and other components of the institution of formal education to which minority children and families must, at least to some degree, adapt (e.g., Erickson, this volume; Ogbu, this volume; D'Amato, this volume); (2) knowledge of minority cultures to aid in the selection of more effective educational practices (e.g., Jordan 1981; Vogt et al., this volume); and (3) strategies with which to approach schooling as a social institution, to facilitate positive, effective interaction between minority communities and their schools (e.g., Gibson, this volume; Harrison, this volume) and promote innovation and responsiveness among practitioners. The remainder of this chapter will discuss examples of the first two; the last will be addressed briefly at the end.

CONTEXTS FOR INTERACTION BETWEEN ANTHROPOLOGY AND EDUCATIONAL PRACTICE

In most cases, educational anthropologists are neither prepared by training nor in professional positions which would allow them to intervene directly in educational practice, at least at the elementary and secondary level. Consequently, if anthropology is to affect practice in a positive way, it will be through the efforts of professional educators. Therefore, educational anthropologists must ask themselves, "How can I make my knowledge of what happens in schools and in minority communities useful to practitioners?" Educators considering the work of educational anthropology might ask, "How can I access and use information and methods from anthropology to help me in shaping my classroom practice, my administrative decisions, my mentoring and training of teachers?" Or a question for both might be, "How can we interact and collaborate so as to learn from each other and thereby produce better education, especially for the children of minority groups?" In this section, examples from each of several application contexts will be discussed to illustrate varieties of interaction between anthropology and educational practice. Many of the examples come from the first-hand experience of the authors, both of whom have been engaged in applied efforts for some years.

Based on the intensity of contact between anthropological perspectives and educational practice and on the amount of access practitioners have to resources and support for applying anthropological perspectives in the classroom, there are four broad categories of contexts in which interaction between anthropology and practice in minority education can take place. These are: (1) practitioner–anthropologist collaborations; (2) formal teacher education; (3) mentoring and networking relationships; and (4) situations in wihch a practitioner is working alone but is able to call on anthropological perspectives to inform practice. We discuss these in descending order of intensity of contact between anthropology and practice.

Practitioner–Anthropologist Collaboration

This is the application context in which usually there is the greatest intensity of contact and the most interaction between anthropological perspectives, in the person of a professional anthropologist or an educator thoroughly trained in the field, and one or more professional practitioners. Generally, such collaborations also involve the presence of both anthropologist and practitioner at the practice site (in the school or classroom), so that both experience the realities of the application process first hand. Collaborations can be of quite limited duration, as in the traditional research project, or they can be longer-lived or even, at least in potential, permanent arrangements.

Permanent Collaborations: The School Anthropologist. The basic idea of creating a permanent collaborative relationship between anthropologist and school is to have an educational anthropologist (or a functional equivalent) operate as a permanent part of the school institution, in the same way as do various kinds of educational specialists, psychologists, and sometimes social workers or even police officers. School anthropologists would be responsible for learning about the community served by a school or school district in a way that, given the current demands on their time, individual practitioners, if they live out of the district or come from very different backgrounds than their students, cannot possibly do. School anthropologists would use ethnographic methods to generate information about the community for the school and about the school for the community, and would attempt to serve as liaisons betwee the two. Ordinarily they would live in the community served and become, as much as possible, participant–observers in the life of the community. In some cases, they might be persons who were already community members, who had or could be provided with the relevant anthropological perspectives and methodological skills.

As far as the authors know, no good examples of this context for the intersection of anthropology and educational practice currently exist. However, a version of it was planned as a long-term undertaking, and actually functioned for over two years in Hawaii, as part of the Kamehameha Elementary Education Program (KEEP) effort. KEEP, at the time of this experiment (1981–1983), was a fairly large-scale, multidisciplinary operation dedicated to improving education for native Hawaiian children. It involved a variety of social science and education researchers, along with a cadre of research and demonstration teachers, as well as teacher consultants working in the public schools. Over a number of years, it had developed ways of teaching Hawaiian children which produced improved achievement for them (Tharp et al. 1984); and in 1981–82, it began to greatly expand what had formerly been a relatively small-scale effort of consultation to public school sites.

A team of two, a woman and a man, both anthropologists, established themselves in an area of high Hawaiian population where it was anticipated there soon would be a large number of KEEP-trained consultants operating. The man, a *haole* (Anglo), rented a house in the heart of the community, on a street where several Hawaiian families were living. The woman (of Chinese ancestry) drove to the community each day, but spent long hours there, and participated in neighborhood and community activities. Both quickly entered into the life of the community and became part of friendship and family networks. The man was "adopted" by one of the neighborhood families. In the time that the team worked in the area, they were able to generate very high-quality ethnographic data, from both community and school, which eventually contributed to the matrix of ideas concerning student compliance (D'Amato, this volume). Simultaneously, they also worked with practitioners in the community's schools on applying theory and the emerging research data to ongoing practice.

Unfortunately, funding for the school anthropologist project was withdrawn before it could be fully developed and tested in other locations. In spite of the fate of this individual effort, having a person (or team of people) assume the permanent role of home-community liaison, especially for schools and districts serving substantial minority populations, seems an idea at least worth considering.

Time-limited Collaborations: Educational Application "Projects."
Projects that are expected to have a limited life span are the much more
common format for anthropology-practice collaboration. Here we present two
examples.

In the work represented in this volume by Moll and Diaz (see also Diaz,
Moll and Mehan 1986), a team of anthropologically oriented researchers
used ethnographic and microethnographic methods to carefully examine
what was happening in settings where minority students were not doing
well and, based on anthropological and sociohistorical theories, to help to
reorganize instruction. The latest work in this line (e.g., Moll 1990) has
added explicit teacher–researcher collaboration to the method. With the goal
of improving Latino students' literacy learning, Moll used ethnographic
methods to document the origin, use, and distribution of knowledge and
skills in Hispanic households. Moll also used these methods (observation and
videotaping) to examine existing methods of instruction. In an after-school
study group, researchers and teachers used the household data, along with
other sets of data, to develop methods of literacy instruction that built on the
resources of the community. "This study group represents a social context for
informing, assisting, and supporting teachers' performances; it is an activity
setting where teachers and researchers get together to study teaching, to
learn about the households, and to develop innovations; it is also a self-
assisting group where teachers help themselves" (Moll 1990: 8).

A second example comes from KEEP. For much of its existence, KEEP was
a collaborative effort in which professional anthropologists provided knowledge of those aspects of the home and community culture of the children
that were felt to be especially important to learning in school, and developed
information about classroom and peer cultures of Hawaiian children at
school (Vogt et al., this volume; Jordan 1984, 1985; Jordan and Tharp 1979;
Tharp et al. 1984). Along with the other members of the project, they worked
on developing methods for translating theory and research into educational
practice (Jordan 1985). Practitioners, including consulting teachers, classroom teachers, and administrators, contributed knowledge of the range of
educational practice available for use in most teachers' repertoires. Research
and demonstration teachers experimented with different practices and
developed on-the-ground knowledge of what worked and what did not. (The
research and demonstration teachers taught a half-time schedule in order to
allow them the time for reflection and collaboration with other workers on
the project, as well as for the painstaking preparation necessary for ongoing
innovative practice.) Out of this collaborative effort came methods for
teaching educationally at-risk native Hawaiian children that were effective
in a variety of contexts (Tharp et al. 1984).

In the initial KEEP collaboration, the knowledge bases called upon were fairly widely distributed among a variety of personnel, and the "anthropological perspectives" were represented mainly by anthropologists. This does not have to be the case. In the instance of the KEEP/Rough Rock collaboration (Vogt et al., this volume; Jordan, Tharp and Vogt 1985), roles were distributed among fewer individuals. Initially, an anthropologist contributed knowledge of anthropological principles and methods and conducted classroom ethnography. A KEEP master teacher contributed knowledge of educational science and the range of available classroom practices, as well as a great deal of experience in classroom operation, albeit in a different student culture. Both master teacher and anthropologist brought knowledge of methods for translating research into practice. A Navajo teacher and her aide, who were the other partners in the collaboration, brought knowledge of the local Navajo culture (in which the anthropologist was experientially naive) and of the community. They needed only to discover that this kind of knowledge was relevant to educational practice in order to begin to apply it. They also brought an intimate personal knowledge of their students (who were the children of the small, though geographically extensive, community of which they were members), and they were expert in day-to-day classroom operation with this population of children.

The point here is that (as was noted above) in some circumstances the anthropologist may not be the most appropriate person to contribute knowledge of local culture or classroom culture to the process of developing educational applications. Practitioners who are culture members and members of the local community may, in many circumstances, much more appropriately fill those roles. Experienced and trained practitioners can also carry out classroom ethnography and undertake translation of anthropological research and theory into classroom practice.

Formal Teacher Education

Another kind of context for interaction and interchange between anthropology and educational practice is one in which there is intensive contact on the level of concepts and ideas, but less involvement of anthropologists or anthropologically sophisticated personnel with actual "on-site" practice. This category encompasses preservice and inservice college and university courses, when such courses are structured appropriately.[2] Through a series of

---

[2] There are many modes of inservice teacher education. Practically any acquisition of knowledge or skills that practitioners encounter after completing their basic degree program can be characterized as inservice training. We will not discuss here what is perhaps the most common mode of inservice training, in which practitioners attend one or a few sessions of a few hours or less in length in which an expert or a trainer presents some specific knowledge or technique. Then the practitioner returns to classroom or administrative office, with little

courses (the ideal) or an individual course, educational anthropologists can work with practitioners to help them develop and use anthropological perspectives, while practitioners bring knowledge of the actualities of their classrooms and schools to the interchange.

A Program-Level Effort. An important and large-scale example of a model for preservice and midservice training based on anthropological perspectives has been developed at the University of Alaska, Fairbanks. The Cross Cultural Educational Development program (X-CED) (R. Barnhardt 1977; C. Barnhardt 1982; Kuhn and Esmailka 1982) was developed to train Native Alaskan teachers (and a smaller number of non-Native teachers) to teach in the rural community schools of Alaska. A field-centered approach, it was designed to allow Native students to learn to be teachers on the home ground of their own villages, to be able to remain natives and community members while becoming teachers. It also was designed to enable Native students to learn in familiar contexts, similar to the ones in which they would eventually work, and to employ familiar learning interaction styles, including those involving cooperation and collaboration.

An assumption behind this effort to train Native teachers was that they would bring to teaching an intuitive understanding of the needs and communication style of the children of their community, an assumption that appears to have at least some support from research data (C. Barnhardt 1982). Also it was assumed that Native teachers would be more likely to stay in their rural teaching jobs for substantial periods and that they would provide more appropriate and pertinent role models for Native children than would non-Native teachers. The approach tended to retain Native students in college who otherwise might have dropped out. However, because Native teachers still represent only a small percentage of the total teacher corps, because institutional pressures to conform to traditional (non-Native) styles of teaching are almost overwhelming, and because of the drop-out of at least some teachers from classrooms because traditional roles and expectations in education do not match well with their alternative style of training (R. Barnhardt 1977; Kuhn and Esmailka 1982), whether an alternative, Native teacher training effort such as X-CED can have a significant impact on Native Alaskan education as a whole is still an open question.

---

or no follow-up service available. As a context for anthropological perspectives and educational practice to meet and interact, this is perhaps the least effective although, at least until very recently, probably the most widespread. It has the advantage of low cost in invested time and energy; but it has the disadvantage of low impact on practice. This should be no surprise since it violates many of the principles of good teaching which flow from both educational science and the anthropological study of enculturation. Knowledge is characteristically presented out of context; there is little opportunity for guided practice; and there is no provision for self-observation or feedback about any attempts to apply any knowledge that has been gained.

A Course-Level Effort. In situations where anthropological perspectives cannot inform an entire teacher education program, a single course may be structured to promote maximum experience with anthropological perspectives for practitioners. A Master's course developed by Jacob at George Mason University is designed to put practitioners in a position to apply anthropological perspectives on their own or in a networking context after the course is finished. To do this, the instructor helps the practitioners in the course acquire anthropological perspectives, application strategies, and skills to evaluate the results of any changes they might make.[3]

To identify perspectives of educational anthropology, the class reads anthropological case studies, which are organized around topics such as culture and learning, culturally-patterned social interaction, variability within cultures, and culture contact in schools. Primary materials are used rather than texts to allow the practitioners to develop their skills in analyzing perspectives, comparing across reports, and inductively developing their own perspectives to take from the readings.[4]

Since anthropological perspectives represent a new way of looking at education for most of the practitioners, care is taken to facilitate their acquisition of anthropological perspectives. Since change is most likely to occur in the context of group support, there is an emphasis on whole-class and small-group discussions.[5]

To create opportunities for the instructor and practitioners to jointly apply these perspectives, application cases (also called teaching cases in the literature) are the primary focus of class sessions five times during the semester. Each case describes a "real-life" dilemma that practitioners might face and that is related to the topics previously discussed in class. Practitioners are asked to write a response to each case before the class meeting. Guidelines for the assignment stress identifying alternative ways to "frame" the dilemma, and discussing and evaluating possible courses of action. In class the practitioners discuss the application case, usually first in small groups and then in the whole class with the instructor. The result of each discussion is that everyone comes away with a broadened view and a range of alternative perspectives, hypotheses, and possible actions. After class

---

[3] The course does not focus on transmitting anthropological knowledge about particular ethnic groups, which tends to be a static approach and could lead to stereotyping.

[4] See Spindler and Spindler (1990) for a related point of view.

[5] Other activities are designed to provide *experiences* of cultural differences. For example, course participants reflect on their own cultural background and cross-cultural experiences before participating in small group discussions that identify similarities and differences among class members. Videos such as "Preschool in Three Cultures: Japan, China, and the United States" (Tobin, Wu and Davidson 1989) and readings that describe alternative approaches to education (e.g., Rohlen 1987; Hostetler 1987) are very useful in putting mainstream American culture into a broader perspective.

discussions all participants make notes of the new perspectives that they learned from the discussions. Although these collaborative problem-solving sessions do not deal with actual practice, the application cases provide simulations and an important opportunity to apply anthropological perspectives.

The course also focuses on application of anthropological perspectives to actual practice. The application case experience culminates in the equivalent of a take-home exam at the end of the semester in which practitioners identify a current or past dilemma or problem from their own practice, describe it, and then analyze it from multiple perspectives.

To address anthropological research methods, which can be used by practitioners to gather information about local cultures or to monitor the effectiveness of particular educational practices that they have implemented, one class session early in the semester is explicitly devoted to anthropological methods, and throughout the semester the instructor highlights methodological features of the studies read. A major paper for the course requires practitioners to conduct a classroom research project using these methods. The focus might be understanding a group of students or evaluation of a solution to a problem they have.

If the approach described here is successful, practitioners should emerge with new ways of looking at classroom dilemmas and new strategies for solving problems. In fact, students from this class report such outcomes. For example, in an anonymous end-of-semester evaluation, practitioners described the most important thing they had learned: One teacher said, "I learned to be more aware of cultural variation among school children and not to disregard culture as a possible reason for many problems encountered by teachers and students." Another practitioner reported, "[I] feel better equipped to work with teacher staff in meetings in discussion and problem solving on students." A third claimed, "I learned new steps to approach a problem." A year and a half later, practitioners reported continued impact. One teacher said, "I have become more sensitive to the needs and offerings of my foreign students and of their relationships to the American students....I use my children's experiences whenever I can. I let them become the teachers since they are the experts. My eyes are always 'open' to these children. I constantly use my observation skills." An ESL teacher responded: "I have reminded myself frequently that all behavior is logical, once the underlying reasons are understood. I have attempted to examine problems from student[s'] viewpoint[s] and recognize antagonisms as cultural, not just personal. I have used informants in my search for insights into student problems—sometimes teachers or parents, on other occasions more advanced ESL students from the same cultural background. Finally, and most importantly, I have used the anthropological principle of identifying the problem, applying a solution and observing and evaluating results." Such feedback suggests that this kind of course is one mechanism, often overlooked by academic anthropologists, for influencing practice.

However, because the course is not site-based and is of relatively short duration, it does not have some of the benefits of long-term involvement at a specific site. For example, practitioners do not have easy access to a support system after the course ends. Moreover, without the structure of the course requirements and with the normal demands of their jobs, most practitioners have reported that they are unlikely to engage in extensive classroom research after the course ends. A site-based course followed by ongoing collaboration between the instructor and practitioners might resolve some of these problems. Another potential solution to this problem, as well as a context for anthropology/practice interaction in its own right, is the presence of mentors and within-system support networks for practitioners.

Networking and Mentoring

Networking and mentoring represent middle-of-the-road contexts in terms of the degree of contact between education and anthropology and in terms of the amount and consistency of support for applying anthropology in education. In these contexts, a number of practitioners interested in applying anthropological principles of data "network" or work together to support each other in this effort. In the examples that are known to the authors, a professional anthropologist or someone with training in anthropology was involved at least at the beginning of the network. Theoretically, this does not have to be the case. A group of practitioners who share some background in anthropology (such as a course of series of courses like the one designed by Jacob, or the X-CED program) could well network with each other to provide mutual support for applying their knowledge to their practice. Networking can be structured through direct day-to-day collaboration (usually within the same school) in which decisions are made to some extent cooperatively, or it can take place through a looser association in which practitioners share what they are doing in their individual classrooms or institutions without any joint decision-making necessarily involved. The term *mentoring* usually indicates a similar, but more one-on-one, relationship, in which someone who is more experienced, at least in terms of a particular technique or process, teams up with someone less experienced. Mentoring can take place within the context of a network, or sometimes a mentoring relationship can evolve into a network.

The Evolution of a Network. At Rough Rock (Vogt et al. this volume; Jordan et al. 1985), the faculty had one semester of continuous interaction with the anthropologist and the KEEP master teacher, both of whom had a good deal of experience in applying anthropology to educational practice in

Hawaiian contexts. The interaction was very intensive for the Rough Rock teacher and aide in whose classroom they were working on a daily basis, and less intensive for the rest of the faculty. Subsequently, there were several years of intermittent contact, at some periods quite minimal, and sometimes, for a few members of faculty and administrative staff, quite intensive, as when delegations from Rough Rock visited Hawaii for periods of a week or more. During the initial semester's visit, a mentoring relationship was set up between the KEEP teacher and the Navajo teacher (and to a lesser extent, the Navajo aide). Both teachers were experienced, but at the start of the relationship, the Rough Rock teacher wanted to learn the specifics of the KEEP program, while the KEEP teacher and the anthropologist were interested in incorporating the Navajo teacher and her aide into the effort to begin development of a culturally compatible Navajo education program. The Rough Rock teacher and aide observed the KEEP teacher's lessons and the KEEP teacher answered questions and provided commentary, often with the aid of videotapes of the lessons. As the semester progressed and the Rough Rock teacher began to take over some of the teaching, the KEEP teacher observed and gave her feedback, again, sometimes with the assistance of videotapes. As the Rough Rock teacher and aide became more sophisticated in the use and adaptation of the KEEP program with their own student population and began to get the idea of applying their knowledge of their own culture, community, and students to their teaching practice, the relationship acquired a more collaborative character. The two teachers observed and commented upon each other's teaching and, with the anthropologist and aide, plotted how to adapt a Hawaiian education program to a population of Navajo children. The rest of the faculty also were involved in a less intensive way. They were given periodic updates on the progress of the work in the Rough Rock KEEP classroom, watched videotapes of the classroom, and provided comments and hypotheses about what would work and what would not. (At least one of these hypotheses turned out to be very important.) The mentoring relationship was gradually beginning to metamorphose into one of greater mutuality and also one of greater inclusion—a network.

After the semester of intensive contact, the Rough Rock teacher and aide and their colleagues continued to organize themselves into a network for change. This effort was facilitated by the coming of a period of relative stability in the administration of their school, which provided the faculty, who were discontented with some aspects of their educational program and outcomes, with the opportunity to undertake serious change efforts.

Among the original bases of their efforts were two principles springing from their exposure to anthropological perspectives. One principle was the relevance of their knowledge of their own culture, community and children to the shaping of their educational practice. In this respect, they were filling a double role, that of practitioner, and also one of the roles that an anthropologist might occupy in other change efforts in minority education, that of bringing knowledge of the local culture of classroom and community to bear on educational practice. The second principle was the necessity of local investigation and local knowledge of educational issues, resulting in local solutions. They were not expecting to produce a program which would be universally "good education" for all children or even all Native American children, but rather hoping to produce some educational solutions which would work for the children of Rough Rock, and which might contribute to applied efforts at other Navajo schools.

A Network for Reflection. Douglas Campbell (1988) and two colleagues began a staff development project in which a small group of teachers were to define the particular focus for staff-development and the anthropologists then would work collaboratively with teachers "in applying the features of ethnographic research as a *process,* not in taking established bodies of research on teaching and translating them for teachers' use" (p.102). This undertaking evolved over several years into something much like a network of practitioners and ethnographers, engaging in reflection on practice and, in the case of the practitioners, developing some changes in practice based on this process of mutual reflection (Berkey et al. 1990). In this particular network organization, the ethnographers' observations and questions remained carefully within the nonjudgmental, noninterventionist tradition of ethnography, but nonetheless helped practitioners "discover tacit knowledge and question previously unexamined assumptions" (Berkey et al. 1990: 231). At the same time, *all* network members, including researchers, teachers and administrators, both supported the work of the rest and focused on opening themselves up to new ideas and the reactions of other network members concerning their own professional practice. For these processes to take place effectively, the participants agreed, certain conditions and undertakings were highly desirable. These included: (1) An institutionalized allowance of *time* for reflection (in this case, one half day of release time per week for practitioners); (2) trust and respect for other network members; (3) an open-ended approach, of the kind associated with ethnography; and (a bit surprising to them) (4) the process of preparing oral and written accounts of their effort, as a way to organize reflection (p.230–231).

The Lone Practitioner

It is possible for anthropological perspectives and cultural knowledge to be applied by practitioners independent of any current contact with either anthropologists or a network of like-minded colleagues. When this happens, it is much to be applauded, since there are currently many more educational practitioners than there are educational anthropologists, or even colleagues with anthropological perspectives. Also, whatever the context, the real act of application, involving as it does the leap from knowledge to action, always has to take place in the person of the practitioner. However, for a single practitioner to operate alone without current support of a project, a mentor, or a network of some kind is difficult, at best. This is not to say it does not happen.

An Anthropologically Sophisticated Practitioner. A research and demonstration teacher for KEEP invented a new program element operating in a "lone practitioner" mode (Jordan et al. 1982; Tharp et al. 1979). She had heard a presentation and had some conversations with an anthropologist about the high degree of responsibility given at quite early ages to Native Hawaiian children. She knew that these children did a large share of the work of their households as part of a cooperating group of siblings, and that they negotiated tasks and roles within the sibling group with little direct supervision from adults. She also knew that the children learned many of their home-based competencies through modeling and observation. When she was asked to pilot a KEEP language arts program in a first-grade classroom in a public school where there was a high proportion of Hawaiian students, she decided to apply this information to her practice. She wanted to involve the children in the life of the classroom, to allow them to have a sense of ownership of the classroom and what happened in it. She also had the very practical problem that, because she was using another teacher's classroom for half of each day, she had to set up 12 language arts centers every morning and take them apart again at lunchtime. She decided to turn this task over to the children. First she opened the doors of the classroom, allowing the children free access to the room in the morning, when ordinarily they would be shut outside while the teacher did her preparation inside. Knowing that Hawaiian children tend to be good at learning through observation, she informally modeled all of the tasks that needed to be done, talking aloud to herself about those tasks where some information was necessary that could not readily be observed visually. Finally, knowing that Hawaiian children are taught to value "helping" and that they are accustomed to organizing their work for themselves, she simply gradually backed off from the classroom tasks and let the children take over, without attempting to direct or organize their participation. This meant giving up a measure of control and trusting the children's competence in a way that she might not have done without her anthropological perspective. It also meant combining that anthropological perspective with her practitioner perspective to produce a knowledge of what was likely to be workable and useful in this particular situation, with the particular individuals who occupied her classroom. Her strategy was very successful, producing eager involvement on the part of her students, as well as highly competent task performance.

This is perhaps the purest kind of example one is likely to find of a practitioner applying anthropological perspectives, and in this case some specific pieces of ethnographic information, with little outside help during the process of application. However, it should be noted that the practitioner was operating in a larger context which encouraged and supported interdisciplinary exchange and educational innovation. So, although the teacher was working independently, she was not completely isolated.

VARIED CONTEXTS, COMMON FACTORS

This chapter has discussed various processes and contexts in which anthropologists and educators can interact to apply anthropological principles, research, theory, and methods in minority education practice. In successful application contexts, certain kinds of expertise, knowledge, and conditions seem to be important.

In all cases, expertise in day-to-day classroom operation is central. In addition, the most important information bases seem to involve knowledge of:

- school and classroom culture, especially the culture of the particular classroom and school which is the site of the application effort
- the culture(s) of the student population[6], especially as it interacts with the school context in the form of a peer culture
- some aspects of the home and community culture(s) of the student population, especially the teaching and learning interactions and processes in which students are socialized in their home cultures
- processes that can be used for translating anthropological data into educational practice (e.g., Jordan 1985)
- research and theory in educational anthropology
- the full range of sound educational practice available for application.

These various knowledge bases may be represented each by a different individual or combined in fewer individuals. Rarely, one worker may possess all of the requisite knowledge bases; more typically, some degree of collaboration, mentoring or networking is necessary. Even where not strictly

---

[6] Because of anthropology's traditional focus on particular cultural groups, most research has concentrated on one cultural group or on situations in which there was one dominant minority group in addition to the majority group. Educational anthropologists have not yet directed much attention to the multiethnic classroom, which is becoming increasingly prevalent in the United States (Jacob 1989). Such situations provide a new frontier for anthropological research and theory and for collaboration between anthropology and practice.

necessary, such links and interchanges are probably desirable, as it strengthens the checks and balances of development work to have two or more people providing and responding to each other's ideas.

In addition to the need for certain bodies of knowledge, certain contextual conditions seem to favor effective application: (1) There needs to be openness to change and mutual influence both on the part of practice and on the part of anthropology. (2) Personnel positions need to be allotted to the application effort. Anthropologists need to be in the schools to influence and be influenced by the realities of school life. Reliable, trained substitute teachers are needed to release classroom practitioners for application and innovation work with the assurance of quality and continuity of educational service to the students. The two-on-one classroom, with two teachers, each teaching half-time while working half time on innovation and application, should be seriously considered as an option in intensive application efforts. (3) Time must be set aside in which the work of innovation and application can take place. This allotment of time must be institutionalized, something that participants in application efforts, particularly practitioners, can count on, and it must be maintained for a significant period, with a year being perhaps the minimum useful time. Such allotment of time must be seen as a necessary condition to producing and maintaining effective education, not a grudgingly given "privilege."

All in all, the people involved in application efforts need to be able to think about what they are doing, to plan and to talk to others operating in similar circumstances, to reflect and reflect again on what is known and on the relationship of knowledge to practice. The process of applying anthropology (or any other body of knowledge) to practice is energy-intensive and time-consuming, demanding concentration and courage. It is not for the faint-hearted. And it is both unkind and unrealistic for institutions trying to promote intervention, change, or application of knowledge, of whatever variety, to do so without making adequate allowances of people, time and energy to the process. Without such allotments, practical applications of high quality simply will not happen or be maintained. To think that we can change any aspect of educational practice, and especially practice in minority education, without some considerable and long-term application of time and effort is to believe in magic.

REFERENCES

Barnhardt, Carol
    1982   Tuning-In: Athabaskan Teachers and Athabaskan Students. *In* Cross-Cultural Issues in Alaskan Education, Vol. II. Ray Barnhardt, ed. Pp. 144–164. Fairbanks, Alaska: Center for Cross-Cultural Studies, University of Alaska, Fairbanks.

Barnhardt, Ray
  1977 Field-Based Education for Alaskan Native Teachers. *In* Cross-Cultural Issues in Alaskan Education. Ray Barnhardt, ed. Pp. 87–98. Fairbanks, Alaska: Center for Northern Educational Research, University of Alaska - Fairbanks.
Berkey, Ramona, Teresa Curtis, Francine Minnick, Kathryn Zietlow, Douglas Campbell, and Becky Wendling Kirschner
  1990 Collaborating for Reflective Practice: Voices of Teachers, Researchers and Administrators. Education and Urban Society 22(2):204–233.
Campbell, Douglas R.
  1988 Collaboration and Contradiction in a Research and Staff-development Project. Teachers College Record 90:99–121.
Diaz, Stephen, Luis Moll, and Hugh Mehan
  1986 Sociocultural Resources in Instruction: A Context-Specific Approach. *In* California State Department of Education. Beyond Language: Social and Cultural Factors in Schooling Language Minority Students. Pp. 187–230. Los Angeles: Evaluation, Dissemination and Assessment Center, California State University.
Hoestetler, John A.
  1987 Education and Communitarian Societies—The Old Order Amish and the Hutterian Brethren. *In* Education and Cultural Processes: Anthropological Approaches. Second edition. George Spindler, ed. Pp. 210–229. Prospect Heights, IL: Waveland.
Jacob, Evelyn
  1989 Students Creating Culture: Cooperative Learning in a Multi-ethnic Elementary School. Paper presented at the annual meetings of the American Anthropological Association, November, New Orleans.
Jordan, Cathie
  1981 The Selection of Culturally Compatible Classroom Practices. Educational Perspectives 20(1):16–19.
  1984 Cultural Compatibility and the Education of Hawaiian Children: Implications for Mainland Educators. Educational Research Quarterly 8(4):59–71.
  1985 Translating Culture: From Ethnographic Information to Educational Program. Anthropology and Education Quarterly 16(2):105–123.
Jordan, Cathie and Roland G. Tharp
  1979 Culture and Education. *In* Perspectives on Cross-Cultural Psychology. Anthony J. Marsella, Roland G. Tharp and Thomas J. Ciberowski, eds. Pp. 265–285. New York: Academic Press.
Jordan, Cathie, Roland G. Tharp and Lynn Vogt
  1982 Just Open the Door: Cultural Compatibility and Classroom Rapport. Technical Report 101. Honolulu: Center for Development of Early Education, Kamehameha Schools/Bishop Estate.
  1985 Compatibility of Classroom and Culture: General Principles with Navajo and Hawaiian Instances. Working Paper. Honolulu: Center for Development of Early Education, Kamehameha Schools/Bishop Estate.

Kuhn, Mark and Wendy Rosen Esmailka
  1982 Promises to Keep. *In* Cross-Cultural Issues in Alaskan Education, Vol. II. Ray Barnhardt, ed. Pp. 133–143. Fairbanks, Alaska: Center for Cross-Cultural Studies, University of Alaska, Fairbanks.
Moll, Luis
  1990 Community-mediated Instruction: A Qualitative Approach. Paper presented at the annual meeting of the American Educational Research Association, Boston.
Rohlen, Thomas
  1987 Seishin Kyoiku in a Japanese Bank: A Description of Methods and Consideration of Some Underlying Concepts. *In* Education and Cultural Processes: Anthropological Approaches. Second edition. George Spindler, ed. Pp. 451–461. Prospect Heights, IL: Waveland.
Spindler, George, and Louise Spindler
  1990 The Inductive Case Study Approach to Teaching Anthropology. Anthropology and Education Quarterly 21:106–112.
Tharp, Roland G. and Ronald Gallimore
  1976 The Uses and Limits of Social Reinforcement and Industriousness for Learning to Read. Technical Report 60. Honolulu: Center for Development of Early Education, Kamehameha Schools/Bishop Estate.
Tharp, Roland G., Cathie Jordan, Larry Loganbill, and Lynn Vogt
  1979 Coming Home to School. Videotape. Honolulu: Center for Development of Early Education, Kamehameha Schools/Bishop Estate.
Tharp, Roland G., Cathie Jordan, Gisela E. Speidel, Kathryn Hu-Pei Au, Thomas W. Klein, Roderick P. Calkins, Kim C.M. Sloat, and Ronald Gallimore
  1984 Process and Product in Applied Developmental Research: Education and the Children of a Minority. *In* Advances in Developmental Psychology, Vol. III. Michael E. Lamb, Ann L. Brown, and Barbara Rogoff, eds. Pp. 91–141. Hillsdale, NJ: Lawrence Erlbaum.
Tobin, Joseph, David Wu, and Dana Davidson
  1989 Preschool in Three Cultures: Japan, China, and the United States (Videotape). New Haven, CT: Yale University Press.

Author Index

A

Abdul-Jabbar, K., 102, *106*
Acland, H., 4, 5, 6, *12*
Allen, C., 226, *228*
Ambron, S., 244, *247*
Angrosino, M., 236n, *247*
Apple, M.W., 34, 44, *48*
Arroyo, W., 131, 132, *141*
Atkinson, P., 182, 188, 189, *205*
Au, K.H., 30, *49,* 56, 57, *64, 106,* 186,
    200, 202, *205,* 258, 259, *271*

B

Bakhtin, M.M., 37n, *49*
Bane, M.J., 4, 5, 6, *12*
Banks, J.A., 4, 5, *11*
Baratz, J., 6, *11,* 28, *49*
Baratz, S., 6, *11,* 28, *49*
Barnhardt, C., 30, *49,* 153, *163,* 261, *269*
Barnhardt, R., 153, *163,* 261, *270*
Barth, F., 38n, *49*
Bashook, P., 237n, *249*
Bateson, G., 40, *49, 205*
Bekker, G.J., 38n, 39, 41, *49*
Bereiter, C., 5, *11,* 27, *49*
Berkey, R., 266, *270*
Bernstein, B., 5, *11*
Bettelheim, B., 134, *142*
Beynon, J., 182, 188, 189, *205*
Bluci-Glucksmann, C., 45, *49*
Bogert, K.Y., 56, *65*
Boggs, J.W., 55, 57, *64,* 197, 198, *206*
Boggs, S.T., 185, 198, 200, *205*
Boissevain, J., 125, *126*
Bonacich, E., 125, *126, 128*
Bond, J.T., 4, *12*
Borko, H., 166, 171n, *178*
Bossert, S., 188, 191, 192, 198, 199, 203,
    204, *205*
Bott, E., 236, *247*
Bourdieu, P., 7, *12*
Bouie, A., 103, *106*
Bowles, S., 7, *12*
Boykin, A.W., 94, *106*
Brace, C.L., 4, *12*

Branch, T., 163, *163*
Brienne, D., 215, *230*
Brown, G.H., 129, 130, *142*
Burger, H.G., 84, *106*

C

Calkins, R.P., 258, 259, *271*
Campbell, D.R., 266, *270*
Campbell, E., 6, *12*
Carter, T.P., 129, *142*
Castenada, A., 94, *109*
Castile, G.P., 95, *106*
Castles, S., 123, *126*
Catto, S., 167, *178*
Cazden, C.B., 62, *64,* 210, 213, *228*
Chesterfield, R., 238, *247*
Clark, W.W., Jr., 197, 199n, *205*
Cohen, D.K., 4, 5, 6, *12,* 123, *126*
Cohen, E., 215, *228*
Cole, M., 18, *23,* 68, *79,* 98, *107,* 211, *230*
Coleman, J.S., 6, *12,* 86, *107*
Collins, J., 30, *51*
Compton, D., 238, *247*
Cook, T., 238, *247*
Cronbach, L., 238, 244, *247*
Crowell, D., 55, 56, *64*
Cummins, J., 117, 123, *126*
Curtis, T., 266, *270*

D

D'Amato, J., 59, *64,* 182n, 183, 184, 188,
    189n, 190, 191, 195-196, 198, 199,
    200, 202, 203, 204, *205,* 212, *228*
Davis, C., 129-130, *142*
Davidson, D., 262n, *271*
Deutsch, M., 5, *12,* 27, *49*
DeVos, G.A., 42, *49,* 87, 91, 95, *107, 108,*
    136, *143*
DeWare, H., 89, *107*
Diaz, R., 68, 76, *79*
Diaz, S., 67, 68, 69, 71, 73, 76, *78, 79,* 85,
    107, 259, *270*
Diskin, M., 130, *142*
Dobbert, M., 237n, *250*
Dornbusch, S., 244, *247*

Subject Index